RAY BRADBURY
R is for Rocket
The Anthem Sprinters
and other antics
by Ray Bradbury
DIAL DRAMA
The Machineries of Joy
BRADBURY
Ray Bradbury's own selection of his best stories With an Introduction by Gilbert Highet
RAY BRADBURY'S
AUTUMN PEOPLE
RAY BRADBURY
TOMORROW MIDNIGHT
RAY BRADBURY'S
two memorable books-
THE GOLDEN APPLES OF THE SUN and
A MEDICINE FOR MELANCHOLY-
forty-four stories in all, complete in one volume.
TWICE 22
S is for space
Ray Bradbury
RAY BRADBURY
THE HALLOWEEN TREE
Illustrated by Joseph Mugnaini
stories by
RAY BRADBURY
I SING THE BODY ELECTRIC!
THE PANDEMONIUM THEATER COMPANY PRESENTS
THE WONDERFUL ICE CREAM SUIT
RAY BRADBURY
RAY BRADBURY
WHEN ELEPHANTS LAST IN THE DOORYARD BLOOMED
Celebrations for almost every day of the year

A Life and Career History, Photolog, and Comprehensive Checklist of Writings

Ray Bradbury (Photo by Michael Childers)

THE RAY BRADBURY COMPANION

Ray Bradbury

1977

A Life and Career History, Photolog, and Comprehensive Checklist of Writings With Facsimiles From Ray Bradbury's Unpublished and Uncollected Work in all Media

by William F. Nolan
Introduction by Ray Bradbury

A Bruccoli Clark Book
Published by Gale Research,
Detroit, Michigan
1975

book designed by Richard Kinney

Library of Congress Cataloging in Publication Data

Nolan, William F. 1928–
The Ray Bradbury companion.

"A Bruccoli Clark book."
1. Bradbury, Ray, 1920– —Bibliography.
I. Title.
Z8113.3.N64 016.813'5'4 74-10397
ISBN 0-8103-0930-0

To DONN ALBRIGHT,

artist, friend, fellow-collector,
for enthusiastic and multitudinous
contributions to this book.

Contents

Illustrations

THE RAY BRADBURY COMPANION

The Inherited Wish
An Introduction by Ray Bradbury

Looking over this prodigious job done by William F. Nolan causes me to think two things:

I'm glad I didn't have to do the research.

I'm glad that I have written every day of my life for forty years in order to make this kind of trouble for Bill Nolan.

And, while I'm at it, I'm glad that my loves were wide-spread and diversified and somewhat crazy, and that I moved into and out of various fields even as a boy so that, later on, I could shift gears, fill my life with new artistic intrigues and never suffer boredom.

I have always been the sort who goes to parties and vanishes to be found in the next room borrowing a typewriter and writing a poem or tale. I have mostly preferred the talk inside my own head rather than share the conversation of others. I have, then, been good company to me. This is not said smugly, for the gods are watching. I observe it as a calm fact, I do indeed get along well with myself. The two of us, the me that writes and the me that watches me write, are a rambunctious pair; I enjoy our twin relationship, not knowing, even at this minute, which of us is in charge, the emotional dynamite-expert, or the quasi-intellectual who occasionally has to say "Calmness" or "Serenity" or "Sit down and be still" when my outbursts get too anarchic.

Looking at all the listings put down here by Bill

Nolan, I am reminded of Dick Cavett's interview not so long back with Lord Laurence Olivier. In the interview, Olivier remarked on the genetics of his acting as some sort of Inherited Wish.

Hearing this, I sat bolt upright. My blood recognized that sound, that turn of phrase, and I knew the truth of my being, my life, and my writing career.

I am one of those whose bloodstream, whose marrow, and whose soul has Wished him into existence.

It seems the only explanation, when environment itself is not enough to explain growth or excuse failure.

I have the feeling that I was born to be me. And if this sounds mystical, no, I don't mean to confound you with that. It is simply that I have had to live inside my skin where every fibre, cell and muscle, every sense, seemed to have partaken of tumult. If someone slapped me on the back the hour I was born, causing me to yell, then every morning I feel the same slap and know some sort of rebirth, simply because I know I am alive for another day and able to write down yet another surprise.

I look back upon myself, then, as some sort of compulsive hysteric. I would have made a fine Holy Roller, to fall on floors, convulse, and speak in tongues.

As it was, I leaped from bed each day waiting for the Universe to fall on me and devour me from toenails to earlobes. I was possessed by this wild thing that tore through my veins and made me want to grow up to be the greatest Mad Scientist who ever blew up a world, the greatest Magician in history who could read all minds, and the greatest Writer in the world who could outwrite even, by god, Edgar Rice Burroughs himself! Unthinkable, but true.

So you could say I caught a fever when I was three and the fever has prolonged itself, increasing by incredible degrees and quadrupling itself every three years since, egged on, pushed on, exploded on by some new hero who ravened at my heels . . .

For, all the things I loved were lonely things. No one else around seemed to share my blind and blithering obsessions with Space, with magic, with Dracula at midnight and Frankenstein at noon. The nearest thing to my outrageous convulsion was my Aunt Neva, but she was a dormouse compared to her nephew. And my friends? Some of them liked Buck Rogers, and liked Blackstone the Magician, and liked Dracula and Lon Chaney and *Science and Invention.* But nobody *loved* them, wildly, with total indiscretion. If any of these grostesques, imaginary or otherwise, had come to the door one night to take me away forever, I would have gone. That is how completely addicted and full of passion my small body was.

I have what might be called almost total recall back to the hour of my birth. I remember suckling, circumcision, and nightmares-about-being-born experienced in my crib in the first weeks of my life. I know, I know, such things are not possible. Most people don't remember. Psychologists say that babies are born undeveloped, and that only after some few days and weeks are they capable of seeing, hearing, knowing. But, I saw, I heard, I knew. And, later in my life, wrote a story about myself called "The Small Assassin," in which a child is born fully aware and sets out to revenge itself on its parents for having thrust it into the world.

I have only the proofs of memory to offer in all this. When I was three I saw Lon Chaney in *The Hunchback of Notre Dame.* I didn't see the film again until I was seventeen. Outside the theatre I told my friends I remembered seeing it as a very small child. They hooted. I then described several basic scenes in the film. Inside the theatre, my friends stopped hooting. What I recalled is what we saw on the screen.

I can only reiterate: I *remember* crawling on floors, walking in snow storms, and being left at someone's house for a few hours one night when I was a year old.

Out of this grand trash heap of recollection, the impact of Chaney, Douglas Fairbanks, Edgar Allan Poe when I was eight, Buck Rogers at nine, Tarzan at ten, and all the science fiction magazines from these same years, my fevers grew and towered and impelled me toward the sort of impulse that only some small hyper-active boys can know.

Aged twelve, I began to write fictions about Mars and the Moon; I predicted to friends at school that within two weeks I would be broadcasting over the radio in Tucson, Arizona. I jogged over to the radio station, hung about, emptied ashtrays, ran for cigarettes, made a pest of myself, and wound up playing bit parts on Station KGAR exactly two weeks later.

What drove me? How much of me is blood and chromosomes shot through and through with combustions that lean toward Art? How much of it is family, mother, father, older athletic brother, town born and grown in? The only available answer seems to be *me.* I could not wait, ever, for anything. Once I fell in love, I seized greedily at all the parts of that love. I stayed on for endless performances of Blackstone the Magician, forcing my father to come drag me whining from the theatre, for I had just discovered how he made a horse disappear center-stage! I walked or skated ten miles a day every day all summer long when I was fourteen to hang around the cinema studios and see famous people. I rummaged trash cans behind the CBS Radio studios to filch out and save (to this day!) scripts broadcast a few hours before by Burns and Allen or Louella Parsons and her guests on *Hollywood Hotel.* When a student talent revue was announced in my High School, I showed up with a complete script and acted out all the parts. Needless to say, the teacher-director selected me to write the show and help produce it.

It should seem obvious by now that I was always out of breath, always going somewhere, always wanting something, and there weren't enough days or hours for me to fill with my loves.

Science fiction was one among half a dozen such grand affairs I had with life. And I wrote it amongst 4,000 students at Los Angeles High School who neither knew nor cared whether or not one damned rocket was ever built or pointed toward the Moon, Mars, or the Universe.

Worse still, I loved and would later write stories

for *Weird Tales*. So, from the beginning, I was headed wrong in two fields that would never prove out. Yet, I plunged ahead, feeling that if I were wrong I would be the *best* creative wrong that ever was.

Which brings us to the years when I began to see my science fiction published.

It is hard for the modern reader, born during the past two decades, to realize how difficult times were in 1949. We so-called science fiction writers have always had doubts about that rather dubious label. Mainly because gangs of intellectual apes have clubbed us for a full lifetime, and when they weren't beating us were busily ignoring us. There seemed no way for us to win or please. Naturally, most of us grew up with at least a tinge of self-doubt and inferiority.

What if what the bright apes said at their literary teas were true? What if science fiction, after all, wasn't even so much as a crippled shadow on the far outside wall of Plato's much-talked-about cave?

What if instead of reality being compassed by our imaginative flights, it had always escaped us, and we were merely kidding ourselves about Space, Time, Eternity, mankind and his robots, humanity and its dreams?

We were outcasts, we strange and eccentric children of *Popular Mechanics*, bastard sons of Jules Verne out of Hugo Gernsback, stuck together in our *ad hoc* church groups of fans and writers here and around the world, uttering equations, occasionally spouting *Esperanto*, assuring ourselves that we and *only* we knew the predicaments of man and could measure his future flights by merely putting our special heads together and circumnavigating the resultant stars.

We were, then, figures of fun. The hilarity surrounding us as ridiculous social outcasts only began to fade in the late 1950s, and at last becalm itself to embarrassment in 1969 when we *did* actually reach up and footprint the Moon.

Meanwhile, there was the problem of the label.

My first book for Doubleday, *The Martian Chron-*

icles, was published with "Doubleday Science Fiction" stamped on it, front and back.

All of which meant instant neglect for any book so published, so weighted down and intellectually wounded. If you were lucky, showing such a company brand on your flank, you got a snappy 75-word review in the rear of the *Picayune Tribune,* or a capsule summation among the *New York Times* obits.

Critics everywhere, as the saying now goes, were underwhelmed with the arrival of my Martians.

But sometimes the more fortunate gods knock elbows in strange ways. Shortly after the publication of the *Chronicles,* I found Christopher Isherwood browsing in a Santa Monica bookshop. On impulse I bought a copy of my own book and shoved it at him. His face clouded, a sigh escaped him: one more unwanted book to be taken home as door-prop.

Three days later, Isherwood telephoned me, excitedly. Did I know what I had done? he said. What? I asked. Written an incredible book! he replied, adding that he had just gotten the job of chief critic for *Tomorrow* magazine.

His first review would be: *The Martian Chronicles.*

Thus it was I began to squeeze out from under the hostile American pastime of labeling-in-order-to-conveniently-dismiss-and-forget.

Isherwood's review was long and full of praise, and changed my life only toward the better. Bright people who had ignored the very mention of Space, Time, and Machines, now came to feed among the robot sheep because Isherwood had said it was permitted.

Armed with Isherwood's review, I wrote to Doubleday and asked that they omit the "Science Fiction" label from my second book, *The Illustrated Man,* and all future editions of *The Martian Chronicles.* After some few exchanges and consistently pleasant arguments, my editor, Walter I. Bradbury (no relation) agreed. From that time on, while others in my field suffered the slings and arrows of outraged critics unable to tell a sewing-machine from a moron computor, I began to collect notices that inclined to find me a trifle better than I deserved.

The proof of all this pudding is, of course, that while the James Bond films, and *The Avengers* series on television are out-and-out science fiction, they are never so labelled. When Michael Crichton publishes *The Andromeda Strain* or Romain Gary writes *The Gasp* or Brian Moore puts *Catholics* in print, the editors are impeccably silent as to the SF content therein, thus insuring front page reviews. Only on rare occasions does a Heinlein, a Clarke, or an Asimov get similar attention, and more often than not only when they publish in scientific journals far afield from the imagined rocket or that amusing and ridiculous future of hydrogen bombs, nuclear policies, smogs, energy crises, herniated ecologies, the muggers' cities that, come off it! will surely *never* arrive.

But while our critics lagged, our children sped ahead.

Very late on in the century, boys and girls, nonreaders all, suddenly took an interest in reading. They actually seized up books, read them in flashes, and ran off, shouting to their teachers and parents. We were witness to the not unpleasant spectacle of teachers being nagged from the broad base below rather than the narrow apex of administration above.

So science fiction crept in through the school basement ventilating systems, and the Sleeping Beauties awoke. Students by the million, long drowsed and napping over curricula systematized when Lincoln advised his generals to drink the same whiskey Grant was drinking, batted their eyes, lit their brains, and tossed copies of Clarke, Asimov, and Sturgeon at English departments until they, too, awoke.

The revolution is in full-flood. Where, five years ago, no courses were being taught, now, in thousands of high schools and colleges across-country, science fiction, former outcast, has become everyone's favorite uncle.

It amuses me to recall that back in 1950 I told friends that if Bertrand Russell ever got around to writing fictions, it would simply *have* to be science fiction, fantasy, or both combined, for it is, after all, the fiction of ideas, the fiction of the dishonorable "gadget". And what are gadgets, finally, but ideas concretized in three-dimensional forms to make or break worlds? The hydrogen bomb is a silly "gadget" that has turned war back toward politics, reversing the old trend of politics exhausting itself and becoming war. When such gadgets proliferate, men like Lord Russell must join hands with such as we.

What happened? Bertrand Russell published two books of fiction in the Fifties. Both were rammed chockful of technological excursions into Gernsback, or if you prefer, C. S. Lewis tomorrow-afternoon Country. I saw Lord Russell for one brief but memorable night in London in the spring of 1953 and he admitted, with quiet humor, that he simply could not resist plunging into our wild meadow, littered with disastrous machines or machines that, paradoxically, might recycle man back toward humanity.

And then, of course, there is the problem of reverse snobbism, encountered among science fiction writers and fans who, over the years, complained that when I wasn't being unscientific (which is an unvariable with me), I wasn't writing science fiction at all.

So I found myself trapped between two alien camps, the Others Out There, and My Own People Here. I felt like Alice sipping from the bottle marked DRINK ME, trying to grow myself large to fit one house, then small to fit yet another. I soon saw the process as a try-out for madness. I went back to my magic realism and simple sauce, which means gazing deeply into my typewriter and glancing up only when an idea flew by.

It was in those confused middle years of publishing-by-the-label that Gerald Heard and Aldous Huxley came to me with a fascinating view of my occupation. Upon our first meeting, later verified by Mr. Huxley, Gerald Heard exclaimed:

"Do you know what you are?"

"What am I?" I asked.

"A poet, oh dear me, yes, a poet!"

"I'll be damned," I said.

"No, saved." And Mr. Heard proceeded to read to me from my own pages. "There. You hear? You see?"

I heard. I saw. And yet one more intuitive surprise filled my life and moved me in new directions. Because of nice literary gentlemen like Mr. Heard and Mr. Huxley I dared test the thin ice and move out, always fearing to fall through, but finally beginning to write not only poems hidden like faces in stories, but real poems written to *be* poems on one or two pieces of paper. Since then, hardly a morning has passed that I haven't gone directly to my typewriter to fire off a gun, scare up birds from hidden trees, hoping to see a flight that is rare and beautiful. Which means, in sum, to write a new poem.

But it is all surprise. If this book means anything at all, it is a record of the surprises I have given myself over a period of more than thirty years. With it I must record the astonishment I felt when older men came to me and told me about my own work, thus surprising me further.

In 1953 I wrote an article for *The Nation* concerning science fiction and my reasons for being in the field. In the article I used the operative terms of my life: love, zest, gusto, enthusiasm.

In the mail, late in May, a letter arrived return-addressed: B. Berenson, I Tatti, Settignano, Firenze, Italia.

Unfolding the letter I found these opening words:

"Dear Mr. Bradbury: This is the first fan letter I have written in 89 years."

The letter was signed by Bernard Berenson, the Italian Renaissance Art Historian. In his note, Mr. Berenson praised my use of those great words: love, enthusiasm, zest, gusto. If I were ever in Italy, he added, I was to come see him.

The point of all this is, of course, that through love and wild enthusiasm, one unlocks the well-springs. Out jumps Surprise.

In the midst of so much rejection, then, from my high school days into my middle thirties, I turned to older men like Mr. Huxley, Mr. Heard, and Mr. Berenson for that approval one needs in order to have a final belief in oneself.

I visited Bernard Berenson twice in Italy. He became my second father. We corresponded until two weeks before his death. One of his letters to me and my wife, when he feared death was imminent, reads: "Children, come home!" I wept, and would have gone. Fortunately, he survived that year and we were able to see him a final time and trade affections.

The capping irony is, of course, that now, today, science fiction has grown respectable enough that one is tempted to have the label stamped back on one's books. Yet, I am not that brave. Snobs still live in the thickets, just beyond the orchard. Better to write science fiction and pretend you are baking your grandma's pies or mowing your dad's front lawn. If this be hypocrisy, it is most amiable, and it is, after all, my turn to laugh.

This seems a good and proper place to list my mentors and teachers, starting with Jennet Johnson who taught me the short story and Snow Longley Housh who taught me poetry at Los Angeles High School. The impact of these two women on me was immense and lasting.

After that, the list is long, and includes many of the most noted writers in science fiction and fantasy. Robert Heinlein welcomed me into his life when I was nineteen and I saw him and his wife on many occasions for several years during which they encouraged me in my writing. At the same time I was receiving help from Jack Williamson, Henry Hasse, Ross Rocklynne, Edmond Hamilton, and Arthur K. Barnes.

But the two people who gave most completely and freely of their time were Henry Kuttner and Leigh Brackett. Henry read and criticized dozens of stories over the years. He wrote a new ending for my story, "The Candle," which was my first appearance in *Weird Tales.* His ending remains on the story to this day. The last three hundred words are his.

As for Leigh Brackett, every Sunday afternoon

for approximately five years we met at Muscle Beach in Santa Monica, where Leigh played volleyball. I read her perfect stories written for *Planet* and she read my inept stories written for God-knows-who. Her writing appears in the first six hundred words of my story "Tomorrow and Tomorrow," and in the first five hundred or six hundred words of "The Scythe." She helped me get both stories going. I could never find a way to better what she had done and got her permission to let those openings stand as written.

I was able to repay my debt to Leigh, and further my own career, an admirable combination, when she called me in 1944 telling me she had to go to work immediately on *The Big Sleep* as a screenplay for Howard Hawks, and would I, *could* I, take over and finish a novella she was writing for *Planet* titled "Lorelei of the Red Mist."

I not only took over but finished the last half of the novella in roughly a week's time. I sent it to Leigh at the studio and she telephoned me later. "You son-of-a-bitch, you did it!" she cried. "The last half is just like the first half. You've got my style down cold!"

"I've been reading your work on the beach for five years," I said. "It'd be a miracle if I hadn't assimilated everything you've ever done!"

Leigh, indeed, had taught me a lot.

Finally, here at the end of the Introduction, I must acknowledge the influence of three remarkable people who have cheered me on over the years.

Don Congdon became my friend back in 1946, a year before he became my agent. We started our literary association in September, 1947, the same month I married Marguerite McClure. It was, then, a month for a double-marriage. I have lived to praise and nurture and appreciate both. Marguerite Susan McClure, brave woman, has been in our home when I came back from the wars. Don Congdon, out on the battlefield, has been right about everything in my career for more than twenty-five years. What other writer can make that outrageous claim about his literary representative? I may have written science fictions, but Don has run ahead to make sure the Future was worth having and come back to report and give me strength.

The third person is the jackdaw gatherer and keeper of data, William F. Nolan, who did all of the incredible work on this book you hold in your hands.

Myth has it that actors, artists, writers are surrounded by admirers, claques, groupies, what-have-you. That is rarely the truth. Most of us are lucky if we have a few friendly individuals who pop up in our lives on occasion to warm a cold day.

Bill Nolan showed up on my doorstep when I was living in a small apartment in Venice, California in mid-1950, a fast-talking, arm-flinging 22-year-old boy who seemed more Fourth of July rocket than human animal, and whose energy, over the years has never diminished. If that old description still fits, he is the Fellow who "leapt on his horse and rode off in all directions!" Except in Bill's case, it *works.* He is madness maddened. Given a job, he fastens to it with bulldog teeth until the last fact is in and the final sum counted. I have always thought of myself as a creature of high energy and much adventurous activity. But I am a maniac Tom Thumb compared to Nolan, who, I imagine, will write a Library by the time he explodes, at ninety-nine, and blows away.

For his continual high spirits, then, his wit, his humor, his nitro-glycerin intellect, his friendly companionship over the early years that were lean and the later years that were harvest, my love and my thanks.

RAY BRADBURY
Los Angeles, California

Preface

Over the past decade and a half, as a professional writer, I have sold thirty books—novels, biographies, anthologies, as well as collected editions of my short stories and articles—but this volume on Ray Bradbury is unique among my works. Even the extensive checklist which I prepared on Dashiell Hammett in my critical/bibliographical study of this writer* did not approach the complexity and latitude of the present project. Here, assembled in these pages, is literally everything I could gather by and about Ray Douglas Bradbury from his birth in 1920 into 1974—a book which is biographical, bibliographical and (through Ray's INTRODUCTION) autobiographical.

A point of clarification is necessary: I am *not* a Bradbury fan. I dislike and reject this simplistic, misleading label. I *am* a Bradbury reader, an abiding supporter, and Ray's good pal of twenty-four years; we are hard-working fellow writers toiling in the same Los Angeles vineyard, and this printed record reflects my enthusiasm and respect for a man I am proud to count among my closest friends. (It also reflects a penchant for compiling and indexing; I've been addicted since childhood and have, in my files, complete lists on favorites such as Hemingway, Steinbeck, Fitzgerald, Thurber—and on the work of most of my

* *Dashiell Hammett: A Casebook.* Santa Barbara, California: McNally/Loftin, 1969.

writer-friends from Richard Matheson to Ron Goulart.)

A word about format. The listings in this book do not represent, in execution or intent, a formal bibliography. They are arranged, in chronological checklist form, as a basic aid to readers, collectors, and researchers interested in first printings of Bradbury's work and in material printed about him. Beyond a few particularly important European editions of *The Martian Chronicles* I have made no attempt to include foreign-language reprint versions of Bradbury books. In the case of Great Britain, I have listed only first British editions and first British paperbacks.

The same situation obtains with regard to Bradbury's magazine reprints. My collection is limited, in the main, to first printings. Therefore, a listing of Bradbury reprints is beyond the scope of this book, since I do not have copies of such material. (I have also been unable to supply page or volume numbers on magazines and newspaper material since much of my collection consists of tearsheets, without page numbers.)

It is hoped that another writer will someday prepare a formal Bradbury bibliography wherein such information will be tracked down and recorded. Bradbury himself has no central file of his work, nor does he keep records of printed titles. Although his cellar overflows with publications containing his stories, essays and articles, and though his shelves bulge with books bearing his byline in various world editions, he has never catalogued this vast output.

Fortunately, I have kept records of his first printings as related to books and magazines, and have published, from time to time since 1952, various Bradbury checklists. But, until this present volume, I have never attempted to cover the full scope of his work.

It is doubtful that any other popular writer of our time has penetrated so many levels of contemporary culture. Here, as this book demonstrates, is a man involved in cantatas and comic strips, stage drama and science fantasy, mysteries and magic, screen vehicles and pulp magazines. He creates Disney robots and television scripts, reviews books and films, writes verse and space-age essays, and is a novelist, lecturer, and social critic.

Most of his readers think of him as a fiction writer—and indeed some 300 pieces of Bradbury fiction have been printed—but he has written at least 150 non-fiction pieces. In all, including his verse, plays, reviews, scripts, etc., his total of original works exceeds 700 items. Thus, he has been far more prolific than his total of books would indicate.

Ray Bradbury's work has appeared in two dozen countries around the world, and his books have sold upwards of twenty million copies. Outside the U.S., Canada, and England, his books and stories have been widely translated in Argentina, Belgium, Czechoslovakia, Denmark, Finland, France, Germany, Hungary, Iceland, Italy, the Netherlands, Japan, Norway, Poland, Portugal, Rumania, Spain, Sweden, Switzerland, the U.S.S.R., and Yugoslavia. In Bantam pocket editions alone some twelve million copies of his books have been sold in the United States.

Bradbury's audience is widely diversified. He attracts a vast number of young readers, pre-teen and teen aged; his books are in constant demand among college students and as teaching aids in secondary schools.

Although he is best known as one of the world's most successful science fiction writers, his work transcends the genre; as a storyteller, he is equally comfortable in Illinois, circa the 1920s, in Ireland, 1954, or on Mars, 2001.

A large number of facsimile pages supplement the listings—and these reflect the full range of Bradbury's creativity. They include working manuscript pages from stories, stage plays, and articles, an operetta, diary notes, high-school juvenilia, letters, sections of unpublished screenplays, television and radio scripts, novels, verse, Bradbury pamphlets, LP records, samples of song lyrics, and comic strips. Here, too, are photos of the author at various stages of his life—and an illustration of several foreign-language editions of *The Martian Chronicles.*

All of these items were photographed from my collection of Ray's work by Morris Scott Dollens, a mutual friend and the man who has been responsible for many Bradbury book-jacket photos.

In addition to these photos, and the listings themselves, I have also provided a detailed life history, covering every major biographical fact in Ray Bradbury's career. Many of the facts in this history appear in print for the first time, revealing much about man and writer.

Academic interest in Bradbury continues to increase, and his work is now being taught in many colleges and high schools in the U.S. and overseas. He began in the nation's lowly pulps to emerge, triumphantly, in the nation's textbooks.

This record is comprehensive—in that amateur as well as professional work is listed, from 1936 (when he had his first poem printed at the age of fifteen) into late 1973. His *full* creative output through thirty-seven years is listed here.

Since I do not have any Bradbury duplicates in my collection, I would ask that fans, students and researchers do *not* write to me requesting copies of items listed in this book. As a fulltime professional, with an active career of my own to pursue, I cannot take time to answer queries, Xerox book or magazine items, or otherwise supply material relating to Bradbury's life or work.

Beyond my obvious debt to the subject of this book, I owe thanks to several others: Donn Albright, whose help was constant and substantial; Ray's wife (and my good friend) Marguerite; his editor at Doubleday, Walter I. Bradbury; his agent Don Congdon; pressman Roy A. Squires; radio buff Ray Stanich; researcher Helen Lewis; science fictioneer Forrest Ackerman; editor C. E. Frazer Clark, Jr.; artist Joseph Mugnaini, and photographer Morris Dollens. Particularly, I wish to express my gratitude to Professor Matthew J. Bruccoli for initial encouragement and solid editorial aid.

William F. Nolan
Woodland Hills, California
1974

RAY BRADBURY PHOTOLOG

Esther Marie Moberg, Ray Bradbury's mother as a girl of 22 in 1910.

The Samuel Bradbury family, circa 1911. Standing on left, Leonard Spaulding Bradbury, age 20 (Ray's father). Standing next to him, Samuel Hinkston Bradbury, Jr. (Ray's uncle). Seated left to right, Minnie Davis Bradbury (Ray's grandmother), Samuel Hinkston Bradbury (his grandfather), Nevada Marian Bradbury (his Aunt "Neva"), Bion Bradbury (his uncle).

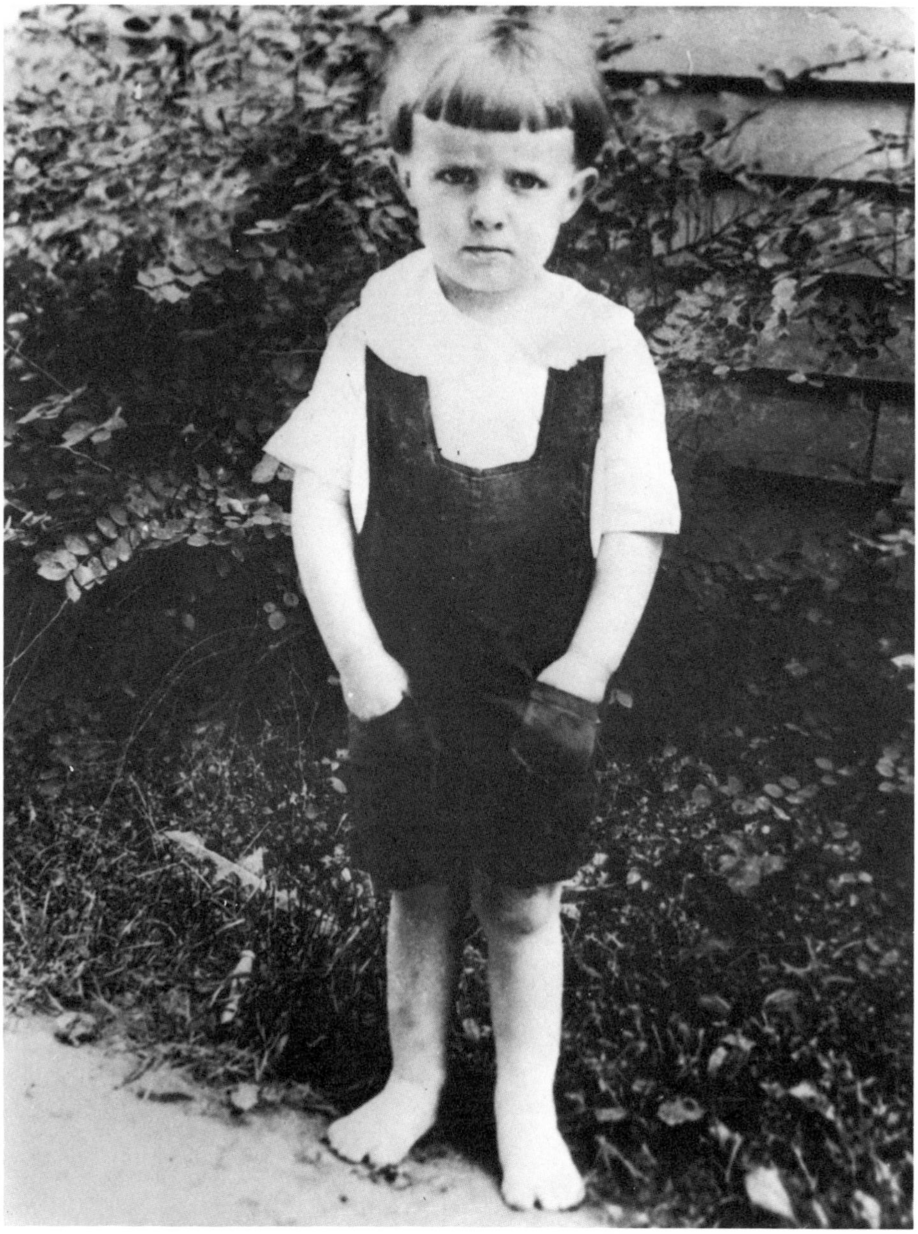

A determined Ray Bradbury at 3, in his yard in Waukegan, Illinois, later summer 1923—the year he was taken to see *The Hunchback of Notre Dame.*

Portrait of Ray's Aunt Neva in 1925, at 16—the year she introduced young Ray to the world of fantasy via the book *Once Upon a Time.*

"Shorty" (Ray) during his first school year, with his brother "Skip" (Leonard) and their father in 1926—the year young Bradbury discovered "Oz" and *The Phantom of the Opera.*

A star-struck 14-year-old, posing in front of Paramount Studios in 1934 with actress Grace Bradley.

With his father and brother in 1938, the year Bradbury graduated from Los Angeles High School.

BRADBURY
Ackerman
Harryhausen
Williamson
Hamilton
Heinlein

At the Los Angeles Science Fiction League, circa 1939. Bradbury, at far left, with Leslyn Heinlein (Mrs. Robert Heinlein). Seated directly to Bradbury's right: Forrest Ackerman (who printed Ray's first short story in the club magazine) and Ray Harryhausen (the animator who would later be best man at Bradbury's wedding). Also in this group: writers Jack Williamson (standing, middle of room), Edmond Hamilton (next to Williamson) and, seated, Robert A. Heinlein.

Bradbury at 25. Portrait taken in September 1945.

Dustjacket portrait for *The Martian Chronicles*, taken in 1949 by Morris Scott Dollens.

In Ireland, working on the screenplay of *Moby Dick* with director John Huston, January 1954.

With his four daughters in 1962. Standing, Susan. Seated, left to right: Ramona, Alexandra and Bettina.

At a publisher's promotional gathering in 1964—with writers Dolph Sharp, Sidney L. Stebel, and William F. Nolan.

With his wife, Marguerite, and his stage director, Charles Rome Smith, 1965.

A nostalgic portrait. In 1968, with "Blackstone the Magician"—the man who gave 10-year-old Bradbury a live rabbit during a 1931 stage appearance in Waukegan.

Bradbury in a recent photo (circa 1970) at his home in Cheviot Hills, with oil painting in background by Joe Mugnaini, the artist who has illustrated several Bradbury books.

THE LIFE AND CAREER OF RAY BRADBURY

A Chronology

1920

Ray Douglas Bradbury born August 22, at 4 P.M. at a maternity hospital one block from his parents' house (11 S. St. James Street) in Waukegan, Illinois.

Middle-named for actor Douglas Fairbanks by his father, Leonard Spaulding Bradbury, who was born December 1, 1890, in Waukegan, descended from English family who settled in America in 1630. Leonard's father and grandfather published a pair of Illinois newspapers at turn of the century as Bradbury & Sons. Leonard ran away from home at sixteen, headed west, spent time in Tucson, Arizona as young man.

Ray Douglas third child born to Esther Marie Moberg Bradbury. In 1916 she gave birth to twins, Leonard and Samuel, the latter dying at age two in 1918. She was born August 18, 1888, in Stockholm, Sweden. Came to Massachusetts in 1890, where her father worked in steel mills. At eight, with her family, moved to Waukegan where she later met and married Leonard Bradbury.

At Ray's birth, in 1920, his father was working as a telephone lineman for Bureau of Power and Light in Waukegan. Raised a Baptist, Ray recalls attending Sunday School each week through age thirteen.

1921

Remembers his first snowfall that winter, as well as many events of his early months. Such memories of infancy later formed basis for "The Small Assassin."

1923

At three, is taken by his mother to see Lon Chaney silent, *The Hunchback of Norte Dame,* and is profoundly affected by this horror film.

1925

At five, given book of fairy tales for Christmas, *Once Upon a Time,* by his Aunt Neva, age sixteen. Book introduces him to the world of fantasy.

1926

Ray's grandfather dies, as he faces reality of death for first time at five-and-a-half.

A daughter, Elizabeth, is born to Mrs. Bradbury—her last child.

Neva begins reading the *Oz* books of L. Frank Baum to Ray at six.

His mother takes him to see Chaney's *The Phantom of the Opera* and this film (combined with another that year, *The Cat and the Canary*) fixes within him a lifelong fascination with horror. He grows up fearing the dark.

In September enters first grade at Central School in Waukegan, but remains there only a month, as his father takes family west in October.

The Bradburys live in a rented house in Roswell, New Mexico, for two weeks, then move on to Tucson, Arizona, where Ray enrolls at Roskruge, a local grammar school.

1927

Bradburys return to Waukegan in May, where Ray re-enters Central.

His year-old sister, Elizabeth, dies of pneumonia

when Ray is seven, and a cousin almost drowns in Lake Michigan; he later uses the incident in his story "The Lake."

1928

Ray is bedded with whooping cough and misses three months of school. His mother reads works of Poe to him by candlelight.

Discovers science fiction in pulp magazine *Amazing Stories,* and is stirred by story in that issue, "The World of Giant Ants."

At eight is terrified to cross the ravine near his house due to rumored presence of man called "The Lonely One." Later uses this fear of the ravine in several stories, notably in *Dandelion Wine.*

1929

Becomes Edgar Rice Burroughs fan as he devours tales of Tarzan and John Carter of Mars at his Uncle Bion's house.

Discovers (and begins collecting) comic-strip adventures of Buck Rogers in local paper.

1930

At age ten, with brother Leonard, Ray spends each Monday night at the town library, acquiring lifelong love of books and libraries.

Is nicknamed "Shorty"—and his brother is "Skip."

1931

Circuses and carnivals exert major influence. That summer he is given live rabbit onstage by Blackstone the Magician.

At eleven, dreaming of magic and fantasy, writes first stories by hand on roll of butcher paper.

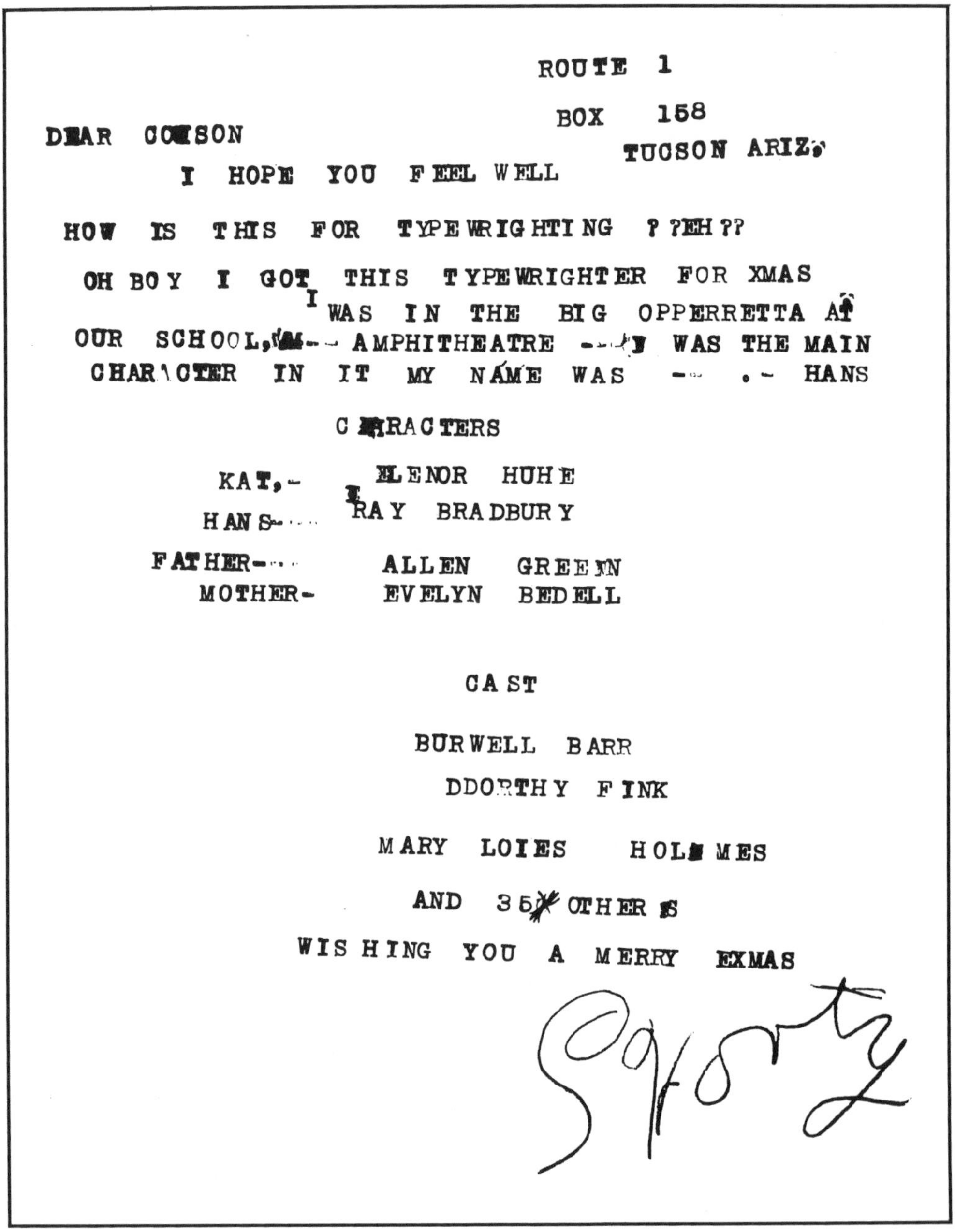

ROUTE 1

BOX 158

TUCSON ARIZ.

DEAR COUSON

I HOPE YOU FEEL WELL

HOW IS THIS FOR TYPEWRIGHTING ? ?EH ??

OH BOY I GOT THIS TYPEWRIGHTER FOR XMAS

I WAS IN THE BIG OPPERRETTA AT

OUR SCHOOL, -- AMPHITHEATRE -- I WAS THE MAIN

CHARACTER IN IT MY NAME WAS -- .- HANS

CHARACTERS

KAT,- ELENOR HUHE

HANS- RAY BRADBURY

FATHER- ALLEN GREEN

MOTHER- EVELYN BEDELL

CAST

BURWELL BARR

DDORTHY FINK

MARY LOIES HOLMES

AND 35 OTHERS

WISHING YOU A MERRY EXMAS

Shorty

Letter written on toy-dial typewriter when Bradbury was 12 in 1932 to a cousin in Waukegan and signed with his nickname, "Shorty."

1932

Determines to become "world's greatest magician." Sends to Chicago for magic tricks. Performs at Oddfellows Hall and at American Legion.

Reads Jules Verne—and copies dialogue, each afternoon, from radio adventures of *Chandu the Magician.*

In midst of Depression, Leonard Bradbury is laid off job as telephone lineman. Moves family to Tucson in hopes of employment. Ray enters Amphitheater School in Arizona.

At twelve, having talked his way into a job with radio station KGAR, Ray reads comic pages aloud over air to children each Saturday. Job lasts four months.

Sings lead in school operetta *A Wooden Shoe Christmas.*

Passion for Burroughs increases as he collects and pastes Sunday Tarzan comic pages in scrapbooks.

Receives toy-dial typewriter for Christmas. Writes stories of Buck Rogers on this machine, as well as his own sequel to *John Carter of Mars.*

1933

In January transfers from Amphitheater back to Roskruge. Remains there for five months.

Avidly reads borrowed copies of *Wonder* and *Amazing Stories.*

Ray's father quits job (selling "chili bricks" to local restaurants) in May. Takes family back to Waukegan. Ray again enrolls at Central.

That summer, at twelve, with Neva, he attends his first World's Fair in Chicago and is fascinated by Century of Progress exhibit, with its "City of the Future."

1934

In January a favorite uncle, Einar, moves to California. (Later, with character "Uncle Einar," Ray transforms him into a winged vampire.)

In mid-April, again jobless, Ray's father drives

MERRY CHRISTMAS

DECEMBER 22nd — 8 O'clock

AMPHITHEATER SCHOOL

PROGRAM

A CHRISTMAS LULLABY	1 B
SANTA'S WORKSHOP	1A-2B
A WONDERFUL TREE	3A-4B-4B
CHRISTMAS READINGS	3B
CHRISTMAS CAROLS	5B-5A

A WOODEN SHOE CHRISTMAS

A Christmas Operetta

6th-7th-8th Grades

Characters

Father	Allen Green	Holland country folks
Mother	Evelyn Bedell	
Hans	* Ray Bradbury	Their children
Katrina	Eleanor Huhn	
John	Clement George	Cousins from America
Helen	Dorothy Hunter	
Martha	Louise Haga	Friends, speaking for girl skaters
Hilda	Dorothy Rockwood	
Hendrick	Herman Schulze	Friend, speaking for boy skaters

Merry England	Stella Colwell	Characters in Katrina's dream
Miss America	Winifred Partridge	
Senorita Spain	Rosemary Gomarro	
Comrade Russia	John Huff	
Honorable Japan	Jean Ross	
Spirit of Christmas	Rita Lux	

St. Nicholas	Ralph Nunnelly
Santa Claus	Andrew Nelson
Black Man	Joseph Smith

Chorus of Girl Skaters.

Florence Carothers, Barbara Pfang, Beatrice Kilbourn Pauline Isbel, Anna Gates, May Egleston, Adabel Gordon Elsie Duke, Dorothy Rockwood, Mardel Eisiminger, Frances Miller, Helen Hodgson, Helen Grissinger, Evelyn Wolf, Viola Colwell, Betty Jo Reece, Louise Haga

Chorus of Boy Skaters

Horance Long, Warren Kersch, Donovan Smith, Edward Sewell; Robert Peery, Herman Schulze, Calvin Vermillion, Fred Squire, Frank Geniec, Myron Mershon, Taylor Moore, Burwell Barr, Jimmie Garison, Harold Drummond Leanard Ramsey, John Rynerson.

Program from a 1932 school presentation in which, at 12, RB sang the lead in this operetta. Note circled name of John Huff, RB's best pal and the boy he later wrote about—under real name—in *Dandelion Wine*.

the Bradburys to Los Angeles, hoping to find work in California. At thirteen, Ray moves with parents and older brother, into 1300 block of Hobart, at Pico.

Recalls roller-skating, each afternoon, to gates of Paramount Studios to get autographs of film stars. Has picture taken there at gate with Marlene Dietrich.

Adds Flash Gordon comic adventures to his scrapbooks.

Is "an audience of one" at Burns and Allen radio show at Figueroa Street Playhouse.

At fourteen, in August, moves with family to 1619 S. St. Andrews in Los Angeles, where they remain through 1938.

In September enters Berendo Junior High.

Dictates stories to girl next door, who types them for him.

1935

Ray sneaks over wall at Paramount to see studio, and is promptly ejected.

Determines to appear in *Saturday Evening Post* and have his fiction selected for *Best American Short Stories.* Begins mailing short stories to major magazines without success.

Leaves Berendo in June.

In September enters Los Angeles High School.

1936

Active in drama club at L.A. High. Decides to become actor.

Writes his first "novel," a 15,000-word anti-war narrative which he never finishes.

In August, four days prior to his sixteenth birthday, a poem of his appears in the *Waukegan News-Sun,* "In Memory to Will Rogers." It is his first printed item.

Enters two career-shaping classes at L.A. High that September: short story class under Jennet Johnson, and poetry class under Snow Longley Housh.

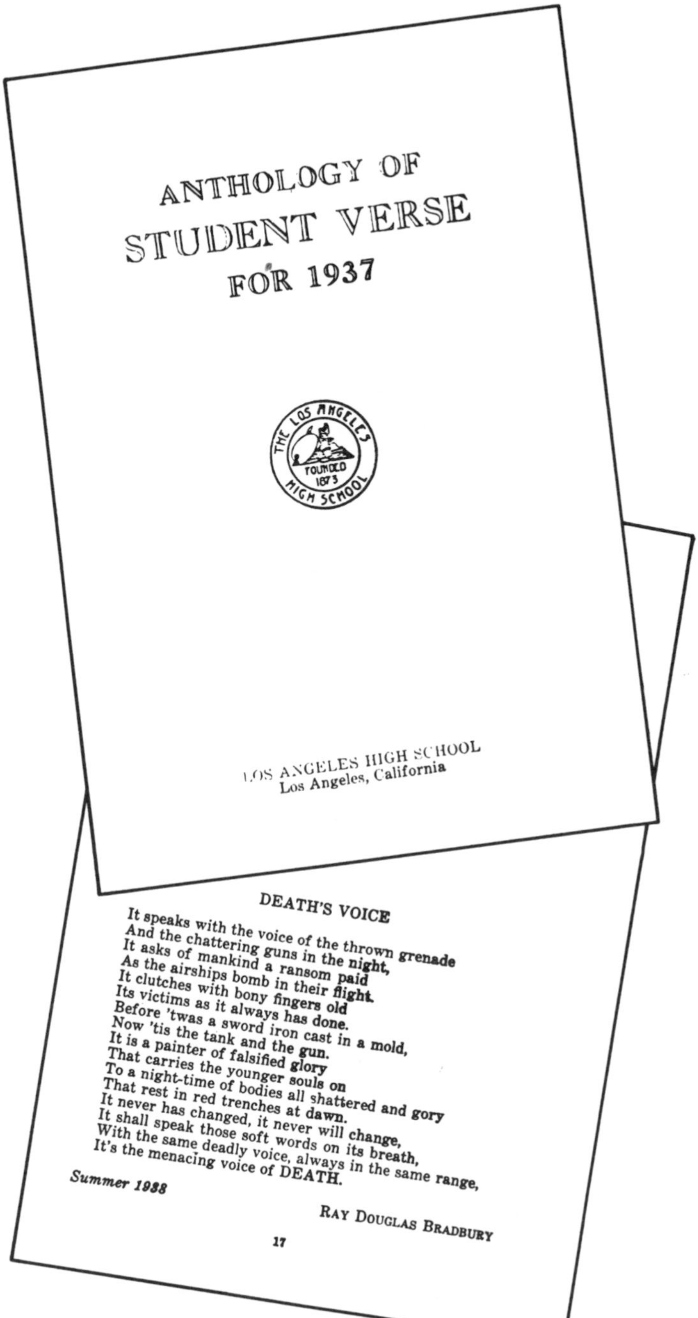

ANTHOLOGY OF
STUDENT VERSE
FOR 1937

THE LOS ANGELES HIGH SCHOOL
FOUNDED 1873

LOS ANGELES HIGH SCHOOL
Los Angeles, California

DEATH'S VOICE

It speaks with the voice of the thrown grenade
And the chattering guns in the night,
It asks of mankind a ransom paid
As the airships bomb in their flight.
It clutches with bony fingers old
Its victims as it always has done.
Before 'twas a sword iron cast in a mold,
Now 'tis the tank and the gun.
It is a painter of falsified glory
That carries the younger souls on
To a night-time of bodies all shattered and gory
That rest in red trenches at dawn.
It never has changed, it never will change,
It shall speak those soft words on its breath,
With the same deadly voice, always in the same range,
It's the menacing voice of DEATH.

Summer 1938

RAY DOUGLAS BRADBURY

17

Booklet cover and poem, 1937.
RB's first book appearance.

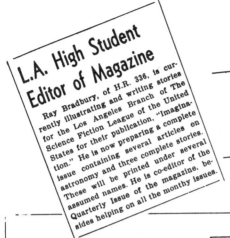

L.A. High Student Editor of Magazine

Ray Bradbury, of H.R. 336, is currently illustrating and writing stories for the Los Angeles Branch of The Science Fiction League of the United States for their publication, "Imagination." He is now preparing a complete issue containing several articles on astronomy and three complete stories. These will be printed under several assumed names. He is co-editor of the Quarterly Issue of the magazine, besides helping on all the monthy issues.

RAY DOUGLAS BRADBURY
L ikes to write stories
A dmired as a Thespian
H eaded for literary distinction.

BLUE AND WHITE DAILY

Los Angeles High School

Obedience To Law ~ Respect For Others — These · Constitute · Life — Mastery Of Self ~ Joy In Service

Vol. XLVII | Friday, March 18, 1938 | No. 22

APHORISMS . .

IN THE NEWS . . . After school dances, which have met with success, have finally been adopted as regular events, according to **Miss Grace Champion**, acting girl's vice-principal . . . The idea of more frequent dances was suggested by this paper on March 15 . . . Among the new personalities who have signed up for work in the student talent aud are: **Harold Haight, Bob Jackson, Shirley Van, Beverly Fest**, and **Camille Fuller**, as dancers . . . **Ed Knowlton, Bud Charlston, Alvin Peoless**, and **Dave Beebe** have been selected to sing . . . It is planned also to present a dramatic highlight written by **Ray Bradbury**, of the **L. A. Players** . . . Plans for a **Senior Ditch Day** have been suggested each year with no success . . . Student officials, as well as **Mr. Oliver**, wish that these plans be abandoned because it costs the school system 50 cents per pupil a day . . . Thus if 700 seniors ditch, the school loses $350, and if it should happen twice, once each semester, it would cost the tax-payers $700 a year.

Two Groups Request Return Showing of "1938 Roman Revue"

"Roman Revue of 1938" has had two requests for return engagements. Excerpts will be given for the Pico Boulevard Chamber of Commerce Wednesday, April 27, at Webster's. Radio KEHE has asked that the program be presented on a Friday night program in the near future. Due to station regulations the studio orchestra will be used to accompany the acts.

Numbers on the program Wednesday will include: Ray Bradbury, master of ceremonies; accordian solo, Tom Johnson; tap dance, Mickey Heeger; Ralph and Tommy, impersonators, who in real life are Tom Low and Ralph Schlain. Bill Hunter is the accompanist.

High school notices concerning Bradbury, including his yearbook photo entry.

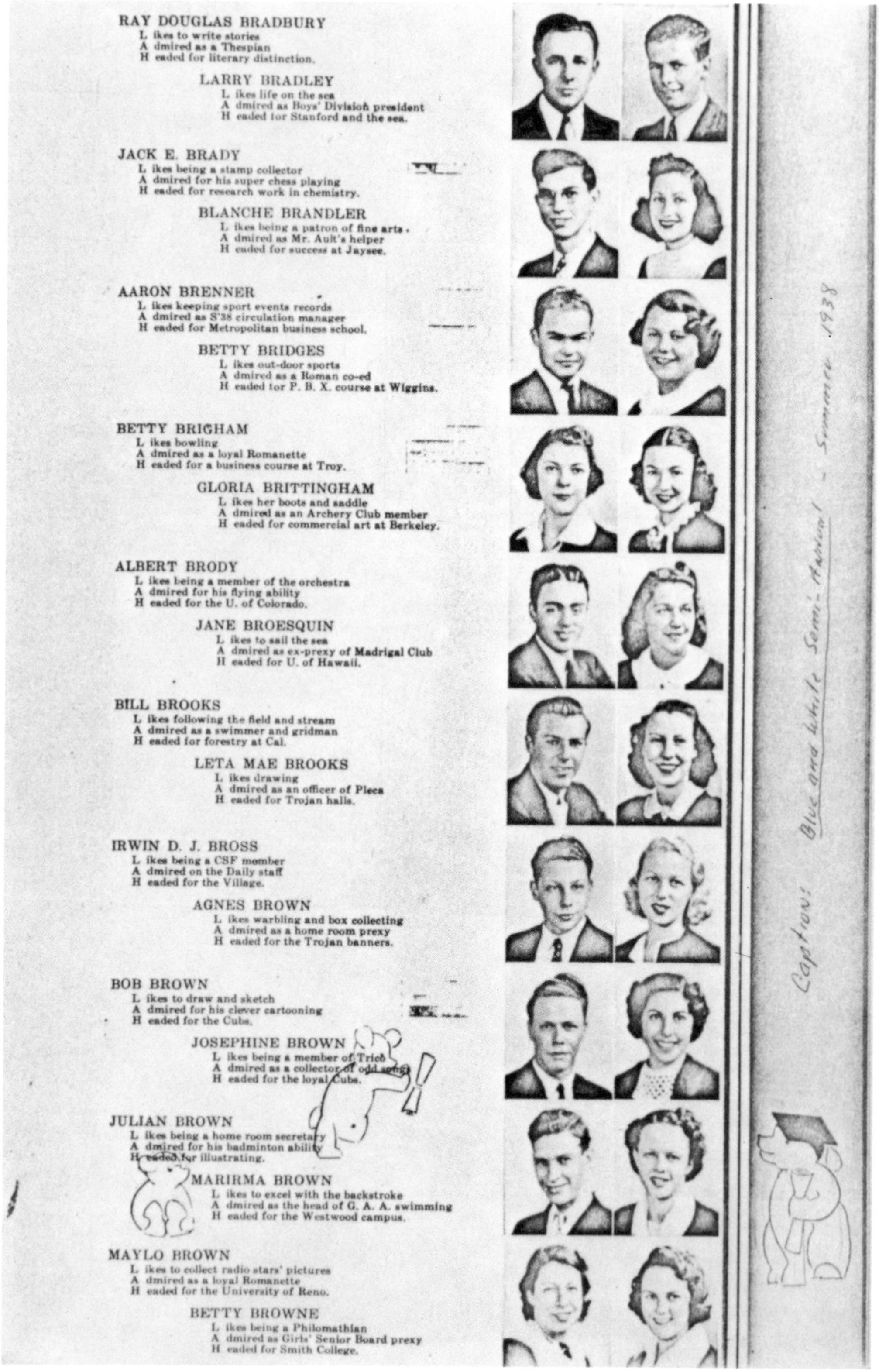

RAY DOUGLAS BRADBURY
L ikes to write stories
A dmired as a Thespian
H eaded for literary distinction.

LARRY BRADLEY
L ikes life on the sea
A dmired as Boys' Division president
H eaded for Stanford and the sea.

JACK E. BRADY
L ikes being a stamp collector
A dmired for his super chess playing
H eaded for research work in chemistry.

BLANCHE BRANDLER
L ikes being a patron of fine arts.
A dmired as Mr. Ault's helper
H eaded for success at Jaysee.

AARON BRENNER
L ikes keeping sport events records
A dmired as S'38 circulation manager
H eaded for Metropolitan business school.

BETTY BRIDGES
L ikes out-door sports
A dmired as a Roman co-ed
H eaded for P. B. X. course at Wiggins.

BETTY BRIGHAM
L ikes bowling
A dmired as a loyal Romanette
H eaded for a business course at Troy.

GLORIA BRITTINGHAM
L ikes her boots and saddle
A dmired as an Archery Club member
H eaded for commercial art at Berkeley.

ALBERT BRODY
L ikes being a member of the orchestra
A dmired for his flying ability
H eaded for the U. of Colorado.

JANE BROESQUIN
L ikes to sail the sea
A dmired as ex-prexy of Madrigal Club
H eaded for U. of Hawaii.

BILL BROOKS
L ikes following the field and stream
A dmired as a swimmer and gridman
H eaded for forestry at Cal.

LETA MAE BROOKS
L ikes drawing
A dmired as an officer of Plecs
H eaded for Trojan halls.

IRWIN D. J. BROSS
L ikes being a CSF member
A dmired on the Daily staff
H eaded for the Village.

AGNES BROWN
L ikes warbling and box collecting
A dmired as a home room prexy
H eaded for the Trojan banners.

BOB BROWN
L ikes to draw and sketch
A dmired for his clever cartooning
H eaded for the Cubs.

JOSEPHINE BROWN
L ikes being a member of Trico
A dmired as a collector of odd songs
H eaded for the loyal Cubs.

JULIAN BROWN
L ikes being a home room secretary
A dmired for his badminton ability
H eaded for illustrating.

MARIRMA BROWN
L ikes to excel with the backstroke
A dmired as the head of G. A. A. swimming
H eaded for the Westwood campus.

MAYLO BROWN
L ikes to collect radio stars' pictures
A dmired as a loyal Romanette
H eaded for the University of Reno.

BETTY BROWNE
L ikes being a Philomathian
A dmired as Girls' Senior Board prexy
H eaded for Smith College.

Caption: Blue and White Semi-Annual - Summer 1938

Blue and White Semi-Annual—Summer 1938

L. A. Players

Mildred Partridge
Lily Johnson

President: Mildred Partridge
Vice-president: Lily Johnson
Secretary: Clarence Sandstrom
Treasurer: Beatrice Davis
Reporter: Robert Johnson
Sponsor: Mrs. Lena Webb

The Drama Club originated with a drama class in 1920. In September, 1921, as the L. A. H. S. Players, this club was opened to the school; and a membership of 1200 was soon reached. A few years later, this club was again reorganized for drama class members only. Gradually, the organization acquired its present form with membership open to all students by tryouts.

At each meeting, plays are presented under student direction. After the performance, members give criticisms; thus they make dramatic education a large part of the club's activities. L. A. H. S. Players sponsor worthy drama in the school and offer opportunities for experience in writing, directing, and participating in dramatic endeavor.

Members: Touba Abrams, Allan Armer, Leah Babitz, Janice Beason, Roberta Bellows, Shirley Ann Blank, Ray Bradbury, June Breedlove, Daniel Brostoff, June Brown, Beverly Chudacoff, Ruth Cohen, Jack Cook, Beatrice Davis, Ethel Dean, Adela de Castro, Lorraine Dunseth, George Eros, Violet Farr, Gerry Fratt, Dyca Ann Frisby, Phyllis Graves, Benny Harris, Frank Holichek, Howard Holtzman, Ralph Hughes, Jean Humble, Marjorie Jarrott, Lily Marie Johnson, Robert Johnson, Betsy Jones, Morton Kroll, Winifred Leftwich, Ida May Marienthal, Roberta McAvoy, Bill McClellan, Marvel McGiboney, Bob Meyer, Kazume Murata, Robert Myers, Jarvis Ofner, Peggy Otes, Jim Parks, Mildred Partridge, Alvin Phillips, Joan Pollak, Muriel Rex, Winton Reynolds, Herbert Rousso, Clarence Sandstrom, Halie May Shearer, Marjorie Stapp, Jean Stern, Frances Stewart, Eleanor Tobin, Patricia Waterman, Jack Whitaker, Betty Mae White, Louise Wilds, Joe Wolf.

Left to right. Bottom row: Rex, Reynolds, Rousso, Shearer, Stapp, Stern, Stewart, Tobin, Waterman, Whitaker, White, Wilds, Wolf. Second row: Jones, Leftwich, Marienthal, McAvoy, Meyer, Murata, Myers, Ofner, Otes, Parks, Phillips, Pollak. Third row: Dunseth, Eros, Farr, Pratt, Frisby, Graves, Harris, Holichek, Holtzman, Hughes, Humble, Jarrott, Johnson. Top row: Abrams, Armer, Beason, Blank, Bradbury, Breedlove, Brosloff, Brown, Chudacoff, Cohen, Davis, Dean, de Castro.

L.A. Players—Summer 1938

Aspiration is to bring forth dramatic talent in students in Los Angeles High School.

Enjoys the privilege of writing, directing, and participation in dramatic endeavors.

Radiates dramatic talent, training, and poise.

Encourages worthy expression of drama and helpful criticism.

Officers:

President: Patricia Waterman
Vice-president: Touba Abrams
Secretary: June Breedlove
Treasurer: Mildred Partridge
Calendar Reporter: Jarvis Ofner
Sponsor: Mrs. Leno C. Webb

Members:

Touba Abrams, Leah Babitz, Ellen Baine, Roberta Bellons, Helen Berman, June Breedlove, Ray Bradbury, June Brown, Don Chapman, Ruth Cohen, Jack Cook, Marguerite Cook, Beatrice Davis, Ethel Dean, Adela de Castro, Lorraine Dunseth, Virginia Lee Ellis, George Eros, Violet Farr, Gerald Fratt, Ruth Friedman, Sandra Friedman, Dyca Ann Frisby, Barbara Gastil, Phyllis Graves, Alvin Greenwald, Frank Holichek, Howard Holtzman, Mary Horton, Carol Imus, Marjorie Jarrott, Lily Marie Johnson, Robert Johnson, Helen Lasarow, Meriam Lasarow, Winifred Leftwich, Morton Levine, Rosalyn Lifshitz, Ida May Marienthal, Roberta McAvoy, Del Morgan, Robert Myers, Jarvis Ofner, Mildred Partridge, Joan Pollak, Virginia Reed, Muriel Rex, Clarence Sandstrom, Joe Schechter, Ralph Schlain, Halie May Shearer, Mary Simpson, Jane Smithwick, Marjorie Stapp, Jean Stern, Frances Stewart, Wilma Taylor, Eleanor Tobin, Beulah Turner, Ann Underhill, Patricia Waterman, Betty Mae White, Louise Wilds, Julie Ann Wright.

L. A. PLAYERS

row: Abrams, Babitz, Berman, Breedlove, Bradbury, Brown, Cohen, Cook, Davis, Dean, de Castro.
ond row: Dunseth, Farr, Frisby, Graves, Holichek, Holtzman, Horton, Imus, Jarrott, V. Johnson, R. Johnson.
ird row: Lasarow, M. Lasarow, Leftwich, Marienthal, McAvoy, Myers, Ofner, Partridge, Pollak, Reed, Rex.
ttom row: Sandstrom, Shearer, Stapp, Stern, Stewart, Tobin, Turner, Waterman, White, Wilds, Wright.

Winter

L.A. Players—Winter 1938

1937

Discovers work of Thomas Wolfe (later paying debt to this author in short story, "Forever and the Earth").

In March achieves school publication with a poem, "Death's Voice," in pamphlet, *Anthology of Student Verse*, published at L.A. High.

Scripts the school's annual talent show, *The 1937 Roman Revue*, and when show is performed in June functions as assistant producer/director. Also plays lead in one-act drama that fall.

Saves lunch money to purchase first typewriter for $10.00 and, by September, is submitting humor and reviews to school paper, *Blue and White Daily*.

In early October discovers science fiction fandom; joins the Los Angeles Science Fiction League, and meets Forrest Ackerman, Henry Kuttner, and Ray Harryhausen.

Contributes humor item to club "fanzine," *Imagination!* Makes debut in November issue.

Best subjects in high school: short story, drama, and astronomy—yet fails English exam.

1938

In January his first short story, "Hollerbochen's Dilemma," is printed in *Imagination*! as he begins to contribute heavily to fan publications. Also functions as co-editor, cartoonist, and columnist for these amateur journals.

Is a leading member of school drama group, the L.A. Players—and is very active in Poetry Club. Acts in school pageant, *Progress of Youth*.

In March attends Jack Benny and Fred Allen radio shows, writing bylined reports on these for school paper.

Is a straight-A student during final semester at L.A. High.

In April serves as Master of Ceremonies for *1938 Roman Revue*.

Has poem, "Truck Driver After Midnight," selected for publication in *Morning Song*, city-wide anthology of best school verse, printed in May.

Graduates in June, wearing bullet-holed jacket of uncle slain in a holdup.

Begins selling newspapers immediately following high school graduation. Undecided between dreams of writing or acting.

Takes night course at L.A. High that summer in the short story—and is helped with his fiction by Henry Kuttner and other local authors. Is influenced by Dorothea Brande's book, *Becoming a Writer.*

1939

Now living with his family at 1841 S. Manhattan Place in Los Angeles.

Earning $10.00 per week as he peddles the *Los Angeles Daily News* at corner of Olympic and Norton.

In June launches his own mimeo fan magazine, *Futuria Fantasia.* Publishes, edits, and contributes fiction, columns, and verse to this publication which eventually runs to four issues.

Attends the first World Science Fiction Convention in New York over Fourth of July weekend. Meets Julius Schwartz. Sees New York World's Fair.

While in New York acts as agent for artist-friend Hannes Bok, selling Bok's work to editor of *Weird Tales.*

In August joins the Wilshire Players Guild, a drama group in Los Angeles led by actress Loraine Day. Writes his first play for this group, but it is not performed.

Absorbed by the work of Hemingway and Steinbeck.

Writes fan letters to professional science fiction and fantasy magazines—and is included in *Who's Who in Fandom.*

1940

Sees Disney's *Fantasia,* a film which influences his life.

Moves with family to 3054 1/2 W. 12th in downtown Los Angeles—and continues to sell papers from corner of 10th and Normandie.

His story, "The Piper," appears in final issue of *Futuria Fantasia.* Concerns man's plunder of Mars which is germination of his *Martian Chronicles.*

Maintains a work room in tenement at Figueroa and Temple which he uses as "office" between newspaper editions. Writes fiction there, befriending several Mexican-Americans who form basis for his stories "I See You Never" and "The Wonderful Ice Cream Suit."

Is aided in his fictional efforts by Robert Heinlein and wife Leslyn Heinlein. They help place his work in West Coast magazine, *Script,* but he receives no money from this publication.

Adapts L. Ron Hubbard's *Fear* as a one-hour radio play for amateur drama group.

1941

Attends a weekly writing class conducted by Heinlein. Meets Leigh Brackett.

Collaborates with professional writer Henry Hasse.

Frequents the apartment of writer Edmond Hamilton and agent Julius Schwartz, seeking help and advice. Also aided by pros Jack Williamson and Ross Rocklynne.

In July makes first story sale (for $27.50) with "Pendulum," a Hasse collaboration, to editor Alden Norton at *Super Science Stories.* Becomes a published professional on his twenty-first birthday, in August, when this story appears on local newsstands.

Abandons acting as career in favor of writing, and leaves Loraine Day drama group to devote full time to fiction.

Writes 52 short stories that year, sells three—and continues to peddle newspapers for income.

The Bradburys move to Venice, California, near the ocean, to 670 Venice Boulevard. Ray sets up workroom there.

1942

Spends each Sunday at Muscle Beach working with Leigh Brackett on "story sessions." Each week brings her new story to criticize.

With help of Henry Kuttner, sells "The Candle" to *Weird Tales,* beginning important relationship with this magazine.

Achieves a quality breakthrough at twenty-two, when he writes "The Lake" (though story does not appear in print for two years).

By end of year is no longer selling newspapers; is able to make a minimal living from his fiction sales.

Attends night class in ceramics at Belmont school in L.A.

1943

Eye trouble keeps him out of service during war years—but he contributes to the war effort by writing radio "spots" for the Red Cross and scripts for the L.A. Department of Civil Defense.

"The Wind," first "classic" Bradbury story, appears that March in *Weird Tales*—and his first quality science fiction story, "King of the Gray Spaces," is printed in the December issue of *Famous Fantastic Mysteries.*

Has now found his style, but his personalized type of science fiction is discouraged by editors seeking formula space fiction; only editorial encouragement comes from detective pulp editor Ryerson Johnson. As result, Bradbury tries writing for detective/suspense publications.

His first autobiographical sketch appears in *Weird Tales* as reader interest in his work increases.

1944

Makes detective pulp debut in mid-year; has fiction accepted by *New Detective, Detective Tales, Dime Mystery,* and *Flynn's Detective Fiction.*

Writes last half of "Lorelei of the Red Mist" for Leigh Brackett, his only novella-length "space opera."

Quality terror story, "The Jar," appears in *Weird Tales.*

Spends summer reading Jessamyn West, Sinclair Lewis, Sherwood Anderson, Eudora Welty, and Katherine Anne Porter. Note to himself, "Do book about people on Mars," results, six years later, in publication of *The Martian Chronicles.*

1945

In January makes first anthology sale—"The Lake" to August Derleth for *Who Knocks*? Derleth also proposes collection of Bradbury stories for publication by Arkham House.

Sells "The Big Black and White Game" to *American Mercury,* and it is selected for *Best American Short Stories.*

Several sales to slick-paper magazines (including "Invisible Boy" to *Mademoiselle*) finance trip to Mexico. Leaves by auto with artist-friend Grant Beach to collect masks for the Los Angeles County Museum. Two-month trip, into late November, provides major fiction material (best exemplified by "The Next in Line").

Receives "fan" letter from New York editor Don Congdon, who asks to see some fiction for possible book publication.

1946

At Fowler's Bookshop, in downtown Los Angeles, meets Marguerite Susan McClure, a U.C.L.A. graduate, working there as a clerk.

On dates at the beach Marguerite ("Maggie") reads poetry aloud to Ray, which forms basis for several stories, including "And the Moon Be Still as Bright" and "There Will Come Soft Rains."

First story in *Martian Chronicles* series, "The Million Year Picnic" is printed in *Planet Stories.*

First radio adaptation of his work is broadcast on *Molle Mystery Theater.*

That September, in New York to meet editors, contacts Don Congdon who plans on becoming an agent and who will represent Bradbury within a year.

Two more quality short stories printed: "Homecoming" and "Small Assassin."

1947

In January his radio drama, "The Meadow," is presented on *World Security Workshop*—and is selected for *Best One-Act Plays of 1947-1948.*

Begins selling material to *Suspense,* CBS radio.

Appears in *Harper's* with "The Man Upstairs."

Writes "Bright Phoenix," the germinal idea he later develops into "The Fireman" and *Fahrenheit 451.*

At twenty-seven marries Marguerite McClure at the Church of the Good Shepherd, Episcopal, on September 27, with Ray Harryhausen as best man. Day before wedding burns a million words of his "bad writing." Sells "I See You Never" to *New Yorker* same week in late September.

Don Congdon joins Harold Matson Company as literary agent, and Bradbury becomes client; Congdon to handle all but pulp sales.

Moves with Maggie to 33 S. Venice Boulevard.

First book, *Dark Carnival,* published by Arkham House in October.

"Homecoming" selected for O. Henry Awards *Prize Stories of 1947.*

1948

Now living on $250 a month: Ray earns half this sum by writing; Maggie works at Hertz to earn the other half.

Business relationship with Julius Schwartz ends in January as Congdon assumes full duties as agent.

Bradbury interviewed by writer R. Walton Williams for *Writers Markets and Methods.*

Completes first book introduction—to Theodore Sturgeon's *Without Sorcery.*

Wins O. Henry Award for "Powerhouse"—named one of three best short stories printed in 1948.

"I See You Never" in *Best American Short Stories 1948,* Bradbury's second appearance in this series.

"Mars is Heaven!" printed in *Planet Stories.*

Dark Carnival released by Hamish Hamilton as Bradbury's first book in England.

"The Million Year Picnic" anthologized by Derleth in *Strange Ports of Call,* Ray's first science fiction story to appear in book format.

Bradbury becomes pivotal member of local writers' group which meets every two weeks to read aloud from works in progress.*

1949

To New York in June, where he meets Doubleday editor Walter Bradbury (no relation) who asks him for book with a "unified theme." Within twenty-four hours Ray is back with outline for *The Martian Chronicles.*

First full profile on him is printed in *Fantasy Review* in England.

Work begins to appear in annual series, *Best Science Fiction Stories,* and his reputation as a quality sf writer begins to equal his reputation for "Weird" fiction.

Martha Foley, August Derleth, Norman Corwin, and Mark Schorer recommend him for Guggenheim Fellowship—which is not granted.

First checklist of his writing is printed in *Fanscient* (an amateur publication), covering his work for nine years.

On November 5 Bradbury's first daughter born: Susan Marguerite.

Week later, to teach her "not to fear the dark," he writes first book for children, *Switch on the Night.*

Selected by the National Fantasy Fan Federation as "best author of 1949" in sf/fantasy field.

*This group was still functioning in 1973.

1950

The Martian Chronicles published by Doubleday in May. To San Francisco to receive "Invisible Little Man Award" from Berkeley sf group, hosted by Anthony Boucher.

Begins to lecture at colleges.

In August he moves family to new home: 10750 Clarkson Road in West Los Angeles.

Radio's *Dimension X* broadcasts several of his stories, as does *Escape.*

"The Veldt" appears that September in *Saturday Evening Post* as "The World the Children Made" and major Bradbury stories are printed in *Collier's, McCall's* and *Esquire.* Has left the pulps; no longer will he write for secondary markets.

In October Bradbury receives first important critical attention in *Tomorrow,* with rave review of *Chronicles* by Christopher Isherwood.

1951

Novella, "The Fireman," appears in *Galaxy.* He will later expand this 25,000-word novella to 50,000-word novel, *Fahrenheit 451.*

Doubleday publishes *The Illustrated Man* in February.

Receives first TV exposure with "Zero Hour" and "Marionettes, Inc." on *Tales of Tomorrow* (ABC).

The Martian Chronicles published in England as *The Silver Locusts* by Rupert Hart-Davis, who becomes Bradbury's primary British publisher.

Second daughter, Ramona Anne Bradbury, born May 17.

In June his first paperback edition appears on newsstands. And, same month, first profile of Bradbury appears in the *Reporter.* Two months later this magazine prints "The Pedestrian."

Receives major coverage in *New York Times Book Review* in August when interviewed by Harvey Breit. First major non-fiction piece appears that month in *Charm*, "The Season of Sitting."

1952

Pamphlet/magazine, *Ray Bradbury Review*, edited by William F. Nolan, published in January, covering first decade as writer and with full index of work through 1951.

Meets Joseph Mugnaini in April, discovering his artwork in a local gallery; writes Doubleday regarding Mugnaini as illustrator for future books.

In June is Guest of Honor at the "Westercon" (Southwest Science Fiction Convention) in San Diego, where he is elected president *pro tem* of newly-formed Science Fiction and Fantasy Writers of America.

Again represented in *Best American Short Stories* with "The Other Foot."

Director John Huston writes him regarding possible film version of *Chronicles*, but project does not materialize.

In September accepts scripting job at Universal Studios. Writes 110-page film treatment, "The Meteor," which is filmed as first 3-D sf picture under title "It Came From Outer Space."

Edits *Timeless Stories For Today and Tomorrow*, collection of fantasy tales, for Bantam.

Works on unproduced screen treatment for 20th Century-Fox—and joins Writers Guild of America.

As follow-up to presidential election, publishes angry open letter "To the Republican Party" in November 10 *Daily Variety*.

Has his speech, "No Man is an Island," printed in pamphlet form.

In December his first illustrated comic book adaptation, "The Coffin," appears on newsstands.

1953

In March Bradbury's first book of "mixed" fiction

(realistic as well as fantastic) published by Doubleday, *The Golden Apples of the Sun,* with Mugnaini illustrations.

Writes major critical piece on science fiction for May issue of *Nation.*

In England his work is praised by J. B. Priestley, Angus Wilson, and Arthur C. Clarke.

John Huston contacts him in August with offer to script *Moby Dick;* Bradbury accepts assignment and leaves for Ireland in September, with wife and daughters, aboard *S.S. United States.*

First novel, the expanded version of "The Fireman," is published by Ballantine that October as *Fahrenheit 451.*

In Ireland, working with Huston on *Moby Dick,* turns out 1500 pages of script over a six month period (into April of 1954).

1954

Wins Annual Gold Medal from Commonwealth Club of California for *Fahrenheit 451.*

Wins Benjamin Franklin Magazine Award for "Best Short Story in an American Magazine During 1953" for "Sun and Shadow."

Wins "The National Institute Award in Literature" from National Institute of Arts and Letters.

Long association with *Playboy* begins as this magazine serializes *Fahrenheit 451* in three issues.

Finishes the final pages of *Moby Dick* in London, in mid-April, and meets Bertrand Russell.

Embarks on European sightseeing trip with family: Sicily, Paris, Florence, Milan, Rome, and Venice. Meets Bernard Berenson in Italy.

First quality verse, "Death in Mexico," printed in *California Quarterly.*

In September, at the World Science Fiction Convention in San Francisco, Anthony Boucher narrates special operatic adaptation of Bradbury's "A Scent of Sarsaparilla."

1955

Children's book, *Switch on the Night,* published by Pantheon in March.

Writes autobiographical sketch for *Twentieth Century Authors,* and reports has had work "in sixty anthologies."

Radio's *X-Minus One* presents several Bradbury adaptations.

Writes his first produced teleplay (for the Alfred Hitchcock show).

Creates TV series, based on *Chronicles,* titled *Report From Space*—optioned but never produced.

"Shopping For Death" is printed in *Best Detective Stories of the Year.*

Work appears for the first time in a textbook—"There Will Come Soft Rains" in *The Informal Reader.*

Third daughter, Bettina Francion Bradbury, born on July 22.

Works with Charles Laughton and producer Paul Gregory on projected Broadway play version of *Fahrenheit 451.* Not produced.

Ballantine releases *The October Country* in November.

1956

In January Bradbury's first Hitchcock TV play is aired: "Shopping For Death."

In February narrates on-the-air introduction to *CBS Radio Workshop* presentation of "Hail and Farewell" and "Season of Disbelief."

In March *Playboy* prints Irish story/article, "The First Night of Lent."

Wins Boys Club of America Book Award for *Switch on the Night.*

Writes science fiction operetta for Elsa Lanchester, *Happy Anniversary: 2116 A.D.*

In June, Huston-directed *Moby Dick* is released across country.

Bradbury has first of several essays on creativity printed in the *Writer.*

Edits second book for Bantam, *The Circus of Dr. Lao and Other Improbable Stories.* Published in October.

1957

"Discovers" Disneyland, with Charles Laughton, in April—beginning Disney relationship.

In May, elected board member of Writers Guild of America West, for two-year term.

Spends summer months in London, scripting *And the Rock Cried Out* as full screenplay for director Carol Reed. Not produced.

In September *Dandelion Wine* published by Doubleday. Based on his Illinois childhood.

That fall first college interview with him is printed (in U.C.L.A.'s *Westwind*). Bradbury's on-campus popularity now established.

Father dies, at sixty-six, in Los Angeles, on October 20.

Works for producer David Susskind on three-act musical, *Rocket Summer.* Never staged.

1958

Again represented in *Best American Short Stories,* with "The Day It Rained Forever."

Works at Hecht-Hill-Lancaster on unproduced screenplay of *The Dreamers.*

Martian Chronicles issued on LP records for the blind, and Doubleday prints a new edition of this book with preface by Clifton Fadiman.

Fourth daughter, Alexandra Allison Bradbury, born on August 13.

In October "The Magic White Suit" appears in *Saturday Evening Post.*

On Thanksgiving day Bradbury moves family into new home at 10265 Cheviot Drive in the Cheviot Hills area of West Los Angeles. Sets up workroom in his cellar.

1959

Writes first of three introductions to works of Jules Verne.

In February Doubleday publishes *A Medicine for Melancholy.* Book published in England by Rupert Hart-David as *The Day It Rained Forever,* containing work not collected in U.S. edition.

"A Wild Night in Galway" printed in *Harper's.*

"Pillar of Fire" selected for *A Treasury of Great Science Fiction.*

1960

First travel piece, on Paris, printed in *Mademoiselle.*

Takes night class at U.C.L.A. in Renaissance history.

Represented (with "The Veldt") in *Britannica Library of Great American Writing.*

First professionally-staged play, *The Meadow,* presented at Huntington Hartford Theatre, Hollywood, in March.

In April *Life* sends him on research trip to interview space experts.

Works on unproduced screenplay of *Martian Chronicles* at M.G.M. for producer Julian Blaustein.

In October his first *Life* article is printed, "A Serious Search for Weird Worlds," and this piece later selected for *Year's Best SF.*

1961

In January wins suit against CBS for *Playhouse 90* TV plagerism of *Fahrenheit 451.*

Is co-founder, with *Saturday Review* critic Arthur Knight, of Writers Guild Film Society.

"The Beggar on the Dublin Bridge" printed by *Saturday Evening Post.*

M.G.M.'s *King of Kings* released, with uncredited narration written by Bradbury.

In September writes first book review (of *Music of the Spheres*) for *Los Angeles Times.*

1962

In February has original teleplay, "The Jail," produced by Alcoa for ABC.

Learns that in Russia he is top-ranked in popularity with Faulkner, Steinbeck, and Hemingway.

Lively Arts releases commercial LP, *Burgess Meredith Reads Ray Bradbury.*

Pamphlet of three Bradbury letters printed by San Antonio Public Library as *The Essence of Creative Writing.*

Icarus Montgolfier Wright, featuring artwork of Joe Mugnaini, released by Format Films.

In September *Life* prints his space essay, "Cry the Cosmos."

Fantasy novel, *Something Wicked This Way Comes,* published in September by Simon and Schuster.

In October *R is For Rocket* published by Doubleday—Bradbury's first collection aimed specifically at young adults.

1963

In April lectures at Royce Hall, U.C.L.A., with Aldous Huxley at conference on cultural arts.

Named "interior design consultant" for the U.S. Government Pavilion at upcoming World's Fair.

Lectures on creativity at California Institute of Technology.

Wins Academy Award Nomination from Motion Picture Academy of Arts and Sciences for *Icarus Montgolfier Wright.*

"The Jail" wins nomination as "Best-Written Script of 1962 in TV Anthology Drama" from Writers Guild of America.

"Bradbury Issue" of *The Magazine of Fantasy and Science Fiction* printed in May—featuring profile and index of work through 1962.

Time/Life publishes special expanded edition of *Martian Chronicles* as part of Reading Program Book Series.

In June three Bradbury plays staged at Desilu Studios as he works, for the first time, with director Charles Rome Smith.

Becomes involved in problems of city's rapid transit system at public hearings in downtown Los Angeles.

Interviewed as part of *Playboy* panel discussion: "1984 and Beyond."

Selected as subject of filmed NBC television special, *The Story of a Writer.*

First book of plays, *The Anthem Sprinters,* published by Dial Press in November.

Works on *Nemo,* a TV drama based on the Verne character. Not produced.

Wins Golden Eagle Film Award from CINE (Council on International Nontheatrical Events) for his film, *Icarus Montgolfier Wright.*

1964

Works on unproduced screenplay of *Martian Chronicles* for Robert Mulligan and Alan Pakula.

Elected chairman of citizens group for rapid transit.

Simon and Schuster publishes his *Machineries of Joy* in February.

In April his *American Journey* opens at New York World's Fair. This film history of the nation is principal attraction at U.S. Government Pavilion.

Makes sentimental return visit to home town of Waukegan with two of his daughters.

October issue of *Playboy* prints "Heavy-Set," fictionalized portrait of his brother. Story achieves runner-up position for the magazine's best fiction award of 1964.

Becomes his own producer that October as *The World of Ray Bradbury* opens at the Coronet Theatre in Los Angeles, with Charles Rome Smith directing.

In December a major interview with Bradbury is presented in *Show.*

1965

In January his fictional tribute to Hemingway, "The Kilimanjaro Machine," appears in *Life.*

In February, directly following successful run of *World of Ray Bradbury,* his dramatic musical, *The Wonderful Ice Cream Suit,* opens at the Coronet.

"The Other Foot" selected for *Fifty Best American Short Stories: 1915–1965.*

Vintage publishes roundup volume of his "best" short fiction in September as *The Vintage Bradbury* with introduction by Gilbert Highet.

Trains to New York, where *World of Ray Bradbury* opens for brief off-Broadway run at the Orpheum.

In October first all-illustrated collection of stories published by Ballantine, *The Autumn People.*

1966

In January Doubleday reprints double-volume of Bradbury as *Twice 22.*

Special section in textbook, *On Writing By Writers,* devoted to Bradbury, with five of his pieces printed, fiction and nonfiction.

Samuel French issues two plays in separate pamphlet editions, *The Pedestrian* and *The Day It Rained Forever.*

Director Francois Truffaut's version of *Fahrenheit 451* released as a major film.

In June second comic book collection from Ballantine is published as *Tomorrow Midnight.*

Doubleday issues second sf collection aimed at young adults in August, *S is For Space.*

Bradbury attends "Vic n' Sadists" informal radio meet in September with Norman Corwin, Stan Freberg, and William Idelson (who played Rush Gook on *Vic and Sade*).

Bradbury introduction to *Fahrenheit 451* published as part of new hardcover edition from Simon and Schuster.

Mother dies, at seventy-eight, in Los Angeles on November 12.

1967

In January, on assignment from *Life,* spends a week with astronauts at Manned Space Center in Houston, Texas.

"The Lost City of Mars" appears in *Playboy.*

Beginning in February, a major two-part interview with RB is printed in *Writer's Digest.*

Student M.A. thesis written on his life and career by Joseph Dauben of Harvard.

To New York in April, where *Dandelion Wine* staged as musical drama at Lincoln Center.

In October Irish play, *The Anthem Sprinters,* staged at Beverly Hills Playhouse.

In November *Life* prints Bradbury space article, "An Impatient Gulliver Above Our Roofs."

1968

Wins Aviation-Space Writers Association Robert Ball Memorial Award for "Gulliver" piece; acceptance speech printed in *Life.*

Works with cartoonist Chuck Jones at M.G.M. on animated history of Halloween. Not produced.

Radio play, *Leviathan '99,* broadcast over BBC in London in May.

In June becomes president of Chamber Symphony Society of California.

First "all fantasy and sf" checklist of work appears in *3 to the Highest Power.*

In August his play, *Any Friend of Nicholas Nickleby's Is a Friend of Mine,* staged at Actors Studio West.

His final essay for *Life,* on trains, appears in August.

College English prints study of *Fahrenheit 451* in September, reflecting growth of academic interest in his work.

Leaves ground for first time as he flies in Goodyear blimp along California coast, "herding whales."

1969

The Illustrated Man released as major film.

Spends summer in London, and is interviewed for *Sight and Sound.*

In July, when U.S. moon landing made, goes on British TV to discuss "man's first step into immortality."

Writes nostalgic introduction to *The Collected Works of Buck Rogers in the 25th Century.*

In October *I Sing the Body Electric*! published by Knopf.

Lectures at U.C.L.A.'s Royce Hall on "Creativity in the Space Age."

Serves on Documentary Awards Committee for the Motion Picture Academy of Arts and Sciences.

In November eldest daughter, Susan, marries at twenty.

In December Bradbury cantata, *Christus Apollo,* performed at Royce Hall, U.C.L.A., with Charlton Heston as narrator.

1970

In April, for *West,* he proposes plan for beautifying city of Los Angeles.

In July works at Disney "robot factory" in Glendale on projected exhibit for Disney World.

"Mars is Heaven!" selected for *Science Fiction Hall of Fame.*

Aids student Richard Dimeo who writes dissertation at University of Utah.

Has eight stories adapted into "narrative songs" and released by Tower on commercial LP, *Songs For a Sideshow of the Mind.*

1971

Involved with First Congress of American Writers (held in New York in April).

First book about him is published, Jose Luis Garci's *Ray Bradbury, Humanista Del Futuro.*

Apollo 15 rocket crew names section of moon "Dandelion Crater" in honor of Bradbury's work.

In November takes part in panel discussion with Arthur C. Clarke and others on "Mars and the Mind of Man" at California Institute of Technology, Pasadena.

1972

West runs portion of projected comic-strip based on *Martian Chronicles.*

Musical stage version of *Dandelion Wine* presented at California State College, Fullerton, where seminar on Bradbury's work is taught. For a semester he is writer-in-residence at Cal State.

Writes lyrics to Lalo Schifrin's music in *Madrigals For the Space Age,* released by Associated Music Publishers.

In April Bantam publishes *The Wonderful Ice Cream Suit and Other Plays.*

In September he speaks as member of Committee For the Future, urging private space probe by 1976.

Feature film, *Picasso Summer,* based on RB short story, released to television.

Book for children, *The Halloween Tree,* published in October by Knopf.

Stages *Leviathan '99* in November at Goldwyn Studios.

Plea for extension of space effort, "From Stonehenge to Tranquillity Base," printed in *Playboy*—to enthusiastic reader response.

1973

Lectures to 700 English teachers at Colorado Springs.

In February *Madrigals For the Space Age* performed at Dorothy Chandler Pavilion at L.A. Music Center.

At work with composer Leonard Rosenman on opera based on Bradbury's "Lost City of Mars."

Adapts his story, "Pillar of Fire," into full-length play—staged at California State College, Fullerton, in December.

Completes first book of collected verse for Knopf, *When Elephants Last in the Dooryard Bloomed*—closing full creative circle in his life, extending back to 1936 when his first poem was printed.

NOTE: In 1974 the Writers Guild of America, West, presented Bradbury with the Valentine Davies Award, for "contributions to the motion picture community which have brought dignity and honor to writers everywhere."

FACSIMILES FROM RAY BRADBURY'S UNPUBLISHED AND UNCOLLECTED WORK

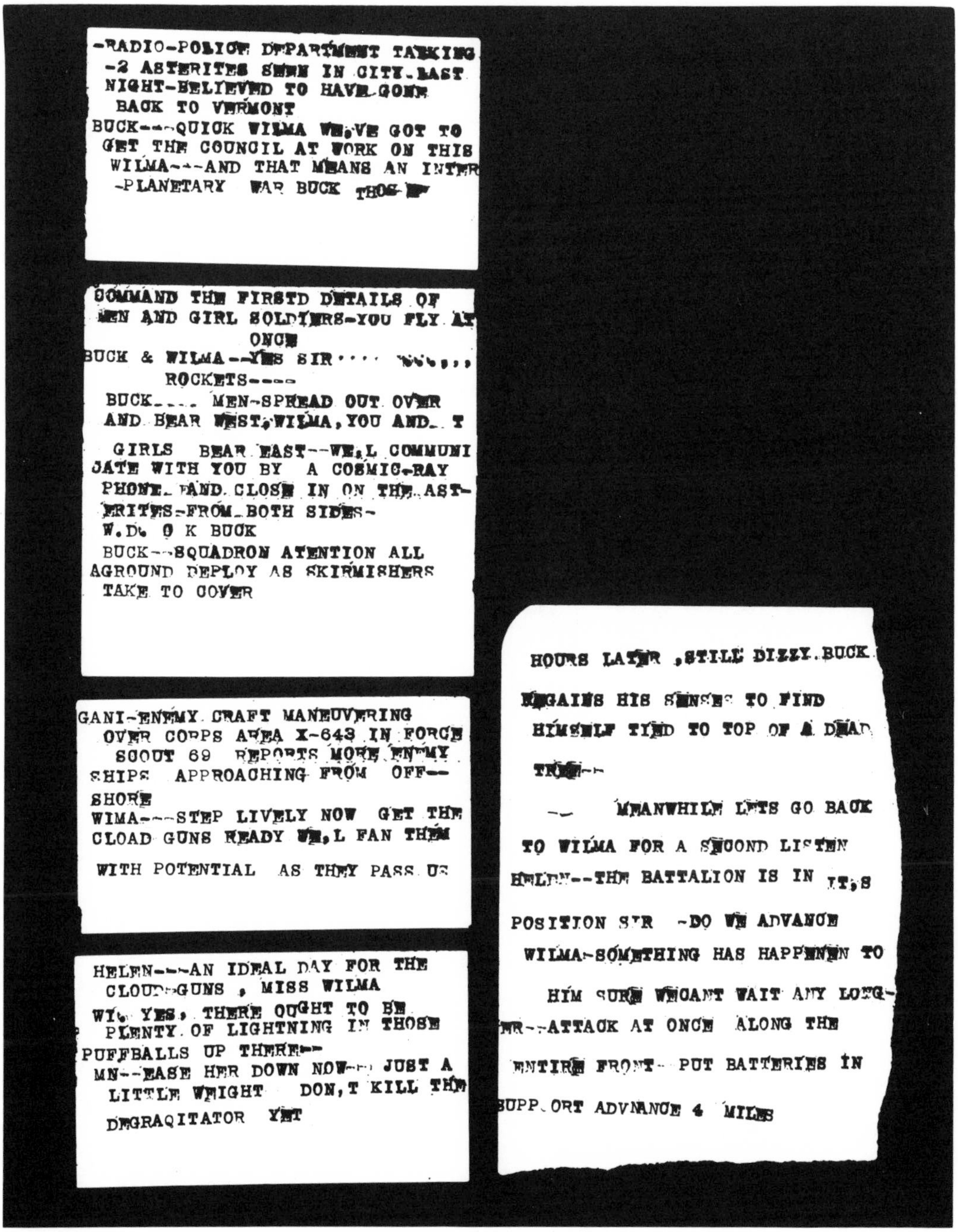

-RADIO-POLICE DEPARTMENT TALKING
-2 ASTERITES SEEN IN CITY LAST
NIGHT-BELIEVED TO HAVE GONE
BACK TO VERMONT
BUCK---QUICK WILMA WE,VE GOT TO
GET THE COUNCIL AT WORK ON THIS
WILMA---AND THAT MEANS AN INTER
-PLANETARY WAR BUCK THOUGHT

COMMAND THE FIRSTD DETAILS OF
MEN AND GIRL SOLDIERS-YOU FLY AT
ONCE
BUCK & WILMA--YES SIR
ROCKETS----
BUCK.... MEN-SPREAD OUT OVER
AND BEAR WEST,WILMA,YOU AND T
GIRLS BEAR EAST--WE,L COMMUNI
CATE WITH YOU BY A COSMIC-RAY
PHONE. AND CLOSE IN ON THE AST-
ERITES-FROM BOTH SIDES-
W.D. O K BUCK
BUCK--SQUADRON ATENTION ALL
AGROUND DEPLOY AS SKIRMISHERS
TAKE TO COVER

GANI-ENEMY CRAFT MANEUVERING
OVER CORPS AREA X-643 IN FORCE
SCOUT 69 REPORTS MORE ENEMY
SHIPS APPROACHING FROM OFF--
SHORE
WIMA---STEP LIVELY NOW GET THE
CLOAD GUNS READY WE,L FAN THEM
WITH POTENTIAL AS THEY PASS US

HELEN---AN IDEAL DAY FOR THE
CLOUD-GUNS , MISS WILMA
WI. YES, THERE OUGHT TO BE
PLENTY OF LIGHTNING IN THOSE
PUFFBALLS UP THERE--
MN--EASE HER DOWN NOW-- JUST A
LITTLE WEIGHT DON,T KILL THE
DEGRAQITATOR YET

HOURS LATER ,STILL DIZZY BUCK
REGAINS HIS SENSES TO FIND
HIMSELF TIED TO TOP OF A DEAD
TREE--
-- MEANWHILE LETS GO BACK
TO WILMA FOR A SECOND LISTEN
HELEN--THE BATTALION IS IN IT,S
POSITION SIR -DO WE ADVANCE
WILMA-SOMETHING HAS HAPPENEN TO
HIM SURE WE CANT WAIT ANY LONG-
ER--ATTACK AT ONCE ALONG THE
ENTIRE FRONT- PUT BATTERIES IN
SUPP. ORT ADVNANCE 4 MILES

Fragments of a "Buck Rogers" story written by RB, age 12, on a toy-dial typewriter, 1932.

"CASTLE DEEP"

JULY—1938

Moving through a deep and verdant forest that lay centuries thick in dust and leaves, three strangers of singular appearance came. Clasped at their waists hung broadswords, about their bodies clung coverings of tight doe skin. They wore jackets of lupine fur, grey and velvety to the touch, and upon their feet were boots of thickest bear skin. They swaggered along the invisible trail in the best of alcoholic spirits, staggering, weaving, and falling hither and yon in the thick of the twigs and leaves.

The first man, tall and lean with years of vagabondry, chuckled as he finished some vile joke, and the second stranger bellowed and fell back in the dust and writhed with laughter, holding his sides and raising a flurry of echoes in the wood.

The third figure, less enebriated than his comrades, a bulging individual of great corpulence, stamped about angrily, pleading with his associates.

"Lords!" he stormed as he shook first one then the other of the two in his fat hands. ""We must hurry from the WOOD! It draws night the setting of the sun! We must not stay longer in this place! Hear me, Lords!" He glanced about with apprehension at the confining closeness of the trees where mottled shadows were collecting.

"My little Ord," laughed the first man loudly, "you worry over fanciful tales! There is nothing wrong with sleeping in a forest at night. If it grows to dark for travel we'll make our bed beneath the leafs!"

"Nay, Lord Naro," gurgled Ord with a terrored look spread across his face. "We may not linger if we value our lives! Did you not hear the story told at the Inn?"

The third man joined the conversation as he heaving laughter subsided. "Ho--you're afraid of this Aratye, are you? The legend of the walking dead in Aratye's castle! Ho!" He burst into another gale of chuckling. "I would snap her bony frame with one finger if she haunted me!"

"You laugh, Titan," spat Ord viciously, "but wait until you see her! It is more than legend, in this, our fifteenth century, that somewhere deep in these woods stands a structure of ill-repute in which she practised her necromancy on unfortunate travellers in life, tortured them on racks, threw their bodies to unreal beasts that she had spawned from the lower regions, and now, in death, she walks again at dusk!" And Ord trembled at the thought.

Naro wrinkled his brows in contemplation of the little Ord, half smiling, half frowning.

"Where is this--this dwelling of Aratye, Ord?" he asked.

Ord pointed ahead. "Lord Naro, perhaps it lies ahead, perhaps behind us. I can only pray we finish with this woodland before dusk!"

The sun was an hour above the horizon and already the forest was shadowed deep and eerie. Nightbirds were stirring tentatively in the trees above. As the trio moved the growths underfoot crackled brittely.

"This--all this," whispered Ord, taking in the whole of the forest with his hands, "is centuries old. Not more than a score of

Original manuscript page from unpublished short story written by RB when he was 17 in July of 1938.

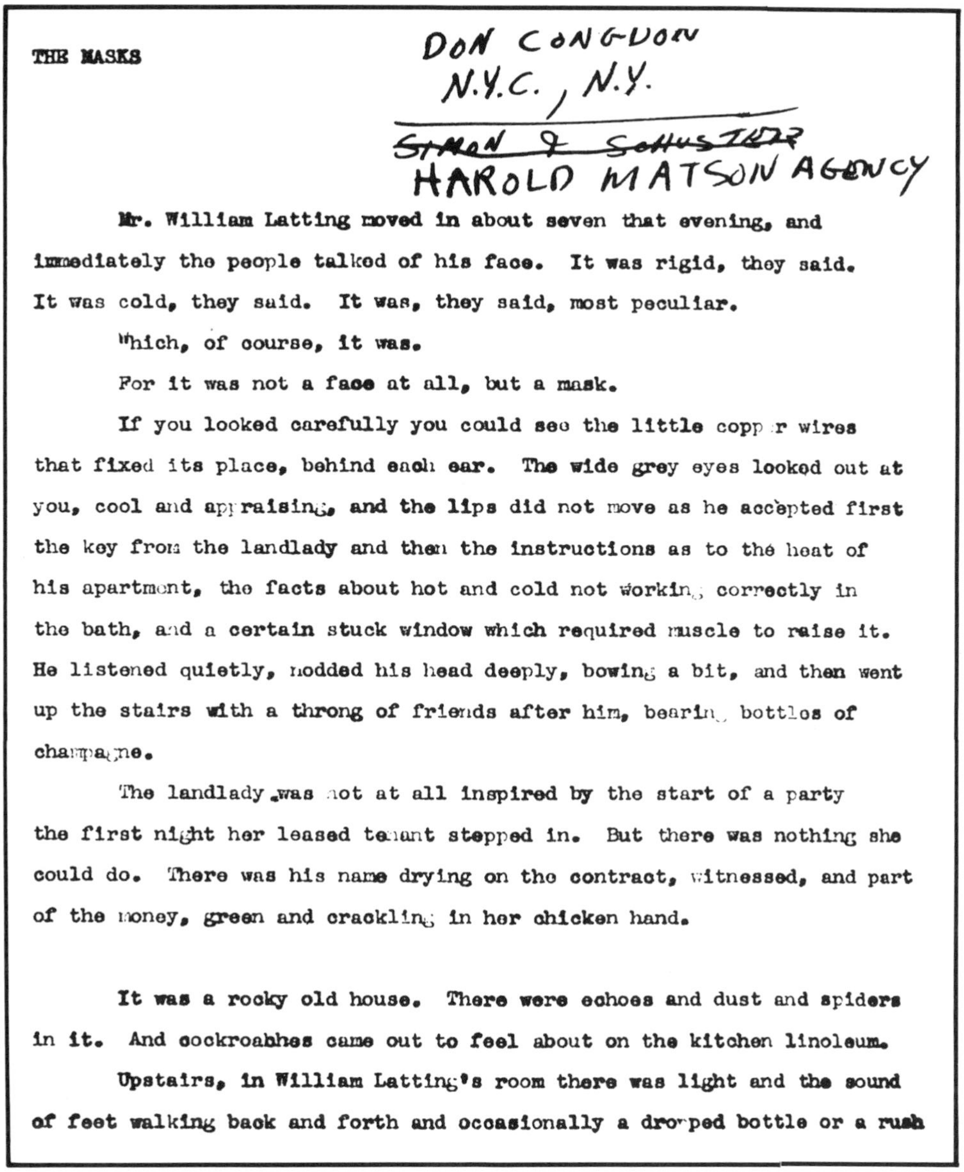

THE MASKS

DON CONGDON
N.Y.C., N.Y.

~~SIMON & SCHUSTER~~
HAROLD MATSON AGENCY

Mr. William Latting moved in about seven that evening, and immediately the people talked of his face. It was rigid, they said. It was cold, they said. It was, they said, most peculiar.

Which, of course, it was.

For it was not a face at all, but a mask.

If you looked carefully you could see the little copp r wires that fixed its place, behind each ear. The wide grey eyes looked out at you, cool and appraising, and the lips did not move as he accepted first the key from the landlady and then the instructions as to the heat of his apartment, the facts about hot and cold not working correctly in the bath, and a certain stuck window which required muscle to raise it. He listened quietly, nodded his head deeply, bowing a bit, and then went up the stairs with a throng of friends after him, bearing bottles of champagne.

The landlady was not at all inspired by the start of a party the first night her leased tenant stepped in. But there was nothing she could do. There was his name drying on the contract, witnessed, and part of the money, green and crackling in her chicken hand.

It was a rocky old house. There were echoes and dust and spiders in it. And cockroabhes came out to feel about on the kitchen linoleum.

Upstairs, in William Latting's room there was light and the sound of feet walking back and forth and occasionally a dropped bottle or a rush

Original manuscript page from an unfinished novel, circa the 1940s.

Saturday, October 16th, 1942

Grant and I to hoffman's - playing Gliere Number Three as background to my OCTOBER. . . Russian movies at night at grand...BATTLE OF SIBERIA, THE GOLDEN KEY (Russian Pinocchio). Downtown for a malt later..calling auntie neva from Bowling Alley..out to sleep at her place for the night..

Sunday, the Seventeenth of October:

Linda, Ray, Grant and I to Mount Wilson observatory. . .having lunch there at Inn..Cadlillac 1942, red upholstery...Neva up at Charlten Flat with Bill Down, but couldn't find her.. wonderful clear warm weather with tops of car down.. home at five thirty...Neva and Grant and I eating tomato soup, walking to Linda's to retrieve Hashie, and then along sunset to have malts, looking at ourselves in mirror behind the counter and laughing hysterically...sitting down in middle of sidewalk with Hashie...telling about time Neva chased a rat into oven where it cooked for a month. . , and Jean urphing when she heard about it.
Into bed at twelve. Out to Venice Monday morning with Neva.

SHOSTAKOVICH'S seventh symphony on radio
worked that morning on lynching story

Manuscript diary notes, unpublished, written in October of 1942.

(O SWEET ELYSIAN (W.C.) FIELDS - CONT.) 2.

Strange rambling ruffian ~~dog~~ CUR, Oh, William Claude
Dear Fields, old W.C. you are our God.
The pontiff of our unresplendent days
Spent in an ice-box gift martini Haze
BECAUSE Reality ~~was~~ IS that stuff which never quite
Finds itself presentable. Reality is grandmas
With a ~~hatchet~~ PICK-AX face, strange WIVES found in
Your bed at three am with cleaver chins, ~~and~~ iguana throats;
Reality is kids who bite your ankles, thieve your
POckets while you nap, bounce balls against
Your ~~unconscious~~ IDs ~~and~~ throw garbage lids like DOLTISH
Discus players in your sleep.
Reality is that blind man, "Here Mr. Towser, no
Mr. Towser honey, sit down, don't move mr Towser!
Watch out for that box of light bulbs,
Give me your cane, honey!"
And a thousand light bulbs exploded before you can stop it.
So you hop it to the keg for a slight infusion of gin.
IS that a sin? IT'S hard for me to knock your life.
I have neither your evil children nor your
Suck-a-sorrow nag-a-worry by-the-hour wife.
They say you started as both knockabout cigarbox
Slinging acrobat [redacted] amidst muggers and thuggees
In East Peoria and fled a father who medalled you with
Bruises as ~~some~~ awards of merit for your goodness AND EUPHORIA
You thought, if goodness wears SUCH epaulettes ~~like~~ AS this,
RIP them off.

Original manuscript page from a Bradbury poem-in-progress, unpublished.

INVASION EVE <u>June 5th-6th, 1944</u>

Somebody said something in a dark room. A kind of fog entered the room while it was being said. Then Douglas turned over and dreamed the words, the strange words he hardly dared touch. He dreamed for ten minutes, then the bed bulked down with a weight and he knew that Skipper was climbing onto the bed with him, all two hundred pink pounds of him.

For a moment they lay there and then Skipper said, "You asleep?"

Douglas cleared his throat before he could speak. "No."

There was a silence for awhile, andSkipper breathed and sighed. Douglas wondered if he had dreamed a dream of if what someone had said in the room and the fog a few minutes ago was true. His heart lay numb, he breathed slowly of the square silence.

"Boy," said Skipper, softly.

"What?" asked Douglas.

Skipper lay listening. "It's so quiet out. Quiet here. Most quiet night I ever heard."

Douglas swallowed. What did the quiet night have to do with it? Why was he apprehensive and tight and waiting for Skipper's next words? Skipper went on, quietly adjusting his big body to the mattress. "All this quiet, and over there, all those guys fighting."

Then Douglas knew what he meant. Then, it WAS true!

The invasion of Europe by American forces.

Original manuscript page from unpublished fragment written during World War II.

EARTHPORT, MARS

by

Ray Bradbury

a series of stories about people on Mars. . .

THE MINISTER

THE DOCTOR

THE LAWYER

THE MERCHANT

THE CHIEF

THE THIEF

THE PROSTITUTE

THE WARRIOR

THE REPORTER

THE GRAVEDIGGER

THE SCIENTIST

THE MOTHER-IN-LAW

THE WIFE

THE CHILDREN

THE MARTIANS

THE LABORER

THE CHEMISTS

THE ARCHAEOLOGIST

THE CLOWN

THE OLD MAN

THE LANDLORD.

Origin of *The Martian Chronicles* is reflected in this early plan made in 1944, when RB formulated his idea for a book of Martian tales.

July 5th, 1985	Rocket Summer
August 10th,1985	Ylla.
October 5th, 1985	Second Expedition The Earth Men
[illegible],	
April 3rd,1986	Mars is Heaven. Third Expedition
April 4th	The Death of the Martians.
July 10th, 1986	MOON BE STILL BRIGHT. 4th Expedition
September, 1986	THE SETTLING IN.
December, 1986	THE NAMING OF NAMES
January, 1997	The Priests.
Spring, 1987	WAY MIDDLE OF THE AIR
Spring, 1987	Sketch: what happened to Negroes?
Autumn, 1987	Mr. Edgar Allan Poe.comes to Mars.
Winter, 1995	The passing years.
SPRING, 1997	The Martian.
Summer, 1998	Usher II
Fall, 1998	Threat of War on Earth.
Fall, 1998	The Off Season.
Fall, 1999	Soft Rains Come
Spring, 1999	The Silent Towns.
Summer, 1999	The Long Years.
FALL, 1999	Million Year Picnic.

Original chronology-page, 1949, in which RB planned the shape and content of *The Martian Chronicles.*

FIRE AND THE STARS

The rockets came in, firebrands, heating the rooves of the houses, baking the children like breadloafs in their silent rooms, turning the populations like sweating half-cows on the spit, bringing them to the window with fire in their eyes. The skies were full of red and yellow and green fountains. The skies were full of sixty billion fireflies and red coins dropping. The sky filtered down a misty crimson rain and there were roads and paths of fire where the rockets lingered and sizzled. The rockets came to Mars to bring the beds and fill the beds, to bring the hammer and wood and go back after the nails. And the towns opened out, slot a fitting the tab b, a house brought in a suitcase, a mansion in a fortnighter, a castle in a trunk.

They gave a party and a free house to the one hundred thousandth immigrant.

Original manuscript page of unpublished "bridge-passage" written for *The Martian Chronicles* and later discarded by Bradbury.

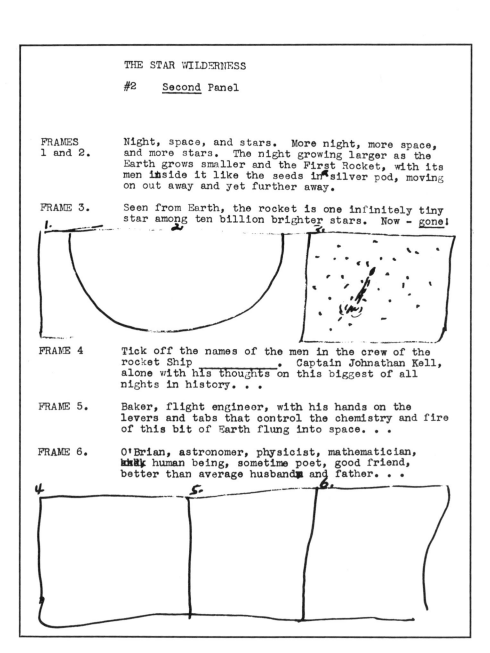

THE STAR WILDERNESS

#2 Second Panel

FRAMES 1 and 2. Night, space, and stars. More night, more space, and more stars. The night growing larger as the Earth grows smaller and the First Rocket, with its men inside it like the seeds in silver pod, moving on out away and yet further away.

FRAME 3. Seen from Earth, the rocket is one infinitely tiny star among ten billion brighter stars. Now - gone!

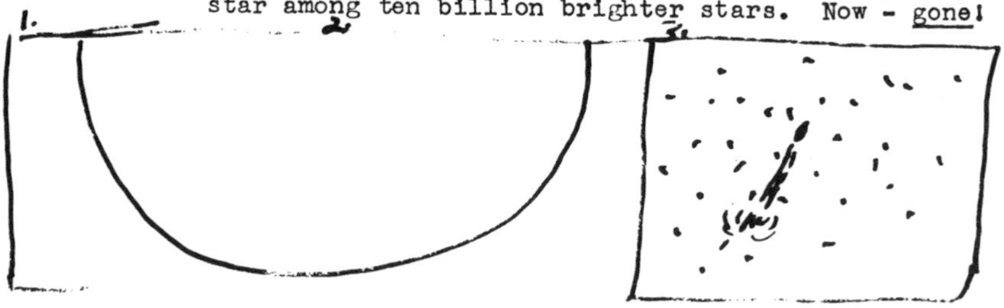

1.
2
3.

FRAME 4 Tick off the names of the men in the crew of the rocket Ship ___________. Captain Johnathan Kell, alone with his thoughts on this biggest of all nights in history. . .

FRAME 5. Baker, flight engineer, with his hands on the levers and tabs that control the chemistry and fire of this bit of Earth flung into space. . .

FRAME 6. O'Brian, astronomer, physicist, mathematician, human being, sometime poet, good friend, better than average husband and father. . .

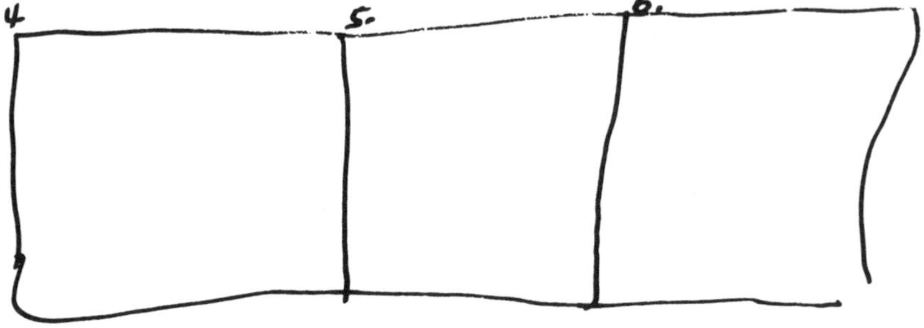

4
5.
6.

Original manuscript page from unpublished comic strip by RB written in the early 1950s and based on *The Martian Chronicles.*

THE GHOSTS

"Did you see what happened to Kemm? He fell dead when the Ghost touched him. Turned black and died away."

In the cell, one ghost turned to the other. "Now see what you did?"

"I did? Both of us."

"You touched him. What've you got, anyway?"

"What've I got, you fool. Nothing. Just some germ, harmless to me, you, everyone in Xxxxx Earth. Too much for him. God he rotted fast. Oh, we're in for it now, just wait."

"Just the same, you shouldn't have touched him!"

The delegation dropped fire on them and after fire, acid. And after acid bullets and after bullets stone and after stones dirt and sand until the vell was buried deep and silent. Then they tore the house down, block by block and strew it to the four directions. The mother and father, screaming for mercy, denying their wickedness, were cut into a thousand pieces and buried in a thousand towns. The children were watched carefully and put in a new home, where often, late of nights they talked about the Ghosts.

"Do you suppose mother and father were witches?"

"I bet they were. How horrid to think."

When the ghosts reappeared on Mars, a year later, it was only natural that the children should be blamed, and promptly killed.

THE END

Original manuscript page of unpublished Martian short story written in the late 1940s.

WAY UP IN THE MIDDLE OF THE AIR 4,000 words

by

Ray Bradbury

Mrs. Tompkins was weeping, "I kept telling her, Lucinda, you stay on and I raise your pay, and you get two nights off a week if you want, but she just looked firm! I never seen her so set, and I said, don't you love me, Lucinda, and she said yes but she had to go because that's the way it was is all. She cleaned the house and dusted it and put supper on the table and then she went to the parlor door and stood there with two bundles, one at each foot and shook my hand and said Goodyb Miss Lavinia. And she went out the door. And there was her supper on the table, and all of us too upset to even eat it. It's still there now, I reckon, last time I looked it was gettin' cold.

"I don't see why they left now with things lookin' up, I mean every day they got more rights, what they want, anyway? Here's the poll tax gone, and more and more states anti-lynching bills passin', and all kinds of equal rights, what more they want? They make good money, almost as good as a white man, but there they go. I offered to give my boy Joseph same money as my son gets there at the mill, you think he'd take it? No. Off he goes!"

Original manuscript page from unpublished early version of "Way in the Middle of the Air," contrasted with the final published version as collected in *The Martian Chronicles.*

June 2003: WAY IN THE MIDDLE OF THE AIR

"Did you hear about it?"

"About what?"

"The niggers, the niggers!"

"What about 'em?"

"Them leaving, pulling out, going away; did you hear?"

"What you mean, pulling out? How can they do that?"

"They can, they will, they are."

"Just a couple?"

"Every single one here in the South!"

"No."

"Yes!"

"I got to see that. I don't believe it. Where they going—Africa?"

A silence.

"Mars."

"You mean the *planet* Mars?"

"That's right."

The men stood up in the hot shade of the hardware porch. Someone quit lighting a pipe. Somebody else spat out into the hot dust of noon.

"They can't leave, they can't do that."

"They're doing it, anyways."

"Where'd you hear this?"

"It's everywhere, on the radio a minute ago, just come through."

THE SHOP OF THE MECHANICAL INSECTS

It was the day after I landed on the planet 11 that I went to the Shop of the Mechanical Insects. There were a thousand of them, scarab beetles, mantisses, grasshoppers, ants, spiders in a hundred varieties or fashion cascading up and down and spilling and tumbling about in the crystal window. Sunlight flushed them up and down their silver twines. Reflected sunlight burnished their wings or their feelers or their mandibles. Their bodies, some of them translucent, were full of mint-ice or ruby claret or amber sherry. Your house could be full of them if you were rich enough, and all one need do is summon them with a call, "Claret! Sherry! Creme of mint!" And they came like jeweled feathers on the floor, touching delicately up your leg, spinning a web upon your nose and letting themselves, like tiny architects down to build you a dream by pouring a drink into your mouth. Of all the things on all the planets, certainly these spiders were the product of the idle, idle rich, none idler, none richer anywhere in the Star System. I have seen rich men of this planet lying for days, attended by a hoard of spiders, spiders at their mouths, spiders at their ears, spiders to climb into their ears, snugly nested, to sing them ancient songs from the interior of their tiny radio bellies. Spiders to give them liquor, spiders to cleanse their bodies even, in a blanket of flickering diamonds.

And most marvelous of all the spiders was the Proprietor of the Mechanical Insects shop himself. His filegree gold

Original manuscript page from unpublished short story written in the 1950s.

Long After Midnight

1.

Mr. Montag dreamed.

He was an old man hidden with six million dusty books. His hands crawled, trembling, over yellow pages, and his face was a smashed mirror of wrinkles by candlelight.

Then, an eye at the keyhole!

In his dream, Mr. Montag yanked the door. A boy fell in.

"Spying!"

"You got books!" cried the boy. "It's against the law! I'll tell my father!"

He grabbed the boy who writhed, screaming.

"Don't, boy," pleaded Mr. Montag. "Don't tell. I'll give you money, books, clothes, but don't tell!"

"I seen you reading!"

"Don't!"

"I'll tell!" The boy ran, shrieking.

A crowd rushed up the street. Health officials burst in. followed by police, fierce with silver badges. And then himself! Himself as a young man, in a Fire uniform, with a torch. The room swarmed while the old man pleaded with himself as a young man. Books crashed down. Books were stripped and torn. Windows crashed inward, drapes fell in sooty clouds.

Outside, staring in, was the boy who had turned him in.

"No! Please!"

Original opening manuscript page from "Long After Midnight," unpublished early version of "The Fireman."

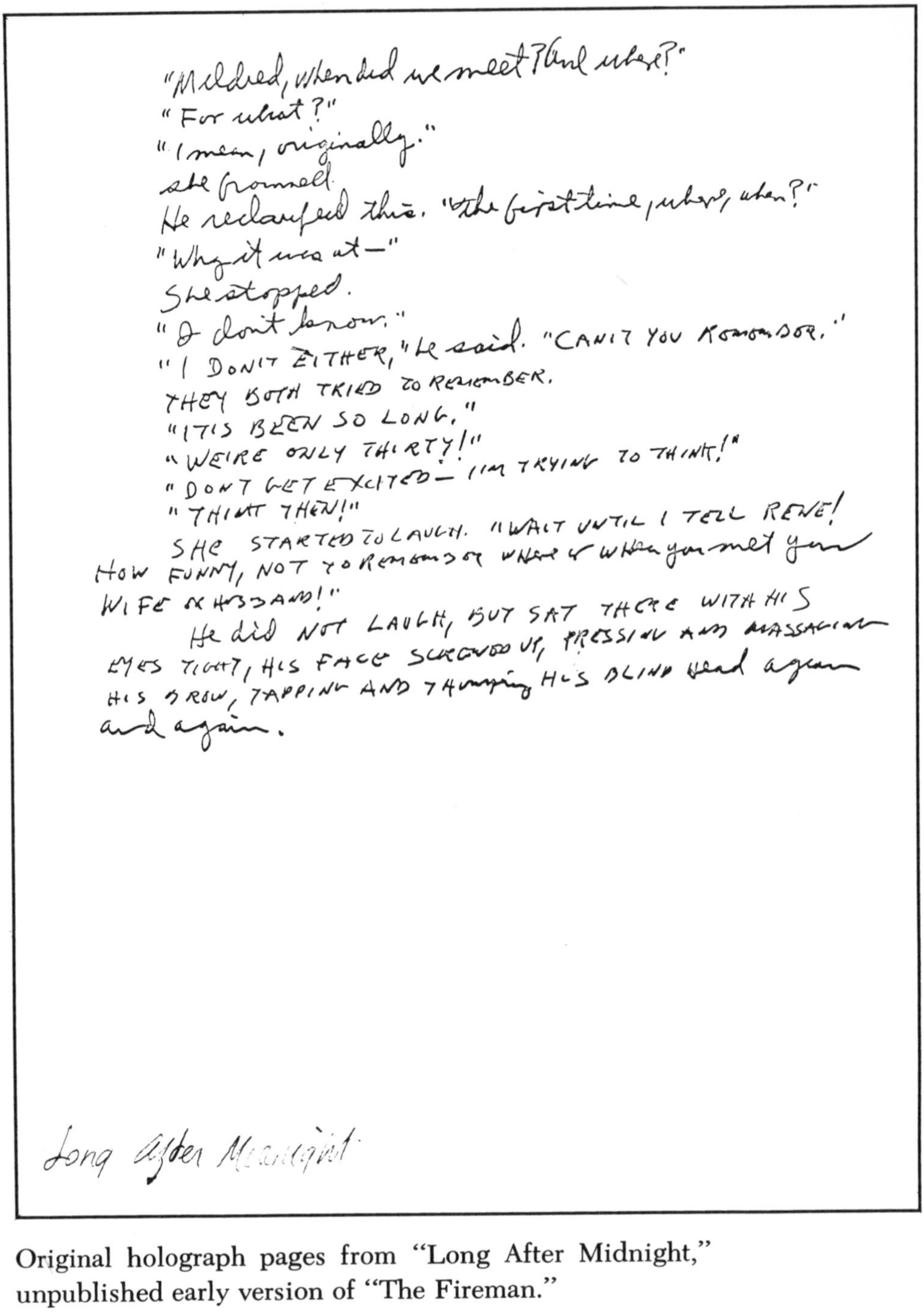
"Mildred, when did we meet? And where?"
"For what?"
"I mean, originally."
She frowned.
He clarified this. "The first time, where, when?"
"Why it was at—"
She stopped.
"I don't know."
"I DON'T EITHER," he said. "CAN'T YOU REMEMBER."
THEY BOTH TRIED TO REMEMBER.
"IT'S BEEN SO LONG."
"WE'RE ONLY THIRTY!"
"DON'T GET EXCITED— I'M TRYING TO THINK!"
"THINK THEN!"
SHE STARTED TO LAUGH. "WAIT UNTIL I TELL RENE! HOW FUNNY, NOT TO REMEMBER WHERE & WHEN you met your WIFE OR HUSBAND!"
He did NOT LAUGH, BUT SAT THERE WITH HIS EYES TIGHT, HIS FACE SCREWED UP, PRESSING AND MASSAGING HIS BROW, TAPPING AND THumping HIS BLIND head again and again.
Long After Midnight

Original holograph pages from "Long After Midnight," unpublished early version of "The Fireman."

How silly — she's too young for you. But so fresh, he thought. If I were five years younger —

Six months had passed.

And then one afternoon he had seen Anna on the street. It was raining again.

"Well, hello, there, it's been a long time!"

"What? Oh, hello."

"How do you like the rain."

"Isn't it terrible?"

"I thought you liked rain."

Her face was pale. She wasn't looking at him.

"What time is it?" she asked.

"Four o'clock, why?"

"There's a T.V. cast at four-thirty — I can't miss."

"SAY, I'VE got a dandelion here," he said.

She looked at it. "There's the snappiest, juiciest program on T.V. TIME FOR TOMASINA!" Her smile was high but her face was set.

"How are things," he said "How's the butterfly collection?"

"Oh, I threw that away, what good was it?"

"It's good to see you."

She wasn't listening.

"I'll take you up on the walk in the woods," he said, carrying the load.

"Don't be silly," she said. "Come over sometime. We just got a new T.V. And we carry good beer."

She walked into the house.

He never spoke to her again. He turned his head when she walked by. And she never looked at him either.

His wife said one day, "That Anna who lived next door?"

"Yes, I knew her once, for awhile."

"Killed in an auto accident yesterday."

"What do you want for dinner?" she asked, a moment later.

Call me Ishmael........and......the sea mist moves in to curtain all as it must have moved ten thousand years ago.

Between these first and last lines the entire philosophical adventure of the White Whale is contained. Between these same first and last lines, the substance of my screenplay holds its shape. Whether I have sustained Melville in this grievous hour of transubstantiation or bled him dry and laid him low, it certainly is not for me to say. So much now lies in the hands of a man who has his own peculiar insanity, who has struck lightning into actors before, and, I hope, will strike them again in directing this film for the screen. I well remember Huston in the center of his living room in Ireland, standing there with the damned face, the rolling wildness in his eye, the ship, the floor of the living room tilting in the storm as he told me how he felt about Ahab and Ahab's insufferable chase. Huston was Ahab. My greatest wish now is that Huston within Peck will make for the Ahab that will drive the film to its finish, inevitably, even as the Pequod, driven by storm and monster, goes to its awesome finale. I want this to be my finest, Huston said. I echo him. Whether our finest is Melville's second-best, November will tell. Like the Pequod, we plunge, like doom, in the cold Atlantic on the long journey off round and about the world. May we come safely to port.

Original manuscript page from unpublished article on *Moby Dick*, written prior to the film's release.

The Mechanical Hound slept but did not sleep, lived but did not live in its gently humming, gently vibrating, softly illuminated kennel back in a dark corner of the firehouse. The dim light of one in the morning, the moonlight from the open sky framed through the great window, touched here and there on the brass and the copper and the steel of the faintly trembling beast. Light flickered on bits of ruby glass and on sensitive capillary hairs in the Nylon-brushed nostrils of the creature that quivered gently, gently, its eight legs spidered under it on rubber-padded paws.

Montag slid down the brass pole. He went out to look at the city and the clouds had cleared away completely, and he lit a cigarette and came back to bend down and look at the Hound. It was like a great bee come home from some field where the honey is full of poison wildness, of insanity and nightmare, its body crammed with that over-rich nectar and now it was sleeping the evil out of itself.

THE MECHANICAL HOUND

It slept. It was not awake, it was only gently humming in its great kennel in the far corner of the police station. The dim light of three o'clock in the morning, the moonlight from the open sky framed through the open window upon its, touched here and there on brass and copper and steel, on bits of ruby glass and on sensitive capillary hairs in the nylon-brushed nostrils of the creature that quivered gently, gently. Its eight legs, with the rubber-padded paws, were spidered under it. It was like a great bee come home from some field where the honey is full of poison wildness, of insanity and nightmare, its body full of that ~~kkkk~~ over-rich nectar, and not it was sleeping the evil out of itself.

The sheriff of the small town lay on his cot, his deputy on another cot across from him, something had kept them awake for an hour now. They both discovered each other with their eyes open. Then they both looked at the metal hound humming in its kennel between them, and at last the sheriff said, "I wonder, sometimes I wonder, what does it think, late nights, or does it think at all? Is it alive, I wonder, or what?"

"It doesn't think anything we don't want it to think."

"Then, that's bad," said the sheriff, quietly, sadly, "for all we put into it is hunting and finding and killing. All we put in it is bad. That's a shame."

Original manuscript page of uncompleted short story in which RB incorporated the opening passage into a section of *Fahrenheit 451.*

FAHRENHEIT 451 -1-
Bradbury

ACT ONE - Scene One.

The lights come slowly up.

On the black stage, nothing but two golden poles.

After a moment, very slowly and with great thought, a man slides down one of the golden poles from above.

This is MONTAG, a man thirty-five, with the look of ashes rubbed into his cheeks, and his hair the color of scorched wood. He looks like what he is - a Fireman. When he reaches the bottom of the pole he does not immediately relinquish it, but looks up into the dark heavens of the Firehouse above him.

A soft gong chimes twelve times, quickly.

VOICE
Midnight. November first. It is now midnight, November first.

Montag lets go of the pole, steps away and stands looking into the darkness.

Down the pole, quickly, drop three men, also in dark uniform. They hit the floor. They move swiftly, nervously, efficiently. One seizes a collapsible card-table out of the wings, unfolds it. The other two set up collapsible chairs. Someone riffles the deck, makes a card appear, disappear. The men laugh. The three men sit. A fourth chair stands empty. The cards are dealt, to the three men, and to the empty place at the table.

The men do not touch their cards. They look up, waiting. They glance at MONTAG. They look at the golden pole which goes up into darkness.

After a moment, down the pole, just as thoughtfully and slowly as MONTAG accomplished it, BEATTY, the Fire Chief slides into view. On his way down the pole, he looks only at MONTAG. When he reaches the floor he stands for a moment leaning against the pole, still fixing MONTAG with his gaze.

MONTAG feels the look, turns. They stare at each other a moment. Then BEATTY turns to sit in the empty chair. Only when he touches his cards, do the men touch theirs.

Original opening manuscript page from RB's unpublished 3-act play of *Fahrenheit 451* completed in November of 1955, but not produced.

MUSIC

A FRONTCLOTH INDICATING A CITY IN 2116

MARIONETTE WALTZ TO CHIMES

THE FRONTCLOTH RISES.
A STREET IS INDICATED AS RUNNING ACROSS STAGE, DOWN STAGE.
ON A SHALLOW ROSTRUM, THE STAGE IS DIVIDED. IN ONE
SECTION, MRS. WYCHERLY LOOKING IN A HAND MIRROR. IN THE
OTHER MR. WYCHERLY LOOKING AT HIMSELF IN A BIG MIRROR.

MRS. WYCHERLY
(SPEAKS)

Happy Anniversary,
Dear Mrs. Wycherly,
Happy Anniversary,
Wycherly, my dear.

(SINGS)

SENTIMENTAL NICKOLODEON

What is it, forty years?
Oh forty, forty years,
Of laughter rinsed with tears,
Of fumbles, foibles, fears;
Forty years of regimen,
And now you're not the specimen,
The gorgeous maid, quite unafraid,
That John took as his wife,
To last him all his life.

(SPEAKS)
To last him all his life?

(SINGS)

MELODRAMATIC

~~Tell me, Mrs. Wycherly,~~
~~Where will you borrow~~
~~Strength to turn a faucet,~~
~~Pull your corset on tomorrow?~~
~~Where strength to squirm and snuggle~~
~~In corset like a gargoyle~~
~~And die after the struggle,~~
~~Before breakfast-time tomorrow.~~

Tell me, Mrs, Wycherly,
Where will you borrow,
A brain self-[illegible] ventilated,
Educated, for tomorrow,
How gain the boon, the benison
Of quaintly quoting Tennyson
Cite THE CHARTERHOUSE OF PARMA
Over jellyrolls and marma-
lade tomorrow.

DIRGE

Oh, what to do for John when I am gone?
What to do for John when he's alone?
Someone must tend his needs
When I'm pushing up the weeds,
What to do for John when I am gone?

CHIMES

MR. WYCHERLY
(SPEAKS)

Happy Anniversary,
Dear Mr. Wycherly,
Happy Anniversary,
Old Wycherly, to you!
(continued)

1

Opening page of unpublished operetta written in 1956, *Happy Anniversary: 2116 A.D.*, showing revision of center lyric.

3.

"Now we must begin the tour," said the first Martian.

In the next hour the Remingtons were whisked through the cool Martian sky on whispering silken nets suspended from the burning wings of a thousand flame-birds. They passed crumbled cities that had lain dead and empty for two hundred centuries, lying like pieces of chalk and salt by the shore of a long-dried sea. They hovered about rivers of blue dust and oceans of cinnamon sand. They saw strange animals like wisps of smoke appearing and vanishing in the forever-twilit land below. And at last the family was deposited upon the bank of an ancient marble canal.

"Then there <u>are</u> canals on Mars!" exclaimed the children.

They walked along the worn stone bed of the silent canal. Here, said the Martians, in the dry season, late, late at night, if you listened you could hear the wind, like a new river flowing in this baked channal. The wind made a sound like water going down to an unknown sea. Listen!

"And here, also, long long ago," said the second Martian, "in the Season of Green Wine, the trees along those far mountain canals would drip a pure fine green liquor into the canals which flowed to twenty directions in a wonderful tide. They say our ancestors, the ancient Martian men and women, with golden-coin eyes in their brown faces, on spring festival midnights would bathe here. They would swim laughing in the green wine, among flower petals. They would sip the wine as they swam. They would float all through the long clear spring nights, idly, lazily, singing, dreaming wine dreams. Dreams of great wars when clouds of metal insects hovered in the dusky sky. Dreams of great loves, too, until the Wine season was

Original manuscript page from short story "Christmas on Mars"—sold to *Esquire* for a holiday issue, but never printed.

January 29th,1945

Dear Augie:

I've spent a lot of time traveling since last September when I wrote you; I've been to Ensenada, Mexico, over to Yuma, to Palm Springs, Lake Arrowhead and Santa Barbara. . .so I must apologize for this long overdue letter.

First, I want to thank you for your suggestion that some time in the next two years Arkham House might try an anthology of Bradbury stories. I certainly hope to continue turning out stories of the calibre necessary to make such a volume possible. Some of my early stories, if ever reprinted, would need quite a bit of rewriting to re-shape them into my present way of thinking and producing. For over a year now I've been working and planning an entire volume of short stories concerning children in fantasy and weird settings... this [redacted] to be titled A CHILDS GARDEN OF TERROR. I hoped to eventually submit the completed book to a publisher in 1946 or 1947, depending on the development and quality of each yarn. And now that you've suggested ARKHAM might be interested later in my work, I hope I shall one day be able to submit the finished work to you. I think it would be a definite off-trail thing, something a little different in the outre pattern. . .and I'm especially pleased with the title. Anyway, the project gives me much to look forward to and work on. Thanks very much for the generous offer.

The above letter, to editor/publisher August Derleth, was followed, a few days later. by the letter below (responding to Derleth's) Both letters are abridged.

Your letter somewhat changes my ideas concerning the proposed volume, and I believe that A CHILDS GARDEN OF TERROR would no longer be a suitable title for such a book, simply because it would restrict the contents. Such stories as THE SCYTHE, THE JAR and THERE WAS AN OLD WOMAN simply would not fit under such a title. Therefore I shall give myself over to the task of worrying out a better one. I can always save the title A CHILDS GARDEN etc., for some time later, if and when all of my child stories are completed and perfected. It will probably be some time, kkkkkk because my present schedule calls for a great deal of Red Cross work, besides my regular output for the pulp magazines to gain an income, and I'm sure you understand the difficulty I have with Weird and the child stories. I hope to write and have accepted a number of very unusual yarns by Weird, this year, though, and these, and kkkk stories already published, and the stories to come in 1946 will probably give you and I plenty of room to move around in in our selection. I'm pleased to know you liked THE JAR, it was one of my favorites. [illegible] S [illegible]. I'll fix up a temporary list of stories sometime this spring or summer, after a few more have appeared, and see [illegible] if they meet with your approval.

Meanwhile, I know little or nothing of the financial side of anthology publication. Could you possible give me an insight into the mechhanisms of Arkham House, copyrights, royalties and sox on?

Hoping this catches you before you answer my first letter, I remain very pleased and flattered by Arkham House's plans.

Sincerely,

Parts of two unpublished letters from RB written in 1945 in which he discusses plans for the future publication of his first book, *Dark Carnival.*

Unpublished cartoon sketches by RB.

THE WRITINGS OF RAY BRADBURY

A Comprehensive Checklist

DARK CARNIVAL

By
RAY BRADBURY

ARKHAM HOUSE • SAUK CITY, WIS.
1947

BOOKS AND PAMPHLETS

All U.S. first editions are listed, with data on U.S. paperback editions through 1972. With the exception of *The Martian Chronicles,* no foreign-language editions are included and only British first editions are listed (first hardcover and first paperback). When a number-letter is attached to a book the number stands for a separate *edition* and the letter indicates a printing *within* that edition. Thus, 1D would signify a fourth printing of the first edition. Change of cover format or fresh binding does *not* constitute a new edition; only a separate setting of type qualifies. Dates in brackets are not on title pages.

Arranged in order of publication.

1 DARK CARNIVAL (1947)

[i-viii] [1-3] 4-21 [22] 23-38 [39] 40-53 [54] 55-60 [61-62] 63-67 [68] 69-77 [78] 79-85 [86] 87-99 [100] 101-119 [120] 121-129 [130] 131-137 [138] 139-147 [148] 149-156 [157] 158 [159] 160-176 [177] 178-191 [192] 193-197 [198] 199-206 [207] 208-217 [218] 219-225 [226] 227-239 [240] 241-250 [251] 252-265 [266] 267-268 [269] 270-278 [279] 280-313 [314-316]

$[1\text{-}8]^{16}$ $[9]^{18}$ $[10]^{16}$

The Wind

By RAY BRADBURY

This is dedicated to those who have lost the game of the elements, by one who has always escaped . . . until tonight.

JOHN COLT was awake and listening. . . .

Moonlight sluiced into his room by the huge triple window fronting the upstairs of the house, fell across his sharp, questioning features.

The wind moved far away in the night, and Colt's lips worked as he listened to it; moving stealthily and mournfully from the sea, approaching the house as surely as mighty horses hooves.

Colt's body shivered, hairs stood erect upon his neck, and goose-pimples clustered on his limbs. He knew why he felt this way. After ten years he could believe nothing else.

He knew the wind was coming toward him—and he slipped from bed, thrust himself tremblingly into a robe, found carpet slippers and ventured downstairs to await its arrival.

He went to the phone, thinking, "This

Bradbury made major changes in the magazine version of "The Wind" (from *Weird Tales*) when he revised the story for inclusion in his first collection, *Dark Carnival.*

is what I've waited for, calmly at first. Curious. Alert. Sure of most factors. But I don't know how much I can stand. I keep losing my grip, gaining it, and losing it again."

His hand shook as he dialed the call through. "Hello, Herb? This is Colt."

"John—how are you?"

"Not so good. And, like a fool, I dismissed my servants today. I'm alone. . . .

All the while he talked, Colt listened. The weird music of the wind was muted by distance. It waxed louder.

"My writing routine for the last week's been shot to hell, Herb. Been trying to get some rest early tonight, but—"

What was that? Colt winced. A tiny breeze, preamble to the wind now on its way, rattled a shutter. Colt thought, did I lock every door, check everything?

"Sorry to hear that, John—" Herb Thompson was talking. Colt gave ear, then:

"Herb, I'd like to have you come for the night. Can you arrange—"

"I'll have to ask the little woman, John. Hold on."

A pause. Thompson was conferring with his wife. And far off the wind rose steadily, rapidly. "Sorry, Colt, Alice says we've got company coming."

"Oh." Colt swallowed. "Look, Herb, it's important. I've got theories about—well." He stopped, groping for words.

"Sounds like a case of nerves," said Thompson. "Why don't *you* come over here?"

"That wouldn't help." Colt shook his head. "I don't know *what* would. I—well —I'll call back in half an hour."

He hung up. What could Herb do? Nothing. It wouldn't be fair to drag an innocent into this set-up. And, anyway, how explain to Herb about the wind? Police help? They'd send a soft-pad squad.

Colt deliberately opened the front door. A lopsided frame of moonlight stroked across the gleaming floor, picked out his wine-colored robe and slippers. He stood, shivering, waiting.

THE great wind could be only a mile away now, soughing through a long high, dim corridor of swaying elms, plunging down the arboreal path toward Colt's lonely country manor.

Colt lit a cigarette, but his dark eyes fastened on the tree lane; eyes that had seen Rangoon, Stockholm, swept from Nairobi to the Amazon.

It was a dark, meaningful wind. Others might have been amused by Colt's wild thoughts. Thompson, for instance, would laugh uproariously.

But Colt was not amused. Alone out here, the nine o'clock countryside steeped in a vast tide of shadowed, eerie silence, this fortress of a house his final refuge, the last roll of dice forced on him, Colt could only wait.

The last stand. Decks cleared for action. Colt dragged on his cigarette, flicked it away, thinking, if I scream no one will hear me. No one. I'm far from town. Too damned far.

He'd phone Herb in twenty minutes. What to say? Something like this: "Herb, it began ten years ago when I was investipating phenomena. I'd been around, seen hurricanes, typhoons and whirlwinds. I knew what wind could do.

"Well, I was in Tibet. I heard of a mountain called the mountain of Winds; the space where the dark winds from all over the earth congregate at one time or other. It's a vast evil mountain, gray and jutting; hard, bony rock without a hand or foothold. Blasphemy to touch it.

"I touched it, Herb. More, I scaled it. Up thousands of sickening, dizzy feet, climbing where only madmen climb to probe into what's better left undissected. I gained its crest raw and wounded.

Of all the high, wild places I've seen

THE WIND

THE PHONE RANG at six thirty that evening. It was December, and already dark as Thompson picked up the phone.

"Hello."

"Hello, *Herb?"*

"Oh, it's you, Allin."

"Is your wife home, Herb?"

"Sure. Why?"

"Damn it."

Herb Thompson held the receiver quietly. "What's up? You sound funny."

"I wanted you to come over tonight."

"We're having company."

"I wanted you to spend the night. When's your wife going away?"

"That's next week," said Thompson. "She'll be in Ohio for about nine days. Her mother's sick. I'll come over then."

"I wish you could come over tonight."

"Wish I could. Company and all, my wife'd kill me."

"I wish you could come over."

"What's it? the wind again?"

"Oh, no. No."

"Is it the wind?" asked Thompson.

The voice on the phone hesitated. "Yeah. Yeah, it's the wind."

"It's a clear night, there's not much wind."

"There's enough. It comes in the window and blows the curtains a little bit. Just enough to tell me."

"Look, why don't you come and spend the night here?" said Herb Thompson looking around the lighted hall.

"Oh, no. It's too late for that. It might catch me on the way over.

Contents:
"The Homecoming"
"Skeleton"
"The Jar"
"The Lake"
"The Maiden"
"The Tombstone"
"The Smiling People"
"The Emissary"
"The Traveler"
"The Small Assassin"
"The Crowd"
"Reunion"
"The Handler"
"The Coffin"
"Interim"
"Jack-In-The-Box"
"The Scythe"
"Let's Play 'Poison' "
"Uncle Einar"
"The Wind"
"The Night"
"There was an Old Woman"
"The Dead Man"
"The Man Upstairs"
"The Night Sets"
"Cistern"
"The Next in Line"

Published October 1947. 3000 copies.

2 ——— London: Hamish Hamilton, [1948]. Abridged from U.S. edition.

3 *The Small Assassin.* London: Ace, 1962. No. H 521. Abridged from U.S. edition. Contents varies from first British edition.

4 ——— London: Four Square, [1964].

Four British Bradbury editions: (upper left) RB's first book published in 1948 by Hamish Hamilton. Seven stories were omitted from the U.S. contents in this British edition. (lower left) RB's first paperback to appear in England, the 1955 Corgi edition. (upper right) The 1959 Rupert Hart-Davis hardback edition. Title and contents varied from the U.S. version, *A Medicine for Melancholy.* (lower right) The 1964 reprint edition, from Four Square, of a collection which contains titles from *Dark Carnival* and *October Country.*

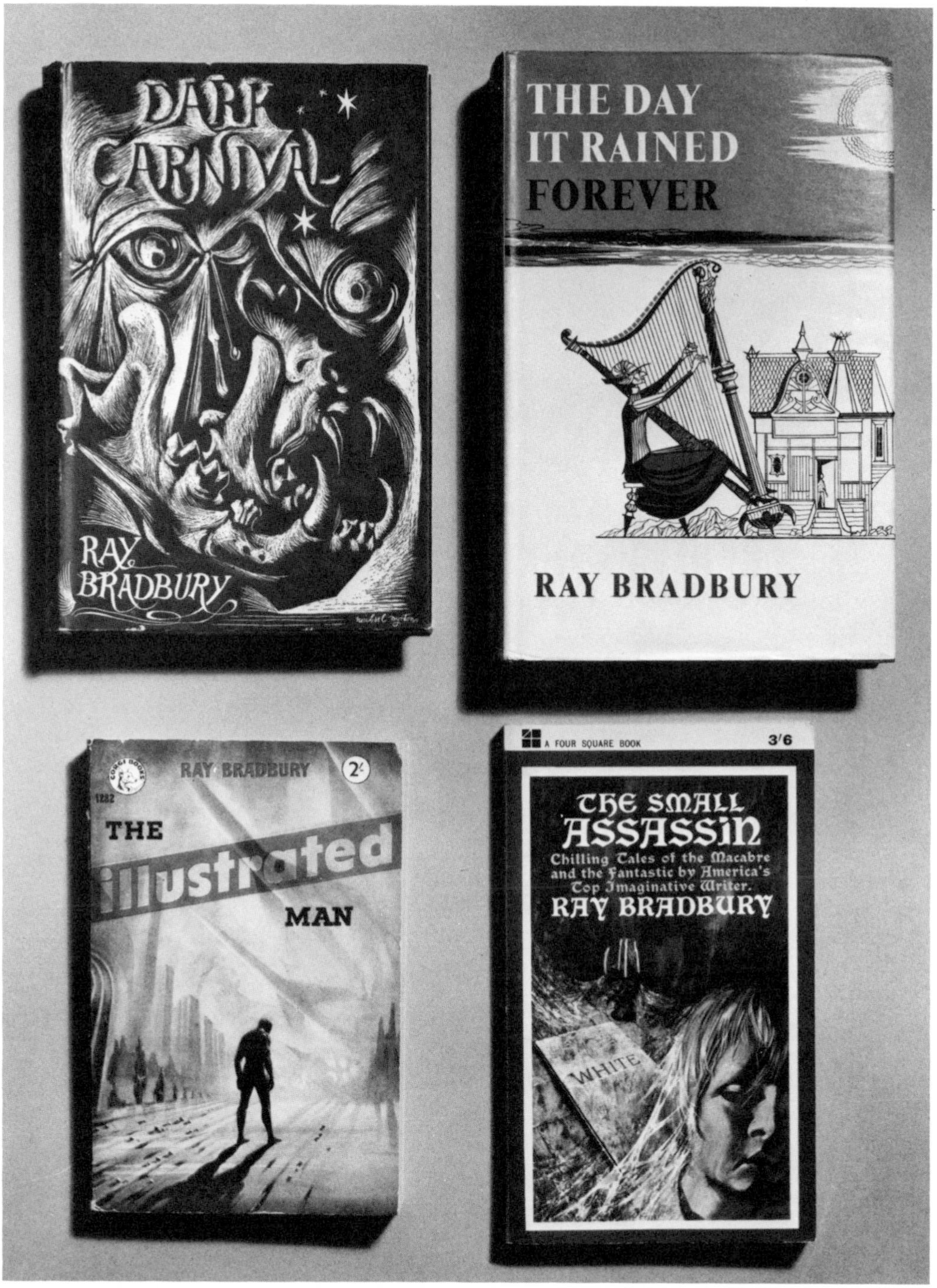
DARK CARNIVAL
RAY BRADBURY
THE DAY IT RAINED FOREVER
RAY BRADBURY
RAY BRADBURY
2/-
THE illustrated MAN
A FOUR SQUARE BOOK
3/6
THE SMALL ASSASSIN
Chilling Tales of the Macabre and the Fantastic by America's Top Imaginative Writer.
RAY BRADBURY
WHITE

THE MARTIAN CHRONICLES

by Ray Bradbury

DOUBLEDAY & COMPANY, INC.

1950

Garden City, N. Y.

1A THE MARTIAN CHRONICLES (1950)
Copyright page: First Edition
[1-12] 13-222 [223-224]

$[1\text{-}7]^{16}$

Contents:
"January 1999: Rocket Summer"
"February 1999: Ylla"
"August 1999: The Summer Night"
"August 1999: The Earth Men"
"March 2000: The Taxpayer"
"April 2000: The Third Expedition"
"June 2001: —And the Moon Be Still As Bright"
"August 2001: The Settlers"
"December 2001: The Green Morning"
"February 2002: The Locusts"
"August 2002: Night Meeting"
"October 2002: The Shore"
"February 2003: Interim"
"April 2003: The Musicians"
"June 2003: Way in the Middle of the Air"
"2004-2005: The Naming of Names"
"April 2005: Usher II"
"August 2005: The Old Ones"
"September 2005: The Martian"
"November 2005: The Luggage Store"
"November 2005: The Off Season"
"November 2005: The Watchers"
"December 2005: The Silent Towns"
"April 2026: The Long Years"
"August 2026: There Will Come Soft Rains"
"October 2026: The Million-Year Picnic"

Published May 1950.

1B ______ New York: Doubleday, 1950. 2nd printing—May.

Variant editions of *The Martian Chronicles:* (top) The dustjacket of the 1950 Doubleday first hardback edition. (center—left to right) RB's first U.S. paperback, published in 1951 by Bantam. First British hardback edition, with title and partial contents change, from Rupert Hart-Davis, 1951. Hardback edition released by Science Fiction Book Club of London, with U.S. title restored and further contents changes. (bottom—left to right) Hardback edition from Doubleday, 1958, with special Fadiman introduction. Expanded paperback edition from Time/Life, 1963, with special introductory material. Illustrated hardback edition from Doubleday, 1973, with expanded contents and biographical/bibliographical data.

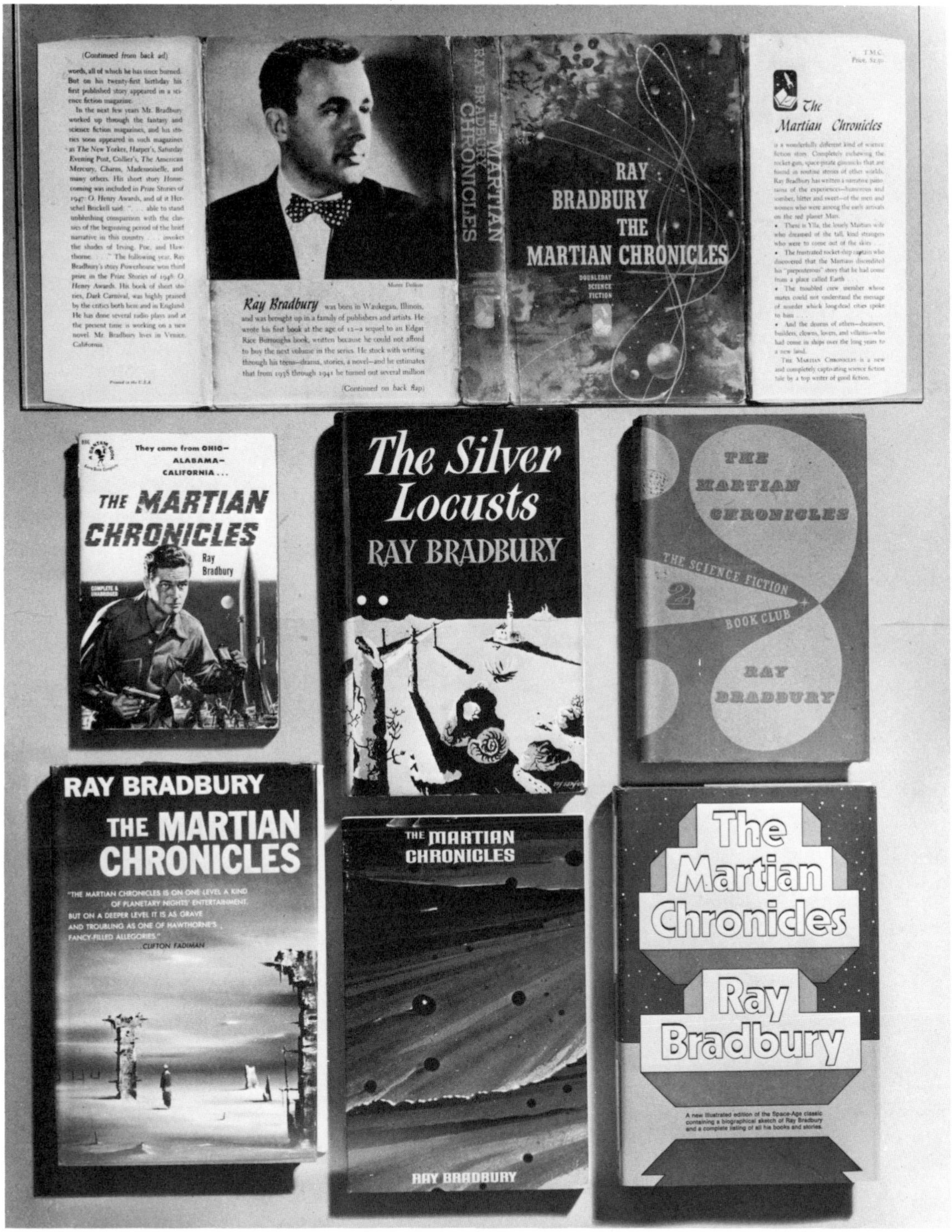
(Continued from back ad)
Ray Bradbury
(Continued on back flap)
THE MARTIAN CHRONICLES
RAY BRADBURY
RAY BRADBURY THE MARTIAN CHRONICLES
DOUBLEDAY SCIENCE FICTION
The Martian Chronicles
They come from OHIO— ALABAMA— CALIFORNIA . . .
THE MARTIAN CHRONICLES
Ray Bradbury
COMPLETE & UNABRIDGED
The Silver Locusts
RAY BRADBURY
THE MARTIAN CHRONICLES
THE SCIENCE FICTION BOOK CLUB
2
RAY BRADBURY
RAY BRADBURY
THE MARTIAN CHRONICLES
"THE MARTIAN CHRONICLES IS ON ONE LEVEL A KIND OF PLANETARY NIGHTS' ENTERTAINMENT. BUT ON A DEEPER LEVEL IT IS AS GRAVE AND TROUBLING AS ONE OF HAWTHORNE'S FANCY-FILLED ALLEGORIES."
. . . CLIFTON FADIMAN
THE MARTIAN CHRONICLES
RAY BRADBURY
The Martian Chronicles
Ray Bradbury
A new illustrated edition of the Space-Age classic containing a biographical sketch of Ray Bradbury and a complete listing of all his books and stories.

1C ——— New York: Doubleday, 1950. 3rd printing—September.

1D ——— New York: Doubleday, [1951]. 4th printing—February.

1E ——— New York: Doubleday, [1951]. 5th printing—December.

1F ——— New York: Doubleday, [1952]. 6th printing—November.

1G ——— New York: Doubleday, [1952]. Science Fiction Book Club.

2 ——— New York: Bantam, [1951]. No. 886. Two printings: June and August.

3 *The Silver Locusts.* London: Rupert Hart-Davis, 1951. Contents vary slightly from U.S. edition.

4 *The Martian Chronicles.* London: Science Fiction Book Club, [1953]. Contents vary slightly from Hart-Davis edition.

5 ——— New York: Bantam, [1954]. Twenty-seven printings: October 1954 through August 1972. Pathfinder edition issued October 1972.

6 *The Silver Locusts.* London: Corgi, [1956]. No. 886.

7 *The Martian Chronicles.* New York: Doubleday, [1958]. Eleven printings: May 1958 through June 1962. With a Prefatory Note by Clifton Fadiman. (See ABOUT BRADBURY IN BOOKS.)

8 ——— New York: Time, [1963]. Contents expanded from first U.S. edition—with Editors' Preface and Time Reading Program Introduction by Fred Hoyle. (See

ABOUT BRADBURY IN BOOKS.)

9 _____ New York: Doubleday, [1973]. Contents expanded to match Time edition—with a profile of RB and checklist of his books and stories by W. F. Nolan. Illustrated. (See ABOUT BRADBURY IN BOOKS.)

Note: Of some thirty foreign-language editions of this book, seven are of special interest:

1 Paperback edition from Argentina: *Cronicas Marcianas.* Buenos Aires: Ediciones Minotauro, [1955].
"Prologo" by Jorge Luis Borges.

2 Hardcover edition from France: *Chroniques Martiennes.* Paris: Le Club Du Meilleur Livre, [1955].
Illustrated, with maps of Mars.

3 Paperback edition from Czechoslovakia: *Martanska Kronika.* Prague: Mlada Fronta, 1959.
With a profile, "Literarni typ Raye Bradburyho," by Josef Skvorecky.

4 Hardcover edition from Czechoslovakia: *Martanska Kronika.* Prague: Mlada Fronta, 1963.
Illustrated, with an article on RB by Frantisek Vrba.

5 Hardcover edition from France: *Chroniques Martiennes.* Paris: Club Des Amis Du Livre, [1964].
Illustrated, with a preface on RB, "Un Marco Polo Du Futur," by Aime Michel, a chronology of RB, and an article on science fiction by Jacques Sternberg.

6 Hardcover edition from Hungary: *Marsbeli Kronikak.* Budapest: Europa Konyvkiado, 1966.
Contains, in addition to *The Martian Chronicles,* eight short stories, *Fahrenheit 451,* and a reprint of his interview in *Show,* "A Portrait of Genius," here titled "Beszelgetes Ray Bradburyvel."

CRONACHE MARZIANE
Bradbury
Marsbéli krónikák
MARŤANSKÁ KRONIKA
Ray Bradbury
Marťanská kronika
ray bradbury
crónicas marcianas
INVASION PÅ
mars
Ray Bradbury
Invasion
på Mars
AVARUUSROMAANI
Ray Bradbury
MARSIN AIKAKIRJAT
OTAVA
CRONACHE MARZIANE
ray bradbury
chroniques martiennes
KRØNIKER FRA MARS
RAY BRADBURY
CRONACHE MARZIANE
RAY BRADBURY
Kom hjem!
Kom hjem!
THE MARTIAN CHRONICLES
by
RAY BRADBURY
RAY BRADBURY
KRØNIKER FRA MARS
Ray Bradbury
Die Mars-Chroniken
Roman/MvS
"Présence du futur"
Chroniques martiennes
de laatste Martiaan
Ray Bradbury
Invasion på Mars
O MUNDO MARCIANO
RAY BRADBURY
RAY BRADBURY
KRONIKI MARSJANSKIE
ФАНТАСТИКА

Twenty-seven foreign-language editions of *The Martian Chronicles,* from France, Italy, Japan, Germany, Hungary, Poland, Portugal, Sweden, Argentina, Russia, etc.

THE ILLUSTRATED MAN

RAY BRADBURY

GARDEN CITY, NEW YORK, 1951

DOUBLEDAY & COMPANY, INC.

7 Hardcover edition from Italy: *Cronache Marziane.* Milano: Arnoldo Mondadori, [1971].
Illustrated, with a checklist of RB works in Italian, plus a profile, "L'Autore" by Giorgio Monicelli.

1A THE ILLUSTRATED MAN (1951)
Copyright page: FIRST EDITION
[i-ii] [1-9] 10-14 [15] 16-30 [31-32] 33-41 [42-43] 44-57 [58] 59-76 [77] 78-92 [93] 94-105 [106] 107-125 [126] 127-130 [131] 132-145 [146] 147-156 [157] 158-173 [174] 175-188 [189] 190-210 [211] 212-219 [220] 221-228 [229] 230-240 [241] 242-251 [252-254]

$[1\text{-}8]^{16}$

Contents:
"Prologue: The Illustrated Man"
"The Veldt"
"Kaleidoscope"
"The Other Foot"
"The Highway"
"The Man"
"The Long Rain"
"The Rocket Man"
"The Fire Balloons"
"The Last Night of the World"
"The Exiles"
"No Particular Night or Morning"
"The Fox and the Forest"
"The Visitor"
"The Concrete Mixer"
"Marionettes, Inc."
"The City"
"Zero Hour"
"The Rocket"
"Epilogue"

Published February 1951.

Timeless Stories FOR TODAY AND TOMORROW

Edited by RAY BRADBURY

BANTAM BOOKS • New York

1B ______ New York: Doubleday, 1951. 2nd printing—March.

1C ______ New York: Doubleday, [1953]. 3rd printing—July.

1D ______ New York: Doubleday, [1958]. 4th printing—April.

1E ______ New York: Doubleday, [1961]. 5th printing—April.

1F ______ New York: Doubleday, [1962]. 6th printing—October.

1G ______ New York: Doubleday, [1969]. Science Fiction Book Club.

2 ______ New York: Bantam, [1952]. No. 991. Two printings in April.

3 ______ London: Rupert Hart-Davis, 1952. Contents vary from U.S. edition.

4 ______ New York: Bantam, [1954]. Three printings: October 1954 through September 1963. Pathfinder edition—five printings August through December, 1965. New printings: twenty-six from June 1967 through July 1972.

5 ______ London: Corgi, [1955]. No. 1282.

1 TIMELESS STORIES FOR TODAY AND TOMORROW (1952)
No. A 944
"Edited and With an Introduction by Ray Bradbury"
Copyright page: First Edition

[I-VI] VII-XIV 1-305 [306]

Perfect binding.

Contents:
"Introduction" by RB (See INTRODUCTIONS.)
"The Hour After Westerly" by Robert M. Coates
"Housing Problem" by Henry Kuttner
"The Portable Phonograph" by Walter Van Tilburg Clark
"None Before Me" by Sidney Carroll
"Putzi" by Ludwig Bemelmans
"The Demon Lover" by Shirley Jackson
"Miss Winters and the Wind" by Christine Noble Govan
"Mr. Death and the Redheaded Woman" by Helen Eustis
"Jeremy in the Wind" by Nigel Kneale
"The Glass Eye" by John Kier Cross
"Saint Katy the Virgin" by John Steinbeck
"Night Flight" by Josephine W. Johnson
"The Cocoon" by John B. L. Goodwin
"The Hand" by Wessel Hyatt Smitter
"The Sound Machine" by Roald Dahl
"The Laocoon Complex" by J. C. Furnas
"I Am Waiting" by Christopher Isherwood
"The Witnesses" by William Sansom
"The Enormous Radio" by John Cheever
"Heartburn" by Hortense Calisher
"The Supremacy of Uruguay" by E. B. White
"The Pedestrian" by Ray Bradbury
"A Note for the Milkman" by Sidney Carroll
"The Eight Mistresses" by Jean Hrolda
"In the Penal Colony" by Franz Kafka
"Inflexible Logic" by Russell Maloney

Published September 1952.

2 ——— New York: Bantam, [1961]. Eleven printings: December 1961 through 1972.

No Man Is An Island

by

RAY BRADBURY

THE GOLDEN APPLES OF THE SUN

by Ray Bradbury

DRAWINGS BY JOE MUGNAINI

Doubleday & Company, Inc.
Garden City, New York, 1953

1 NO MAN IS AN ISLAND (1952)

[1-2] 3-10 [11-12]

[1]^{6}

". . . an address delivered by the author, Ray Bradbury, at the Annual Meeting, November 7, 1952, before the Los Angeles Chapter of the National Women's Committee of Brandeis University."

Published in 1952—in Beverly Hills, California. (See PUBLISHED SPEECHES.)

1A THE GOLDEN APPLES OF THE SUN (1953)
Illustrated by Joe Mugnaini
Copyright page: FIRST EDITION
[i-ii] [1-15] 16-24 [25] 26-30 [31] 32-43 [44-45] 46-56 [57] 58-70 [71] 72-82 [83] 84-89 [90-91] 92-100 [101] 102-107 [108-109] 110-113 [114-115] 116-119 [120-121] 122-134 [135] 136-150 [151] 152-165 [166-167] 168-178 [179] 180-184 [185] 186-194 [195] 196-213 [214-215] 216-221 [222-223] 224-231 [232-233] 234-242 [243] 244-250 [251-254]

[1-8]^{16}

Contents:
"The Fog Horn"
"The Pedestrian"
"The April Witch"
"The Wilderness"
"The Fruit at the Bottom of the Bowl"
"Invisible Boy"
"The Flying Machine"
"The Murderer"
"The Golden Kite, the Silver Wind"
"I See You Never"
"Embroidery"

FAHRENHEIT 451

RAY BRADBURY

ILLUSTRATED BY JOE MUGNAINI

FAHRENHEIT 451—
the temperature at which book-paper catches fire, and burns . . .

BALLANTINE BOOKS, INC.
NEW YORK

"The Big Black and White Game"
"A Sound of Thunder"
"The Great Wide World Over There"
"Powerhouse"
"En La Noche"
"Sun and Shadow"
"The Meadow"
"The Garbage Collector"
"The Great Fire"
"Hail and Farewell"
"The Golden Apples of the Sun"

Published March 1953.

1B ——— New York: Doubleday, 1953. 2nd printing—April.

2 ——— London: Rupert Hart-Davis, 1953. Slightly abridged from U.S. edition.

3 ——— New York: Bantam, [1954]. No. A 1241. Eleven printings—November 1961 through 1972.

4 ——— London: Corgi, [1956]. No. 1241.

5 *Twice 22.* New York: Doubleday, 1966. Combined with *A Medicine for Melancholy.*

1A FAHRENHEIT 451 (1953)
Illustrated by Joe Mugnaini
[i-vi] 1 [2] 3-147 [148] 149 [150] 151-169 [170-172] 173-199 [200-202]

$[1\text{-}5]^{16}\ [6]^{8}\ [7]^{16}$

Contents:
"Fahrenheit 451:
"Part One: The Hearth and the Salamander"

"Part Two: The Sieve and the Sand"
"Part Three: Burning Bright"
"The Playground"
"And the Rock Cried Out"

Published October 1953.

Note: 200 numbered and signed copies of this 4500-copy first printing were bound in ". . . an asbestos material with exceptional resistance to pyrolysis."

1B ______ New York: Ballantine, [1953]. No. 41. This paperbound edition was released at the same time Ballantine released the hardcover edition—both from the same set of plates.

2 ______ London: Rupert Hart-Davis, 1954. Title novel only.

3 ______ London: Science Fiction Book Club, [1955]. Title novel only.

4 ______ London: Corgi, [1957]. No. T 389. Title novel only.

5 ______ New York: Ballantine, [1960]. No. 382 K. Title novel only. Twenty-nine printings April 1960 through September 1972. Bal-Hi Edition in 1967, with "Note to Teachers and Parents" by Richard H. Tyre. Nine printings through June 1972. (See ABOUT BRADBURY IN BOOKS.)

6 ______ New York: Simon and Schuster, [1967]. Full contents, plus new Introduction by RB. (See INTRODUCTIONS.)

Shorter version of novel: "The Fireman," *Galaxy*, February 1951.

Variant editions of ***Fahrenheit 451:*** (top) The dustjacket of the 1953 Ballantine first hardback edition. (center—left to right) First 1953 U.S. paperback from Ballantine. First U.S. edition to print title novel *only,* from Ballantine, 1960. Motion-picture edition, from Ballantine, 1966. Bal-Hi school edition, with special introduction, from Ballantine, 1967. (bottom—left to right) Hardback edition from Simon and Schuster, with full contents and a new introduction by RB, 1967. Limited-edition hardback from Ballantine, 1953, bound in asbestos material. First British hardback edition, title novel only, from Rupert Hart-Davis, 1954.

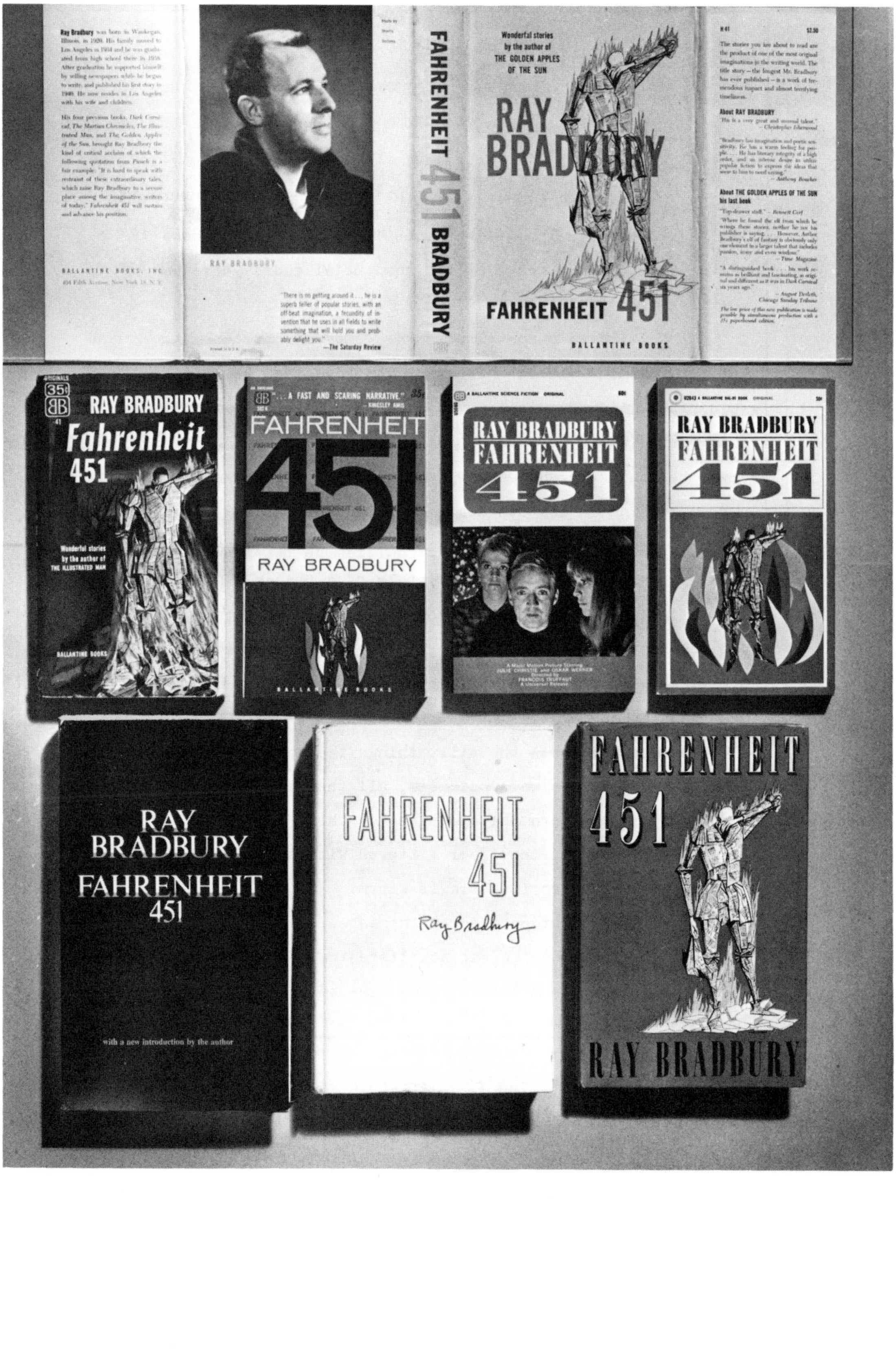

RAY BRADBURY
"There is no getting around it . . . he is a superb teller of popular stories, with an off-beat imagination, a fecundity of invention that he uses in all fields to write something that will hold you and probably delight you."
—The Saturday Review
FAHRENHEIT 451 BRADBURY
Wonderful stories by the author of THE GOLDEN APPLES OF THE SUN
RAY BRADBURY
FAHRENHEIT 451
BALLANTINE BOOKS
$2.50
About RAY BRADBURY
About THE GOLDEN APPLES OF THE SUN his last book
BALLANTINE BOOKS, INC.
35¢
RAY BRADBURY
Fahrenheit 451
Wonderful stories by the author of THE ILLUSTRATED MAN
BALLANTINE BOOKS
"... A FAST AND SCARING NARRATIVE." —KINGSLEY AMIS
FAHRENHEIT
451
RAY BRADBURY
BALLANTINE BOOKS
A BALLANTINE SCIENCE FICTION ORIGINAL
60¢
RAY BRADBURY
FAHRENHEIT
451
A Major Motion Picture Starring JULIE CHRISTIE and OSKAR WERNER
Directed by FRANÇOIS TRUFFAUT
A Universal Release
A BALLANTINE BAL-HI BOOK ORIGINAL
50¢
RAY BRADBURY
FAHRENHEIT
451
RAY BRADBURY
FAHRENHEIT
451
with a new introduction by the author
FAHRENHEIT
451
Ray Bradbury
FAHRENHEIT
451
RAY BRADBURY

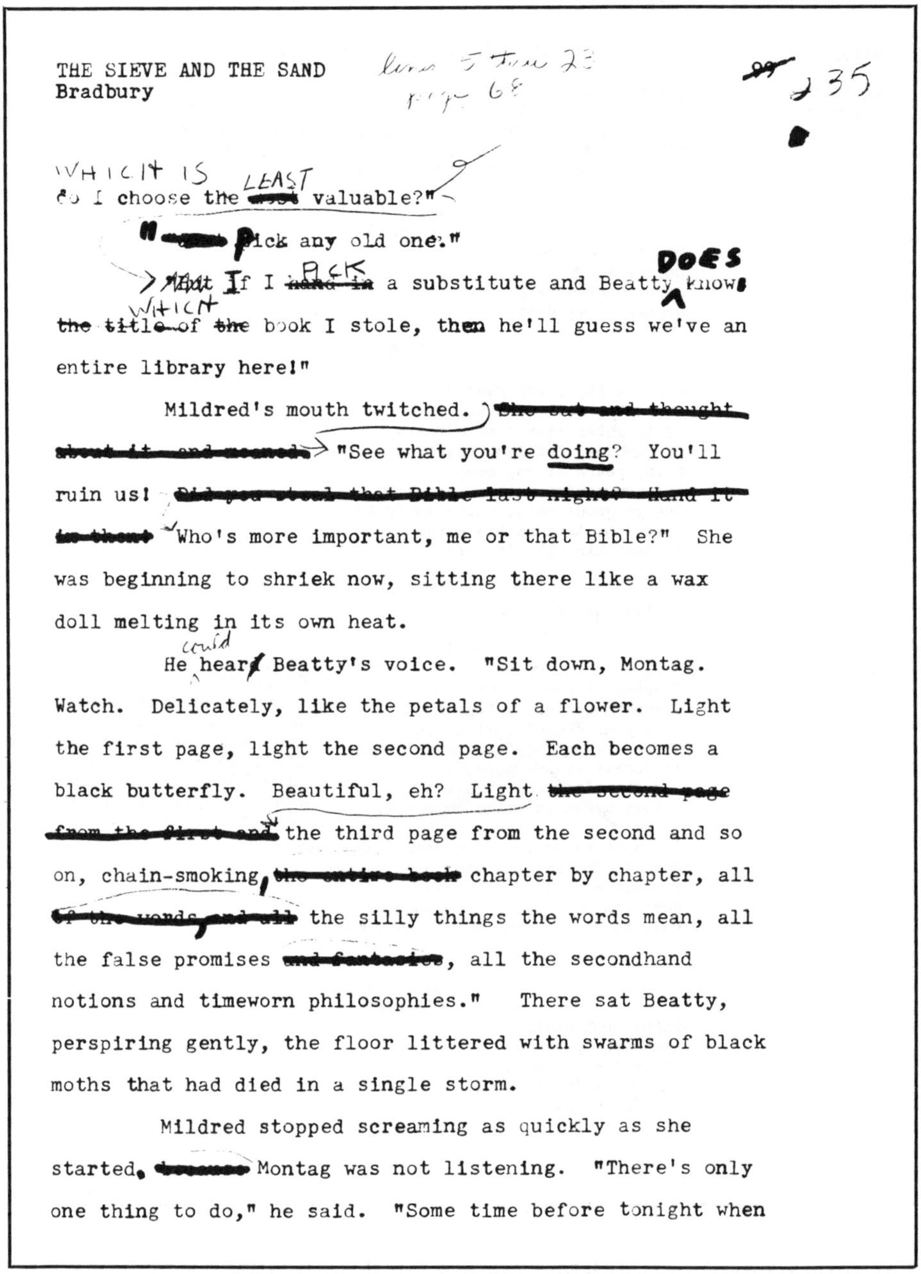

THE SIEVE AND THE SAND
Bradbury

~~34~~ 235

WHICH IS LEAST
do I choose the ~~most~~ valuable?"

"Pick any old one."

"~~But~~ If I ~~hand in~~ BACK a substitute and Beatty DOES know~~s~~ WHICH ~~the title of the~~ book I stole, ~~then~~ he'll guess we've an entire library here!"

Mildred's mouth twitched. ~~She sat and thought about it and moaned.~~ "See what you're doing? You'll ruin us! ~~Did you steal that Bible last night? Hand it in then!~~ Who's more important, me or that Bible?" She was beginning to shriek now, sitting there like a wax doll melting in its own heat.

He could hear~~d~~ Beatty's voice. "Sit down, Montag. Watch. Delicately, like the petals of a flower. Light the first page, light the second page. Each becomes a black butterfly. Beautiful, eh? Light ~~the second page from the first and~~ the third page from the second and so on, chain-smoking, ~~the entire book~~ chapter by chapter, all ~~of the words, and all~~ the silly things the words mean, all the false promises ~~and fantasies~~, all the secondhand notions and timeworn philosophies." There sat Beatty, perspiring gently, the floor littered with swarms of black moths that had died in a single storm.

Mildred stopped screaming as quickly as she started. ~~because~~ Montag was not listening. "There's only one thing to do," he said. "Some time before tonight when

Original manuscript pages from final typescript of *Fahrenheit 451*, showing last-minute revisions by Bradbury.

F 451

"Only the 'family' is 'people'."

"I beg pardon?"

"My wife says books aren't 'real'."

¶ "~~Yes, and~~ Thank God for that. ~~Though a book creates people in the mind, still~~ You can shut ~~it~~ THEM, say, "Hold on, ~~I don't believe you, give me~~ a moment.' ~~You throw the book down. It is not irresistible.~~ You play God to it. ~~do with it as you like.~~ But who has ever ~~successfully~~ torn himself from the ~~weight~~ claw that encloses you when you drop like a seed in ~~the center of~~ a tv parlor? It ~~can~~ grow~~s~~ you any shape it wishes! It is an environment as real as ~~any in~~ the world. It becomes and is the truth. ~~Books are cowards by contrast.~~ Books can be beaten down with reason. But with all my knowledge and skepticism, I have never ~~yet~~ been able to argue with a one hundred-piece symphony orchestra, full color, three dimensions, and being in and part of those incredible parlors. As you see, ~~I am a very odd fellow indeed. My~~ my parlor is nothing but four plaster walls. And here." He held out two small rubber plugs. "For my ears when I ride the subway-jets."

"Denham's Dentifrice; they toil not, neither do they spin," said Montag, eyes shut. "Where do we go from here? Would ~~it help to have more of the right kind of books?~~ BOOKS HELP US?"

SWITCH ON THE NIGHT

by RAY BRADBURY

Illustrations by MADELEINE GEKIERE

Library of Congress Card No. 55-5545
Printed in the United States of America
by Graphic Offset Company, New York, N. Y.

PANTHEON BOOKS

THE
OCTOBER COUNTRY

BY

RAY BRADBURY

Illustrated

by Joe Mugnaini

BALLANTINE BOOKS
NEW YORK

Magazine serialization: "Fahrenheit 451," *Playboy*, March, April, and May 1954.

1A SWITCH ON THE NIGHT (1955)
Illustrated by Madeleine Gekiere

[1-52]

$[1]^{28}$

Published March 1955.

1B _____ New York: Pantheon, [1955]. Library edition.

2 _____ London: Rupert Hart-Davis, 1955.

1 THE OCTOBER COUNTRY (1955)
Illustrated by Joe Mugnaini

[i-xii] [1] 2-306 [307-308]

$[1\text{-}10]^{16}$

Contents:
"The Dwarf"
"The Next in Line"
"The Watchful Poker Chip of H. Matisse"
"Skeleton"
"The Jar"
"The Lake"
"The Emissary"
"Touched With Fire"
"The Small Assassin"
"The Crowd"
"Jack-in-the-Box"
"The Scythe"
"Uncle Einar"
"The Wind"

the circus of dr. lao

and other improbable stories

edited by

ray bradbury

bantam books new york

"The Man Upstairs"
"There Was An Old Woman"
"The Cistern"
"Homecoming"
"The Wonderful Death of Dudley Stone"

Published October 1955.

Note: Fifteen of the twenty-seven stories from RB's first book, *Dark Carnival,* were reprinted here, many revised—along with four previously uncollected stories.

2 _____ New York: Ballantine, [1956]. No. F 139. Nine printings through June 1972.
With an untitled prefatory note added by RB.

3 _____ London: Rupert Hart-Davis, 1956.

4 _____ London: Ace, 1961.

5 _____ London: Four Square, [1963].

6 _____ New York: Knopf, 1970.

1 THE CIRCUS OF DR. LAO AND OTHER IMPROBABLE STORIES (1956)
No. A 1519
"Edited by Ray Bradbury"
Copyright page: PUBLISHED OCTOBER 1956

[i-vi] vii-xi [xii] 1-210 [211-212]

Perfect binding.

Contents:
"Introduction" by RB (See INTRODUCTIONS.)
"The Circus of Dr. Lao" by Charles G. Finney

RAY BRADBURY

SUN AND SHADOW

BERKELEY : 1957

Title, SUN AND SHADOW, printed in red.

"The Pond" by Nigel Kneale
"The Hour of Letdown" by E. B. White
"The Wish" by Roald Dahl
"The Summer People" by Shirley Jackson
"Earth's Holocaust" by Nathaniel Hawthorne
"Buzby's Petrified Woman" by Loren Eiseley
"The Resting Place" by Oliver LaFarge
"Threshold" by Henry Kuttner
"Greenface" by James H. Schmitz
"The Limits of Walter Horton" by John Seymour Sharnik
"The Man Who Vanished" by Robert Coates

1 SUN AND SHADOW (1957)
[i-iv] [1] 2-19 [20-24]

$[1]^{12}$

A short story by RB, printed for members of the Roxburghe Club of San Francisco by Kenneth J. Carpenter.

Issued in 1957 by The Quenian Press, Berkeley, California. Ninety copies.

1A DANDELION WINE (1957)
Copyright page: First Edition
[i-ii] [1-10] 11-13 [14] 15-23 [24] 25-31 [32] 33-43 [44] 45-97 [98] 99-109 [110] 111-125 [126] 127-137 [138] 139 [140] 141-157 [158] 159-165 [166] 167-189 [190] 191-213 [214] 215-223 [224] 225-261 [262] 263-275 [276] 277-281 [282-286]

Perfect binding.

 Note: Although published as a "novel"—without a contents

DANDELION WINE

A Novel by

RAY BRADBURY

Doubleday & Company, Inc., Garden City, New York 1957

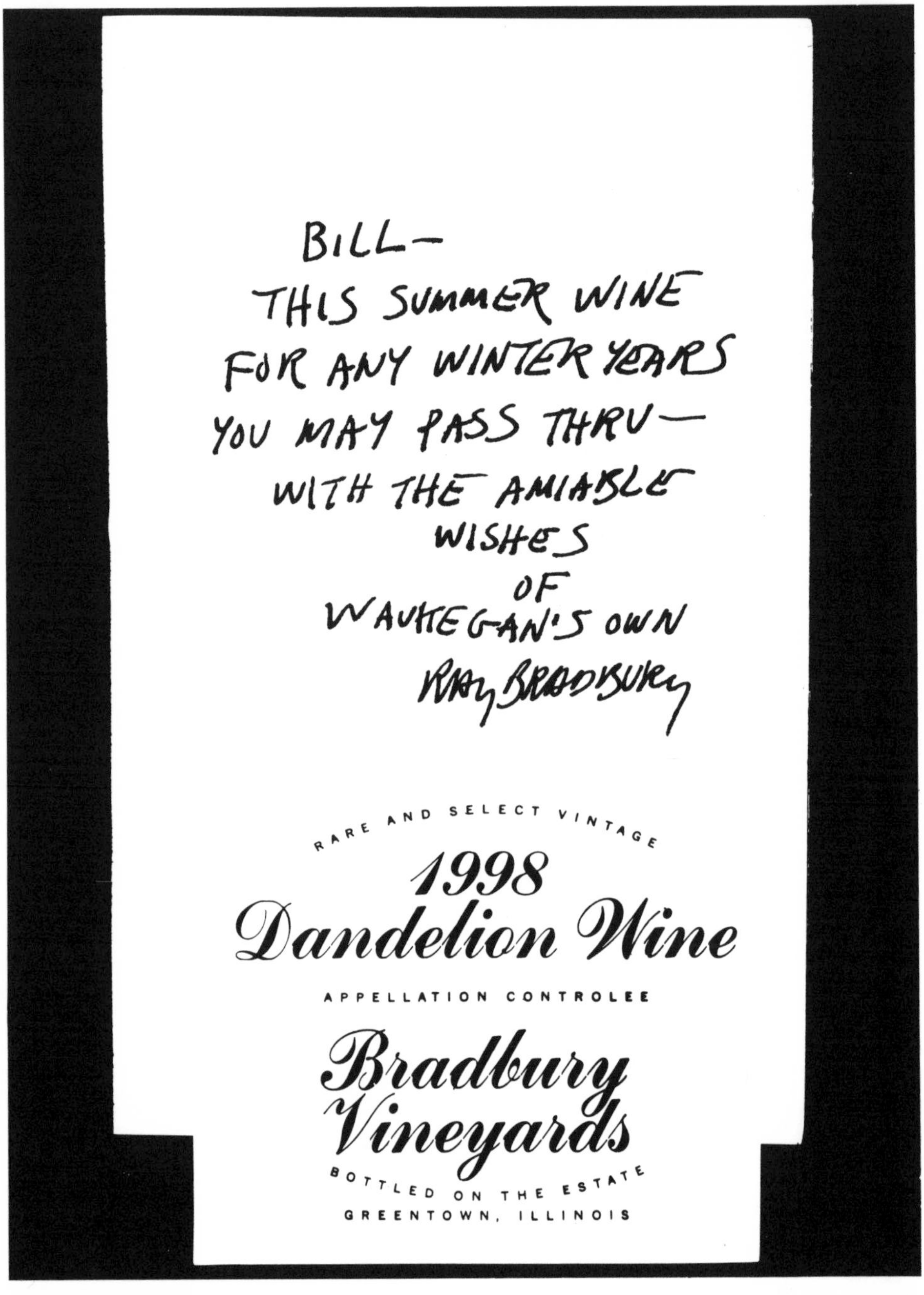
BILL—
THIS SUMMER WINE
FOR ANY WINTER YEARS
YOU MAY PASS THRU—
WITH THE AMIABLE
WISHES
OF
WAUKEGAN'S OWN
RAY BRADBURY
RARE AND SELECT VINTAGE
1998
Dandelion Wine
APPELLATION CONTROLEE
Bradbury
Vineyards
BOTTLED ON THE ESTATE
GREENTOWN, ILLINOIS

RB inscription, undated, attached to publisher's promotion slip for *Dandelion Wine.*

listing—this book is made up of the following integrated short stories (many revised from their original printings), plus new between-chapters "linking" material:

"Illumination"
"Dandelion Wine"
"The Sound of Summer Running"
"The Season of Sitting"
"The Night"
"The Lawns of Summer"
"The Happiness Machine"
"Season of Disbelief"
"The Last, the Very Last"
"The Green Machine"
"The Trolley"
"Statues"
"Magic!"
"The Window"
"The Swan"
"The Whole Town's Sleeping"
"Good-by, Grandma"
"The Tarot Witch"
"Green Wine for Dreaming"
"Dinner at Dawn"

Published September 1957.

1B _____ New York: Doubleday, 1957. 2nd printing—September.

1C _____ New York: Doubleday, 1957. 3rd printing—October.

2 _____ London: Rupert Hart-Davis, 1957.

3 _____ New York: Bantam, [1959]. No. A 1922. Pathfinder edition issued 1964. Twenty printings: February 1964 through 1972.

A Medicine For Melancholy

by
Ray
Bradbury

Doubleday & Company, Inc.
Garden City, New York, 1959

4 _____ London: Corgi, [1965]. No. GN 7240.

1 A MEDICINE FOR MELANCHOLY (1959)
Copyright page: First Edition
[1-11] 12-17 [18-19] 20-22 [23-25] 26-35 [36-37] 38-42 [43-45] 46-70 [71-73] 74-80 [81-83] 84-87 [88-89] 90-98 [99-101] 102-108 [109-111] 112-116 [117-119] 120-127 [128-129] 130-145 [146-147] 148-152 [153-155] 156-162 [163-165] 166-172 [173-175] 176-181 [182-183] 184-185 [186-187] 188-194 [195-197] 198-202 [203-205] 206-215 [216-217] 218-226 [227-229] 230-240

Perfect binding.

Contents:
"In a Season of Calm Weather"
"The Dragon"
"A Medicine for Melancholy"
"The End of the Beginning"
"The Wonderful Ice Cream Suit"
"Fever Dream"
"The Marriage Mender"
"The Town Where No One Got Off"
"A Scent of Sarsaparilla"
"Icarus Montgolfier Wright"
"The Headpiece"
"Dark They Were, and Golden-Eyed"
"The Smile"
"The First Night of Lent"
"The Time of Going Away"
"All Summer in a Day"
"The Gift"
"The Great Collision of Monday Last"
"The Little Mice"
"The Shore Line at Sunset"
"The Strawberry Window"
"The Day It Rained Forever"

the

essence

of creative

writing

Quill is printed in red.

a novel by

RAY BRADBURY

SIMON AND SCHUSTER

NEW YORK

1962

SOMETHING WICKED THIS WAY COMES

Published February 1959.

2 *The Day It Rained Forever.* London: Rupert Hart-Davis, 1959. Contents vary considerably from U.S. edition. Four stories have been eliminated and five other stories added, making this virtually a new RB book.

3 *A Medicine for Melancholy.* New York: Bantam, [1960]. No. A 2069. Twelve printings: April 1960 through 1972.

4 *The Day It Rained Forever.* London: Science Fiction Book Club, [1960].

5 ______ London: Penguin, [1963]. No. 1878.

6 *Twice 22.* New York: Doubleday, 1966. Combined with *The Golden Apples of the Sun.*

1 THE ESSENCE OF CREATIVE WRITING (1962)
[1-12]

$[1]^{6}$

A selection of three letters, slightly abridged, from RB to Clinton Lenoir, and sub-titled "Letters to a Young Aspiring Author."

Published in 1962 by the San Antonio Public Library, San Antonio, Texas. (See PUBLISHED LETTERS.)

1A SOMETHING WICKED THIS WAY COMES (1962)
Copyright page: FIRST PRINTING
[1-12] 13-14 [15-16] 17-134 [135-136] 137-253 [254-256] 257-317 [318-320]

$[1\text{-}10]^{16}$

R IS FOR ROCKET

RAY BRADBURY

DOUBLEDAY & COMPANY, INC.
GARDEN CITY, NEW YORK

Contents:
"Prologue"
I—"Arrivals"
II—"Pursuits"
III—"Departures"

Published September 1962.

1B ——— Simon and Schuster, 1962. 2nd printing—September.

2 ——— London: Rupert Hart-Davis, 1963.

3 ——— New York: Bantam, [1963]. No. H 2630. Eleven printings: September 1963 through January 1972. Pathfinder edition issued 1972.

4 ——— London: Corgi, [1965].

1A R IS FOR ROCKET (1962)
Copyright page: FIRST EDITION
[i-ii] [1-5] 6 [7-11] 12-29 [30] 31-35 [36] 37-45 [46] 47-57 [58] 59-70 [71] 72-78 [79] 80-93 [94] 95-110 [111] 112-126 [127] 128-142 [143] 144-152 [153] 154-156 [157] 158-159 [160] 161-208 [209] 210-217 [218] 219-226 [227] 228-233 [234-238]

Perfect binding.

Contents: Compiled by RB for Young Adult library sections, the book contains fifteen stories from earlier RB collections, and two previously uncollected stories.
Untitled Introduction by RB. (See INTRODUCTIONS.)
"R is For Rocket"
"The End of the Beginning"
"The Fog Horn"
"The Rocket"

"The Rocket Man"
"The Golden Apples of the Sun"
"A Sound of Thunder"
"The Long Rain"
"The Exiles"
"Here There Be Tygers"
"The Strawberry Window"
"The Dragon"
"The Gift"
"Frost and Fire"
"Uncle Einar"
"The Time Machine"
"The Sound of Summer Running"

Published October 1962.

1B _____ New York: Doubleday, [1962]. 2nd printing—November.

1C _____ New York: Doubleday, [1962]. 3rd printing—December.

1D _____ New York: Doubleday, [1963]. 4th printing—May.

1E _____ New York: Doubleday, [1964]. 5th printing—September.

1F _____ New York: Doubleday, [1965]. 6th printing—November.

1G _____ New York: Doubleday, [1967]. 7th printing—May.

1H _____ New York: Doubleday, [1969]. 8th printing—July.

1I _____ New York: Doubleday, [1971]. 9th printing—November.

THE ANTHEM SPRINTERS

And Other Antics

by

Ray Bradbury

THE DIAL PRESS NEW YORK 1963

the machineries of joy

SHORT STORIES BY

RAY BRADBURY

SIMON AND SCHUSTER • NEW YORK • 1964

2 _____ New York: Bantam, [1965]. No. 2915. Two printings: March through May. Pathfinder edition 1966—Twelve printings: September 1966 through 1972.

3 _____ London: Rupert Hart-Davis, 1968.

4 _____ London: Pan, [1972]. No. 0 330 23166 9.

1A THE ANTHEM SPRINTERS AND OTHER ANTICS (1963)
[1-12] 13-28 [39-40] 41-65 [66-68] 69-120 [121-122] 123-148 [149-150] 151-159 [160]

$[1\text{-}5]^{16}$

Contents:
"The Great Collision of Monday Last"
"The First Night of Lent"
"A Clear View of An Irish Mist"
"The Anthem Sprinters"
"The Queen's Own Evaders," An Afterword. (See INTRODUCTIONS.)

Published November 1963.

1B _____ New York: Dial, 1963. No. A 75. Apollo paperback edition. (See PUBLISHED PLAYS.)

1 THE MACHINERIES OF JOY (1964)
Copyright page: FIRST PRINTING
[1-11] 12-24 [25] 26-32 [33] 34-46 [47] 48-54 [55] 56-60 [61] 62-78 [79] 80-87 [88-89] 90-93 [94-95] 96-103 [104-105] 106-115 [116-117] 118-128 [129] 130-140 [141] 142-156 [157] 158-170 [171] 172-187 [188-189] 190-198 [199] 200-210 [211] 212-218 [219] 220-229 [230-231] 232-241 [242-243] 244-255 [256]

$[1\text{-}8]^{16}$

THE PEDESTRIAN
by Ray Bradbury

drawing by
Joe Mugnaini

Dark blue lettering within black frame on grey paper.

Contents:
"The Machineries of Joy"
"The One Who Waits"
"Tyrannosaurus Rex"
"The Vacation"
"The Drummer Boy of Shiloh"
"Boys! Raise Giant Mushrooms in *Your* Cellar!"
"Almost the End of the World"
"Perhaps We Are Going Away"
"And the Sailor, Home From the Sea"
"El Dia De Muerte"
"The Illustrated Woman"
"Some Live Like Lazarus"
"A Miracle of Rare Device"
"And So Died Riabouchinska"
"The Beggar on O'Connell Bridge"
"Death and the Maiden"
"A Flight of Ravens"
"The Best of All Possible Worlds"
"The Lifework of Juan Diaz"
"To the Chicago Abyss"
"The Anthem Sprinters"

Published February 1964.

2 ——— London: Rupert Hart-Davis, 1964. Omits one story, "Almost the End of the World," from U.S. edition.

3 ——— New York: Bantam, [1965]. No. H 2988. Thirteen printings: July 1965 through 1972.

4 ——— London: Corgi, [1966]. No. GN 7489.

1 THE PEDESTRIAN (1964)
[1-16]

$[1]^8$

A short story by RB.

The Vintage Bradbury

Ray Bradbury's own selection

of his best stories

With an Introduction by **Gilbert Highet**

VINTAGE BOOKS

A Division of Random House · New York

"Two hundred eighty copies of this edition . . . have been hand-printed by Roy A. Squires . . ."

No date of publication given beyond author's copyright date, 1951, but printer has elsewhere listed date as September 6, 1964. Issued from 1745 Kenneth Road, Glendale, California.

1A THE VINTAGE BRADBURY (1965)
No. V 294
"Ray Bradbury's Own Selection of His Best Stories"
Copyright page: FIRST VINTAGE EDITION
[i-vii] viii-x [xi-xii] [1-3] 4-12 [13] 14-28 [29] 30-37 [38] 39-48 [49] 50-61 [62] 63-75 [76] 77-81 [82] 83-101 [102] 103-113 [114] 115-139 [140] 141-150 [151] 152-160 [161] 162-178 [179] 180-196 [197] 198-231 [232] 233-242 [243] 244-251 [252] 253-265 [266] 267-274 [275] 276-288 [289] 290-296 [297] 298-321 [322] 323-329 [330-340]

Perfect binding.

Contents: Contains a selection of twenty-five stories from earlier RB collections, plus one previously uncollected story. "Introduction" by Gilbert Highet. (See ABOUT BRADBURY IN BOOKS.)
"The Watchful Poker Chip of H. Matisse"
"The Veldt"
"Hail and Farewell"
"A Medicine for Melancholy"
"The Fruit at the Bottom of the Bowl"
"Ylla"
"The Little Mice"
"The Small Assassin"
"The Anthem Sprinters"
"And the Rock Cried Out"
"Invisible Boy"
"Night Meeting"

THE AUTUMN PEOPLE

RAY BRADBURY

Adapted for E. C. Comics by
Albert B. Feldstein

BALLANTINE BOOKS • NEW YORK

"The Fox and the Forest"
"Skeleton"

Selections from *Dandelion Wine:*
"Illumination"
"Dandelion Wine"
"Statues"
"Green Wine for Dreaming"

"Kaleidoscope"
"Sun and Shadow"
"The Illustrated Man"
"The Fog Horn"
"The Dwarf"
"Fever Dream"
"The Wonderful Ice Cream Suit"
"There Will Come Soft Rains"

Published September 1965.

1B ______ New York: Vintage, [1965]. Library edition—with buckram reinforced binding.

1 THE AUTUMN PEOPLE (1965)
No. U 2141
"Adapted for E. C. Comics by Albert B. Feldstein"
(See COMIC BOOK APPEARANCES.)
Copyright page: First Ballantine Printing
[1-8] 9-189 [190-192]

Perfect binding.

Contents:
All illustrated comic book versions.
"Foreword" by RB. (See INTRODUCTIONS.)
"There Was An Old Woman"
"The Screaming Woman"
"Touch and Go"

Twice Twenty-two

THE GOLDEN APPLES OF THE SUN

A MEDICINE FOR MELANCHOLY

by Ray Bradbury

DRAWINGS BY JOE MUGNAINI

1966

Doubleday & Company, Inc., Garden City, New York

TOMORROW MIDNIGHT

Ray Bradbury

Adapted for E.C. Comics by
Albert B. Feldstein

Illustrated by

Will Elder • Wally Wood • Joe Orlando •
Al Williamson • Jack Kamen • John Severin

BALLANTINE BOOKS • NEW YORK

"The Small Assassin"
"The Handler"
"The Lake"
"The Coffin"
"Let's Play Poison"

Published October 1965.

1A TWICE 22 (1966)
Illustrated by Joe Mugnaini
Contents: "Ray Bradbury's Two Memorable Books—THE GOLDEN APPLES OF THE SUN and A MEDICINE FOR MELANCHOLY—Forty-four Stories in All, Complete in One Volume"

Published January 1966.

1B _____ New York: Doubleday, [1967]. 2nd printing—May.

1C _____ New York: Doubleday, [1968]. 3rd printing—March.

1D _____ New York: Doubleday, [1969]. 4th printing—September.

1E _____ New York: Doubleday, [1971]. 5th printing—October.

1 TOMORROW MIDNIGHT (1966)
No. U 2142
"Adapted for E. C. Comics by Albert B. Feldstein" (See COMIC BOOK APPEARANCES.)
Copyright page: First Ballantine Printing
[1-9] 10-188 [189-192]

Perfect binding.

The Day it Rained Forever

A COMEDY IN ONE ACT

By Ray Bradbury

SAMUEL FRENCH, INC.

25 West 45th Street New York 10036
7623 Sunset Boulevard Hollywood 90046
LONDON *TORONTO*

The Pedestrian

A FANTASY IN ONE ACT

By Ray Bradbury

SAMUEL FRENCH, INC.
25 West 45th Street New York 10036
7623 Sunset Boulevard Hollywood 90046
LONDON *TORONTO*

Contents:
All illustrated comic book versions.
"Introduction" by RB. (See INTRODUCTIONS.)
"Punishment Without Crime"
"I, Rocket"
"King of the Grey Spaces"
"The One Who Waits"
"The Long Years"
"There Will Come Soft Rains"
"Mars is Heaven!"
"Outcast of the Stars"

Published June 1966.

1 THE DAY IT RAINED FOREVER (1966)
[1-2] 3 [4] 5-24 [25-32]

$[1]^{16}$

A Play by RB.

"A COMEDY IN ONE ACT"

Published in 1966 by Samuel French, Inc., New York. With "Author's Production Note" by RB. (See INTRODUCTIONS and PUBLISHED PLAYS.)

1 THE PEDESTRIAN (1966)
[1-2] 3 [4] 5-22 [23-32]

$[1]^{16}$

A play by RB.

"A FANTASY IN ONE ACT"

Published in 1966 by Samuel French, Inc., New York. With "Production Note" by RB. (See INTRODUCTIONS and PUBLISHED PLAYS.)

S

IS FOR SPACE

Ray Bradbury

DOUBLEDAY & COMPANY, INC., GARDEN CITY, NEW YORK

1966

1A S IS FOR SPACE (1966)
Copyright page: First Edition
[1-7] 8 [9-13] 14-38 [39] 40-83 [84-85] 86-96 [97] 98-111 [112-113] 114-118 [119] 120-124 [125] 126-133 [134-135] 136-145 [146-147] 148-165 [166-167] 168-178 [179] 180-194 [195] 196-201 [202-203] 204-220 [221] 222-225 [226-227] 228-232 [233] 234-238 [239-240]

Gathered and glued, but not sewn.

Contents: This book, compiled by RB for Young Adult library sections, contains thirteen stories from earlier RB collections, plus three previously uncollected stories.
"Introduction" by RB. (See INTRODUCTIONS.)
"Chrysalis"
"Pillar of Fire"
"Zero Hour"
"The Man"
"Time in Thy Flight"
"The Pedestrian"
"Hail and Farewell"
"Invisible Boy"
"Come Into My Cellar"
"The Million-Year Picnic"
"The Screaming Woman"
"The Smile"
"Dark They Were, and Golden-Eyed"
"The Trolley"
"The Flying Machine"
"Icarus Montgolfier Wright"

Published August 1966.

1B _____ New York: Doubleday, [1967]. 2nd printing—January.

"CREATIVE MAN AMONG HIS SERVANT MACHINES"

by Ray Bradbury

A Luncheon Address at the 5th Annual Meeting of
Users of Automatic Information Display Equipment

Vacation Village, Mission Bay
San Diego, California
Wednesday, November 2, 1966

ALFRED · A · KNOPF
NEW YORK
1969

I SING THE BODY ELECTRIC!

STORIES BY
RAY
BRADBURY

1C _____ New York: Doubleday, [1967]. 3rd printing—July.

2 _____ London: Rupert Hart-Davis, 1968.

3 _____ New York: Bantam, [1970]. No. S 5621. Four printings: November 1970 through March 1972. Pathfinder edition November 1972.

4 _____ London: Pan, [1972]. No. 0 330 23167 7.

1 CREATIVE MAN AMONG HIS SERVANT MACHINES (1967)
Xeroxed typescript: 12 leaves, stapled [1] 2-23 [24]

"A Luncheon Address at the 5th Annual Meeting of Users of Automatic Information Display Equipment"

Published in 1967 by Stromberg Datagraphix, Vacation Village, Mission Bay, San Diego, California.

Introduction by Marvin J. Kaitz. (See PUBLISHED SPEECHES.)

1A I SING THE BODY ELECTRIC! (1969)
Copyright page: First Edition
[i-xii] [1-3] 4-14 [15] 16-31 [32] 33-49 [50] 51-60 [61] 62-71 [72] 73-89 [90] 91-99 [100] 101-118 [119] 120-131 [132] 133-149 [150] 151-190 [191] 192-199 [200] 201-229 [230] 231-240 [241] 242-253 [254] 255-261 [262] 263-295 [296] 297-305 [306-308]

$[1\text{-}10]^{16}$

Contents:
"The Kilimanjaro Device"

"The Terrible Conflagration up at the Place"
"Tomorrow's Child"
"The Women"
"The Inspired Chicken Motel"
"Downwind From Gettysburg"
"Yes, We'll Gather at the River"
"The Cold Wind and the Warm"
"Night Call, Collect"
"The Haunting of the New"
"I Sing the Body Electric!"
"The Tombling Day"
"Any Friend of Nicholas Nickleby's Is a Friend of Mine"
"Heavy-Set"
"The Man in the Rorschach Shirt"
"Henry the Ninth"
"The Lost City of Mars"
"Christus Apollo"

Published October 1969.

1B ——— New York: Knopf, 1969. 2nd printing—November.

1C ——— New York: Knopf, 1969. 3rd printing—December.

1D ——— New York: Knopf, [1970]. 4th printing—January.

1E ——— New York: Knopf, [1970]. 5th printing—September.

1F ——— New York: Knopf, [1970]. Science Fiction Book Club.

2 ——— London: Rupert Hart-Davis, [1970].

3 ——— New York: Bantam, [1971]. No. N 5752. Four

Old Ahab's Friend,

and Friend to Noah,

Speaks His Piece

A CELEBRATION

BY RAY BRADBURY

Apollo Year Two

Words, A CELEBRATION, printed in red.

THE WONDERFUL ICE CREAM SUIT AND OTHER PLAYS

BY RAY BRADBURY

BANTAM PATHFINDER EDITIONS
TORONTO / NEW YORK / LONDON

A NATIONAL GENERAL COMPANY

Madrigals for the Space Age

FOR MIXED CHORUS AND NARRATOR
WITH PIANO ACCOMPANIMENT

Music by
LALO SCHIFRIN

Text by
RAY BRADBURY

ASSOCIATED MUSIC PUBLISHERS
New York / London

First nine lines printed in grey.

printings: January 1971 through 1972.

4 ______ London: Corgi, [1971].

1 OLD AHAB'S FRIEND, AND FRIEND TO NOAH, SPEAKS HIS PIECE (1971)
[1-16]

[1]^{8}

Verse by RB. "485 copies of this first edition of Ray Bradbury's celebration have been printed during May and June of . . . 1971 by Roy A. Squires . . ."

Issued from 1745 Kenneth Road, Glendale, California.

(See VERSE.)

1 THE WONDERFUL ICE CREAM SUIT AND OTHER PLAYS (1972)
No. SP 7297 (Pathfinder edition)
Copyright page: . . . published April 1972
[i-iv] vi-xiv [1-2] 3-72 [73-74] 75-125 [126-128] 129-161 [162]

Perfect binding.

Contents:
"Introduction" by RB. (See INTRODUCTIONS.)
"The Wonderful Ice Cream Suit"
"The Veldt"
"To the Chicago Abyss"

(See PUBLISHED PLAYS.)

1 MADRIGALS FOR THE SPACE AGE (1972)
[1] 2-43 [44]

Ray Bradbury

THE HALLOWEEN TREE

Illustrated by Joseph Mugnaini

Alfred A. Knopf · New York

NUMBER THIRTEEN: YES! CAPRA CHAPBOOK SERIES

RAY BRADBURY

Zen and the Art of Writing

AND

The Joy of Writing

TWO ESSAYS

CAPRA PRESS 1973 SANTA BARBARA

Butterfly design printed in red.

[1]^{22}

"The Phi Mu Alpha SINFONIA SERIES . . . commissioned by the Sinfonia Foundation . . . to inagurate the observance of the Fraternity's Diamond Anniversary Year, 1972-73"

New York: Associated Music Publishers, 1972.

1 THE HALLOWEEN TREE (1972)
Illustrated by Joseph Mugnaini
Copyright page: First edition
[i-viii] [1-2] 3-7 [8] 9-21 [22] 23 [24] 25-33 [34] 35 [36-37] 38-39 [40] 41-43 [44] 45-60 [61] 62-63 [64] 65-89 [90] 91-119 [120] 121 [122] 123-136 [137] 138-143 [144] 145 [146-152]

[1-5]^{16}

Published October 1972.

2 ——— London: Hart-Davis, MacGibbon, [1973].

1 ZEN AND THE ART OF WRITING (1973)
[1-6] 7-24 [25-26]

Perfect binding.

"Yes! Capra Chapbook Series."

Contents:
Two Essays:
"Zen and the Art of Writing"
"The Joy of Writing"

Published November 1973.

Note: Special handbound edition of 250 numbered copies,

Alfred A. Knopf
New York 1973

RAY BRADBURY

WHEN
Celebrations
ELEPHANTS
for
LAST
almost
IN THE
any day
DOORYARD
in the year
BLOOMED

signed by the author, issued at date of publication.

1 WHEN ELEPHANTS LAST IN THE DOORYARD BLOOMED (1973)

Note: RB's collected verse, publication by Knopf in November 1973. (See VERSE for fifty poems known to be included.)

Other Forthcoming Bradbury Books:

THE DOGS THAT EAT SWEET GRASS (in progress)
Autobiographical account of RB's life and career in question-answer format (with Don Congdon)—to be published by Doubleday.

FAREWELL SUMMER (in progress)
A "sequel" to *Dandelion Wine*—nearing the final-manuscript stage.

FUTURIA FANTASIA
sum. 39
vol. 1 no. 1
ray d. bradbury-editor
HANS BOK

Green ink on white cover stock.

FUTURIA FANTASIA
vol. 1 no. 2 fall 1939
10 cents
BOK.

Green ink on orange cover stock.

BRADBURY'S MAGAZINE

In June of 1939, when he was eighteen, Bradbury began editing and publishing his own mimeo-run science fiction "fan magazine." In all, he completed four issues into September of 1940.

Bradbury's contributions to each issue are marked # in this listing. They include unsigned and pseudonymous work.

FUTURIA FANTASIA (Summer 1939)
Cover drawing by Hans Bok
Typed mimeo in green ink throughout, cover and interior pages: six leaves, stapled: [1-12]
Contents:

"Greetings! At Long Last—Futuria Fantasia!" Editorial.
"The Revolt of the Scientists" by Bruce Yerke. Article.
"Don't Get Technatal" by RB as "Ron Reynolds." Short story.
"The Record" by Forrest J. Ackerman. Short story.
"Thought and Space." Verse.

Issued "Summer" [June] 1939, from 1841 S. Manhattan Place, Los Angeles, California.

FUTURIA FANTASIA (Fall 1939)
Illustrated by Hans Bok
Front cover on dark orange stock

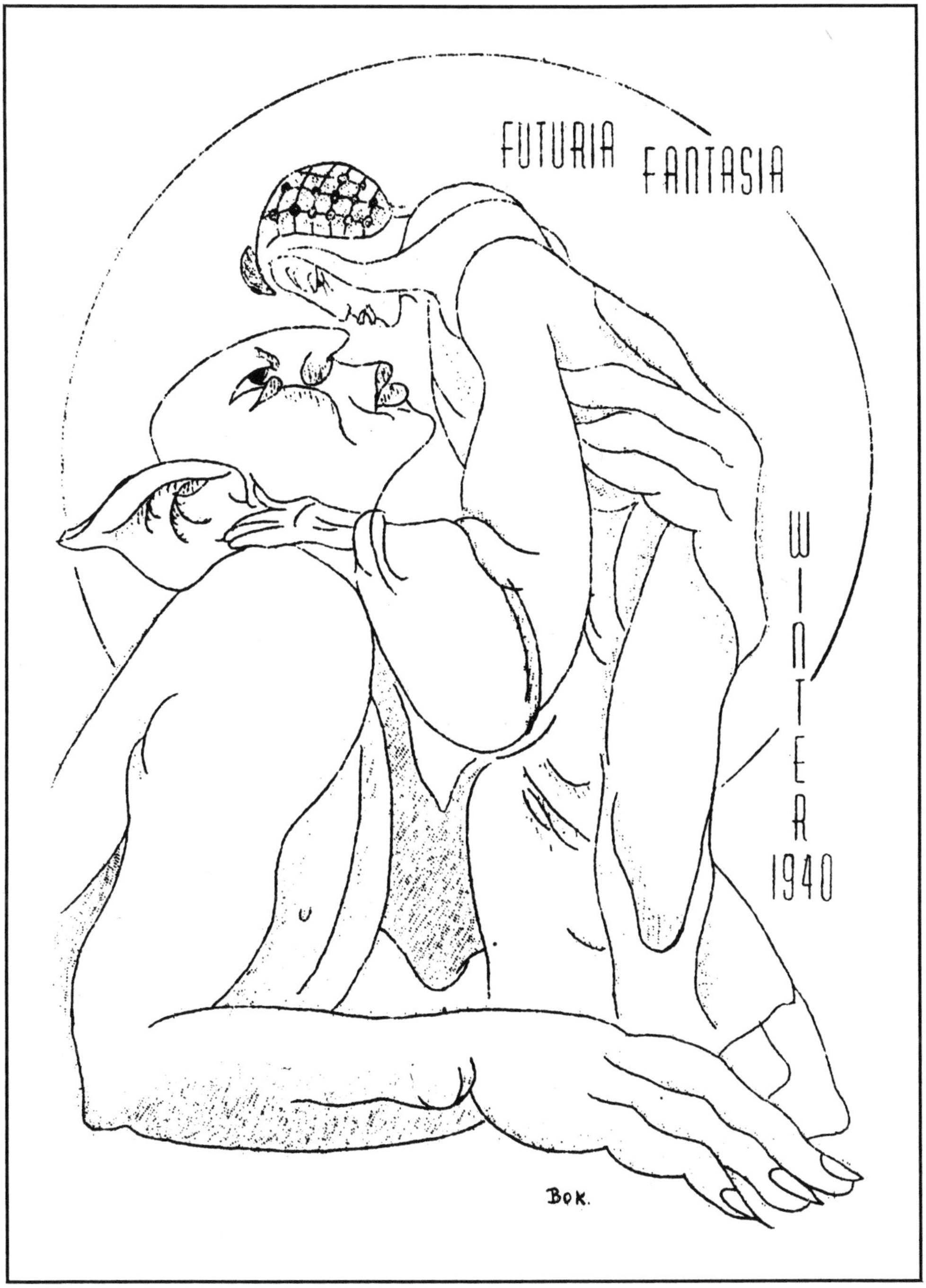
FUTURIA FANTASIA
WINTER
1940
BOK.

Green ink on orange cover stock.

Typed mimeo in green ink throughout, cover and interior pages: ten leaves, stapled: [1-3] 4-18 [19-20]

Contents:

"Worry!!!" Editorial.
"The Galapurred Forsendyke" by H. V. B. (Hans Bok). Humor.
"I'm Through!" by "Foo E Onya." Article.
"Satan's Mistress" by RB as "Doug Rogers." Verse.
"Lost Soul" by Henry Hasse. Verse.
"The Truth About Goldfish" by Henry Kuttner. Short story.
"God Busters" by Erick Freyor. Article.
"The Pendulum." Unsigned. Short story.
"Is It True What They Say About Kuttner?" by RB as "Guy Amory." Article.
"Analysis" in letters to the editor.
"Return From Death" by RB as "Anthony Corvais." Short story.
"Conventional Notes." Unsigned report.
"Local League Life." Unsigned report.

Issued "Fall" 1939, from 3054-1/2 W. 12th St., Los Angeles, California.

FUTURIA FANTASIA (Winter 1940)
Illustrated by Hans Bok
Front cover on dark tan stock
Typed mimeo in green ink throughout, cover and interior pages: ten leaves, stapled: [1-3] 4-19 [20]

"Last Issue . . . This Issue . . . Next Issue." Editorial.
"The Voice of Scariliop" by H.V.B. (Hans Bok). Short story.
"Aw, G'wan!" by Henry Hasse. Article.
"The Flight of the Good Ship Clarissa." Unsigned short story.
"The Intruder" by Emil Petaja. Short story.
"Asphodel" by E. T. Pine. Verse.
"Marmok" by Emil Petaja. Verse.
"Hades." Unsigned verse.

Futuria Fantasia

"The Best Ways to Get Around" by Ross Rocklynne. Article.
"The Symphonic Abduction." Unsigned short story.
"As I Remember" by RB as "Omega." Commentary.

Issued "Winter" 1940, from 3054-1/2 W. 12th St., Los Angeles, California.

FUTURIA FANTASIA (1940)
Illustrated by Hans Bok
Typed mimeo in green ink, interior pages: ten leaves, stapled: [1-3] 4-18 [19-20]
Contents:
"Gorgono and Slith." Editorial.
"Heil!" by "Lyle Monroe" (Robert A. Heinlein). Short story.
"The Phantoms" by Joseph E. Kelleam. Verse.
"Thoughts on the Worldstate" by Henry Kuttner. Short story.
"Would You?" by J. Harvey Haggard. Verse.
"The Piper" by RB as "Ron Reynolds." Short story.
"The Itching Hour" by Damon Knight. Short story.
"I've Never Seen" by Hannes Bok. Verse.
"Ninevah" by J. E. Kelleam. Verse.

Issued in September 1940, from 3054-1/2 W. 12th St., Los Angeles, California.

FICTION

Includes: Short stories, Novels, Bridge-passages and Fragments.

Beginning in late 1937, when he was seventeen, Ray Bradbury began contributing material, without payment, to amateur "fanzines" (science fiction fan publications). Privately printed on mimeo machines in clubrooms, and extremely limited in circulation, these magazines provided young Bradbury with an outlet for his work. He continued with them into 1941 until he began selling professionally. I have eliminated several "humor" items from Bradbury's fanzine contributions, listing only those which may be justly considered short stories.

Stories collected by Bradbury in his books are located by the following symbols:

DC—DARK CARNIVAL
MC—MARTIAN CHRONICLES
IM—ILLUSTRATED MAN
GA—GOLDEN APPLES OF THE SUN
F4—FAHRENHEIT 451
OC—OCTOBER COUNTRY
DW—DANDELION WINE
MM—MEDICINE FOR MELANCHOLY
SW—SOMETHING WICKED THIS WAY COMES
RR—R IS FOR ROCKET
MJ—MACHINERIES OF JOY
VB—VINTAGE BRADBURY

SS—S IS FOR SPACE
IS—I SING THE BODY ELECTRIC!

In order to record fiction in book format, if a story has been anthologized but *not* collected, the anthology title is listed. See ANTHOLOGY APPEARANCES for full data on editor and publisher. Pseudonyms and alternate titles are noted; reprintings and revisions are not. Arranged by date of publication.

** denotes a privately-printed amateur magazine or "fanzine."

"Hollerbochen's Dilemma," ***Imagination!* January 1938. Uncollected, but anthologized in *Horrors Unseen,* 1974. RB's first printed short story.

"Hollerbochen Comes Back," ***Mikros,* November 1938.

"How to Run a Successful Ghost Agency" (as "Brian Eldred"), ***D'Journal,* March 1939.

"Don't Get Technatal" (as "Ron Reynolds"), ***Futuria Fantasia,* Summer 1939.

"Gold," ***Science Fiction Fan,* August 1939.

"The Pendulum" (anon.), ***Futuria Fantasia,* Fall 1939. Uncollected, but anthologized in *Horrors Unknown,* 1971.

"Return From Death" (as "Anthony Corvais"), ***Futuria Fantasia,* Fall 1939.

"The Maiden of Jirbu" (with Bob Tucker), ***Polaris,* March 1940.

"Tale of the Tortletwitch" (as "Guy Amory"), ***Spaceways,* April 1940.

"Luana the Living," ***Polaris,* June 1940. Uncollected, but anthologized in *Horrors in Hiding,* 1973.

"The Flight of the Good Ship Clarissa" (anon.), ***Futuria Fantasia,* Winter 1940.

"The Symphonic Abduction" (anon.), ***Futuria Fantasia,* Winter 1940.

"The Piper" (as "Ron Reynolds"), ***Futuria Fantasia,* No. 4 [September 1940]. Uncollected, but anthologized in

PENDULUM

Prisoner of Time was he, outlawed from Life and Death alike—the strange, brooding creature who watched the ages roll by and waited half fearfully for—eternity?

By RAY BRADBURY and HENRY HASSE

"I THINK," shrilled Erjas, "that this is our most intriguing discovery on any of the worlds we have yet visited!"

His wide, green-shimmering wings fluttered, his beady bird eyes flashed excitement. His several companions bobbed their heads in agreement, the greenish-gold down on their slender necks ruffling softly. They were perched on what had once been a moving sidewalk but was now only a twisted ribbon of wreckage overlooking the vast expanse of a ruined city.

102

From *Super Science Stories*, November 1941. This story marked RB's first professional sale, the issue appearing on his 21st birthday. The illustration was by his artist/friend, Hannes Bok.

Futures to Infinity, 1970.

"The Last Man," ***Damn Thing,* November 1940.

"It's Not the Heat, It's the Hu—," *Script,* November 2, 1940.

"The Tale of the Terrible Typer," ***Fantasite,* November 1940.

"Genie Trouble," ***Damn Thing,* December 1940.

"How Am I Today, Doctor?" ***Damn Thing,* February 1941.

"The Trouble With Humans is People," ***Damn Thing,* March 1941.

"Tale of the Mangledomvritch," ***Snide,* 1941.

"To Make a Long, Long Story Much, Much Shorter," *Script,* July 5, 1941.

"Pendulum" (with Henry Hasse), *Super Science Stories,* November 1941.Uncollected, but anthologized in *Horrors Unknown,* 1971. RB's first story sale.

"Eat, Drink and Be Wary," *Astounding Science Fiction,* July 1942.

"The Candle," *Weird Tales,* November 1942.

"The Piper," *Thrilling Wonder Stories,* February 1943. Uncollected, but anthologized (England), in *The Future Makers,* 1969.

"The Wind," *Weird Tales,* March 1943. Collected in DC and OC.

"Subterfuge," *Astonishing Stories,* April 1943. Uncollected, but anthologized in *Assignment in Tomorrow,* 1954.

"The Crowd," *Weird Tales,* May 1943. Collected in DC and OC.

"Gabriel's Horn" (with Henry Hasse), *Captain Future,* Spring 1943.

"The Scythe," *Weird Tales,* July 1943. Collected in DC and OC.

"Doodad," *Astounding Science Fiction,* September 1943. Uncollected, but anthologized in *Strange Signposts,* 1966.

"And Watch the Fountains," *Astounding Science Fiction*, September 1943.

"Promotion to Satellite," *Thrilling Wonder Stories*, Fall 1943.

"The Ducker," *Weird Tales*, November 1943.

"King of the Gray Spaces," *Famous Fantastic Mysteries*, December 1943.Collected in RR—as "R is For Rocket."

"The Sea Shell," *Weird Tales*, January 1944.

"Reunion," *Weird Tales*, March 1944. Collected in DC.

"The Monster Maker," *Planet Stories*, Spring 1944.

"I, Rocket," *Amazing Stories*, May 1944. Collected, in illustrated comic book version, in *Tomorrow Midnight* by RB. Uncollected in prose version, but anthologized in *The Human Zero*, 1967.

"The Lake," *Weird Tales*, May 1944. Collected in DC and OC.

"There Was An Old Woman," *Weird Tales*, July 1944. Collected in DC and OC.

"Killer, Come Back to Me!" *Detective Tales*, July 1944.

"The Long Night," *New Detective*, July 1944.

"Yesterday I Lived!" *Flynn's Detective Fiction*, August 1944.

"Morgue Ship," *Planet Stories*, Summer 1944.

"The Trunk Lady," *Detective Tales*, September 1944. Uncollected, but anthologized in *Horror Times Ten*, 1967.

"Bang! You're Dead!" *Weird Tales*, September 1944.

"Half-Pint Homicide," *Detective Tales*, November 1944.

"The Jar," *Weird Tales*, November 1944. Collected in DC and OC.

"It Burns Me Up!" *Dime Mystery*, November 1944. Uncollected, but anthologized in *Hauntings and Horrors*, 1969.

"Undersea Guardians," *Amazing Stories*, December 1944.

"Four-Way Funeral," *Detective Tales*, December 1944.

"Lazarus Come Forth," *Planet Stories*, Winter 1944.

"The Poems," *Weird Tales,* January 1945.

" 'I'm Not So Dumb!' " *Detective Tales,* February 1945.

"Hell's Half-Hour," *New Detective,* March 1945.

"The Tombstone," *Weird Tales,* March 1945. Collected in DC.

"Skeleton," *Script,* April 28, 1945.

"The Watchers," *Weird Tales,* May 1945. Uncollected, but anthologized in *Rue Morgue No. 1,* 1946.

"Dead Men Rise Up Never," *Dime Mystery,* July 1945.

"Corpse-Carnival" (as "D. R. Banat"), *Dime Mystery,* July 1945.

"The Dead Man," *Weird Tales,* July 1945. Collected in DC.

"The Big Black and White Game," *American Mercury,* August 1945. Collected in GA.

"Skeleton," *Weird Tales,* September 1945. (Not to be confused with earlier story in *Script.*) Collected in DC, OC and VB.

"The Long Way Home," *Dime Mystery,* November 1945.

"Invisible Boy," *Mademoiselle,* November 1945. Collected in GA, VB and SS.

"Final Victim" (with Henry Hasse), *Amazing Stories,* February 1946.

"The Traveller," *Weird Tales,* March 1946. Collected in DC.

"One Timeless Spring," *Collier's,* April 13, 1946.

"The Miracles of Jamie," *Charm,* April 1946.

"The Smiling People," *Weird Tales,* May 1946. Collected in DC.

"Defense Mech," *Planet Stories,* Spring 1946.

"Rocket Skin," *Thrilling Wonder Stories,* Spring 1946.

"Her Eyes, Her Lips, Her Limbs" (as "William Elliott"), *Californian,* June 1946.

"Chrysalis," *Amazing Stories,* July 1946. Collected in SS.

"The Night," *Weird Tales,* July 1946. Collected in DC and, untitled, in DW.

"The Electrocution" (as "William Elliott"), *Californian,* August 1946.

"Lorelei of the Red Mist" (with Leigh Brackett), *Planet Stories,* Summer 1946. Uncollected, but anthologized in *The Human Equation,* 1971.

"The Million Year Picnic," *Planet Stories,* Summer 1946. Collected in MC and SS.

"Homecoming," *Mademoiselle,* October 1946. Collected in DC and OC, as "The Homecoming."

"The Creatures That Time Forgot," *Planet Stories,* Fall 1946. Collected in RR, as "Frost and Fire."

"Let's Play 'Poison,'" *Weird Tales,* November 1946. Collected in DC.

"The Small Assassin," *Dime Mystery,* November 1946. Collected in DC, OC and VB.

"A Careful Man Dies," *New Detective,* November 1946.

"The Handler," *Weird Tales,* January 1947. Collected in DC.

"The Man Upstairs," *Harper's,* March 1947. Collected in DC and OC.

"Tomorrow and Tomorrow," *Fantastic Adventures,* May 1947. Uncollected, but anthologized in *Untamed,* 1967.

"The Cistern," *Mademoiselle,* May 1947. Collected in DC and OC.

"Rocket Summer," *Planet Stories,* Spring 1947.

"Interim," *Weird Tales,* July 1947. Collected in DC.

"Wake for the Living," *Dime Mystery,* September 1947. Collected in DC, as "The Coffin."

"El Día De Muerte," *Touchstone,* Fall 1947. Collected in MJ.

"Interim," *Epoch,* Fall 1947. AKA: "Time Intervening." (Not to be confused with earlier story in *Weird Tales.*)

"Zero Hour," *Planet Stories,* Fall 1947. Collected in IM and SS.

"The Emissary," first printed in *Dark Carnival,* [October] 1947. Collected in OC.

July 48

The Undead Die

BY E. EVERETT EVANS

There is no resignation for true members of the confraternity of the Undead

—This section written by Bradbury

HE WAS a Jack-in-the-box. Sunset up, sunrise down. And repeat, forever and forever. He was a thing in a box in a cold deep cellar. He was a container for red wines. There was no label on him, but there were little drops of red liqueur upon his sleeping lips. He was the contents of a mahogany box, in a cellar of webs and upside-down things hooked to the ceilings. He lived in a land of dropping midnight waters and soft gray web. He was a white hand, a rouged mouth, a glass eye, a set of white teeth, and a cold heart. He was a pedestrian who walked the nights. He was a sleeper with original ideas as to hours. He was a leaf, a pelt, a flame, a wing. He was Robert Warram, dead these hundreds of years.

"Lisa."

In the cellar came the sound of a woman's name.

"Lisa."

His white hand lifted from his bosom. He put it against the lid firmly. His eyes opened whitely. He pressed upward.

The lid would not open.

"It has *always* opened." He lay back a moment, waiting.

"It *must* open," he declared. With a sudden movement of strength he pushed. The lid gave. Things fell with a loud roar in the cellar world. He was free of the coffin in an instant. He was the only moving thing, the only white thing in the crypt. And he was afraid.

He turned to Lisa's coffin.

It was covered with ash and leaf and

Heading by Boris Dolgov

84

Page from *Weird Tales,* demonstrating RB's help to beginning writers. Entire opening paragraph ghost-written by Bradbury for E. Everett Evans.

"Uncle Einar," first printed in *Dark Carnival,* [October] 1947. Collected in OC and RR.

"The Next in Line," first printed in *Dark Carnival,* [October] 1947. Collected in OC.

"The Maiden," first printed in *Dark Carnival,* [October] 1947.

"The Night Sets," first printed in *Dark Carnival,* [October] 1947.

"Jack-in-the-Box," first printed in *Dark Carnival,* [October] 1947. Collected in OC.

"I See You Never," *New Yorker,* November 8, 1947. Collected in GA.

"The Irritated People," *Thrilling Wonder Stories,* December 1947.

"The Candy Skull," *Dime Mystery,* January 1948. Uncollected, but anthologized in *Masters of Horror,* 1968.

"The Shape of Things," *Thrilling Wonder Stories,* February 1948. Collected in IS, as "Tomorrow's Child."

"The October Game," *Weird Tales,* March 1948. Uncollected, but anthologized in *Alfred Hitchcock Presents: Stories They Wouldn't Let Me Do on TV,* 1957.

"Powerhouse," *Charm,* March 1948. Collected in GA.

"The Black Ferris," *Weird Tales,* May 1948. Uncollected, but anthologized in *The Dark Side,* 1965.

"Jonah of the Jove Run," *Planet Stories,* Spring 1948.

"—And the Moon be Still as Bright," *Thrilling Wonder Stories,* June 1948. Collected in MC.

"The Earth Men," *Thrilling Wonder Stories,* August 1948. Collected in MC.

"Pillar of Fire," *Planet Stories,* Summer 1948. Collected in SS.

"The Long Years," *Maclean's* (Canada), September 15, 1948. AKA: "Dwellers in Silence." Collected in MC.

"Fever Dream," *Weird Tales,* September 1948. Collected in MM and VB.

"End of Summer," *Script,* September 1948.

"Mars is Heaven!" *Planet Stories,* Fall 1948. Collected in MC, as "The Third Expedition."

"Referent"(as "Brett Sterling"), *Thrilling Wonder Stories,* October 1948. Collected in *The Day It Rained Forever* (England) by RB, 1959.

"The Square Pegs," *Thrilling Wonder Stories,* October 1948.

"The Women," *Famous Fantastic Mysteries,* October 1948. Collected in IS.

"Touch and Go," *Detective Book,* November 1948. Collected in GA and VB, as "The Fruit at the Bottom of the Bowl."

"The Visitor," *Startling Stories,* November 1948. Collected in IM.

"The Off Season," *Thrilling Wonder Stories,* December 1948. Collected in MC.

"Asleep in Armageddon," *Planet Stories,* Winter 1948. Collected in *The Day It Rained Forever* (England) by RB, 1959, as "Perchance to Dream."

"The Silence," *Super Science Stories,* January 1949.

"The Man," *Thrilling Wonder Stories,* February 1949. Collected in IM and SS.

"The Great Fire," *Seventeen,* March 1949. Collected in GA.

"The Silent Towns," *Charm,* March 1949. Collected in MC.

"Marionettes, Inc." *Startling Stories,* March 1949. Collected in IM.

"The Concrete Mixer," *Thrilling Wonder Stories,* April 1949. Collected in IM.

"I, Mars," *Super Science Stories,* April 1949. Collected in IS, as "Night Call, Collect."

"The Lonely Ones," *Startling Stories,* July 1949.

"Changeling," *Super Science Stories,* July 1949. Uncollected, but anthologized in *The Pseudo-People,* 1965.

"The One Who Waits," *Arkham Sampler,* Summer 1949. Collected in MJ.

"The Naming of Names," *Thrilling Wonder Stories,* August 1949. Collected in MM and SS, as "Dark They Were, and Golden-Eyed."

"Holiday," *Arkham Sampler*, Autumn 1949. Uncollected, but anthologized in *Far Boundaries*, 1951.

"The Mad Wizards of Mars," *Maclean's* (Canada), September 15, 1949. Collected in IM and RR, as "The Exiles."

"Kaleidoscope," *Thrilling Wonder Stories*, October 1949. Collected in IM and VB.

"Impossible," *Super Science Stories*, November 1949. Collected in MC, as "The Martian."

"A Blade of Grass," *Thrilling Wonder Stories*, December 1949.

"The Spring Night," *Arkham Sampler*, Winter 1949. Collected in MC, as "The Summer Night."

"I'll Not Look for Wine," *Maclean's* (Canada), January 1, 1950. Collected in MC and VB, as "Ylla."

"All on a Summer's Night," *Today*, January 22, 1950.

"Payment in Full," *Thrilling Wonder Stories*, February 1950. Uncollected, but anthologized in *Man Against Tomorrow*, 1965.

"Outcast of the Stars," *Super Science Stories*, March 1950. Collected in IM and RR, as "The Rocket."

"Punishment Without Crime," *Other Worlds*, March 1950. Collected, in illustrated comic book version, in *Tomorrow Midnight* by RB. Uncollected in prose version, but anthologized in *Science Fiction Terror Tales*, 1955.

"Carnival of Madness," *Thrilling Wonder Stories*, April 1950. Collected in MC, as "Usher II."

"Miss Bidwell," *Charm*, April 1950.

"There Will Come Soft Rains," *Collier's*, May 6, 1950. Collected in MC and VB.

"The Green Morning," first printed in *The Martian Chronicles*, [May] 1950.

"Night Meeting," first printed in *The Martian Chronicles*, [May] 1950. Collected, also, in VB.

The following "bridge-passages" appeared in print for the first time in *The Martian Chronicles*, but are *not* complete stories:

"Rocket Summer" (no relationship to work with same title in *Planet Stories*)
"The Taxpayer"
"The Settlers"
"The Locusts"
"The Shore"
"Interim" (no relationship to work with same title in *Weird Tales*)
"The Musicians"
"The Naming of Names" (no relationship to work with same title in *Thrilling Wonder Stories*)
"The Old Ones"
"The Luggage Store"
"The Watchers" (no relationship to work with same title in *Weird Tales*)

"To the Future," *Collier's*, May 13, 1950. Collected in IM and VB, as "The Fox and the Forest."

"The Highway" (as "Leonard Spaulding"), *Copy*, Spring 1950. Collected in IM.

"Forever and the Earth," *Planet Stories*, Spring 1950. Uncollected, but anthologized in *Big Book of Science Fiction*, 1950.

"The Illustrated Man," *Esquire*, July 1950. Collected in VB.

"Way in the Middle of the Air," *Other Worlds*, July 1950. Collected in MC.

"Purpose," *Startling Stories*, July 1950. Collected in IM, as "The City."

"The Window," *Collier's*, August 5, 1950. Collected, untitled, as part of DW.

"Death-by-Rain," *Planet Stories*, Summer 1950. Collected in IM and RR, as "The Long Rain."

"The Whole Town's Sleeping," *McCall's*, September 1950. Collected, untitled, as part of DW.

"The World the Children Made," *Saturday Evening Post*, September 23, 1950. Collected in IM and VB, as "The Veldt."

THE BLUE BOTTLE 5

"Which building do we try?"

"This one here. But wait."

Beck cupped his hands to his mouth and gave a great shout.

"YOU, THERE!"

"There," said an echo, and towers fell. In shattering flights, stone animals with vast granite wings dived to strike the courtyards and fountains. His cry summoned them like living beasts and the beasts indeed gave answer, groaned, cracked, leaned up, tilted over, trembling, hesitant, then split the air and came hard down in evil masks and terrible faces, with grimaced mouths and empty eyes, with vast and eternally hungry teeth suddenly seized out and strewn like shrapnel against their shins, bulleting the two men's arms and chests. A stampede of high creatures, panicked at a cough, took flight. A moment later the bones, buried in bones, were self-made funeral mounds. The dust settled. Two structures remained intact.

Beck moved, nodding to his friend.

"You take that [illegible] one. I'll go here."

THEY MOVED IN SEARCH.

AND, SEARCHING, CRAIG PAUSED, A FAINT SMILE ON HIS LIPS.

Original manuscript page from short story, "The Blue Bottle," a revised version of "Death Wish."

the Playgoer
THE WORLD OF RAY BRADBURY
THE FIREMAN
By RAY BRADBURY
RAY BRADBURY review
edited by WILLIAM F. NOLAN
Galaxy SCIENCE FICTION
FEBRUARY 1951
THE FIREMAN
By Ray Bradbury
JOSE LUIS GARCI
RAY BRADBURY, HUMANISTA DEL FUTURO
Editorial Helios
Fantasy AND Science Fiction
RAY BRADBURY:
TO THE CHICAGO ABYSS
FAHRENHEIT 451
FICTION
by
RAY BRADBURY
PART ONE
THE CONCLUSION OF A FRIGHTENING THREE PART FANTASY
FAHRENHEIT 451
by Ray Bradbury
THE SECOND PART OF A FRIGHTENING THREE PART FANTASY
WHAT HAS COME BEFORE
FAHRENHEIT 451

Material by and about RB, including tearsheets on "The Fireman"—and the 3-part serialization of its expanded version ("Fahrenheit 451") from *Playboy.* Cover of special "Bradbury issue" of *The Magazine of Fantasy and Science Fiction* (center right) was painted by Joe Mugnaini.

"Death Wish," *Planet Stories*, Fall 1950. Uncollected, but anthologized in *A Sea of Space*, 1970, as "The Blue Bottle."

"Season of Disbelief," *Collier's*, November 25, 1950. Collected, untitled, as part of DW.

"The Bonfire," ***Torquasian Times*, Winter 1950.

"The Year 2150 A.D." ***Shangri-LA*, (undated) 1950.

"The Fireman," *Galaxy*, February 1951. This short novel formed basis for *Fahrenheit 451*, but has not been collected or anthologized in its original version.

"The Last Night of the World," *Esquire*, February 1951. Collected in IM.

"No Particular Night or Morning," first printed in *The Illustrated Man*, [February] 1951.

"The Illustrated Man: Prologue/Epilogue," first printed in *The Illustrated Man*, [February] 1951.

"The Rocket Man," *Maclean's* (Canada), March 1, 1951. Collected in IM and RR.

"The Other Foot," *New Story*, March 1951. Collected in IM.

"The Green Machine," *Argosy* (England), March 1951. Collected, untitled, as part of DW.

"In This Sign," *Imagination*, April 1951. Collected in IM, as "The Fire Balloons."

"The Pumpernickel," *Collier's*, May 19, 1951.

"These Things Happen," *McCall's*, May 1951.

"The Screaming Woman," *Today*, May 27, 1951. Collected in SS.

"The Beast From 20,000 Fathoms," *Saturday Evening Post*, June 23, 1951. Collected in GA, RR and VB, as "The Fog Horn."

"The Pedestrian," *Reporter*, August 7, 1951. Collected in GA and SS.

"A Little Journey," *Galaxy*, August 1951. Uncollected, but anthologized in *Galaxy Reader of Science Fiction*, 1952.

"Embroidery," *Marvel Science Fiction*, November 1951. Collected in GA.

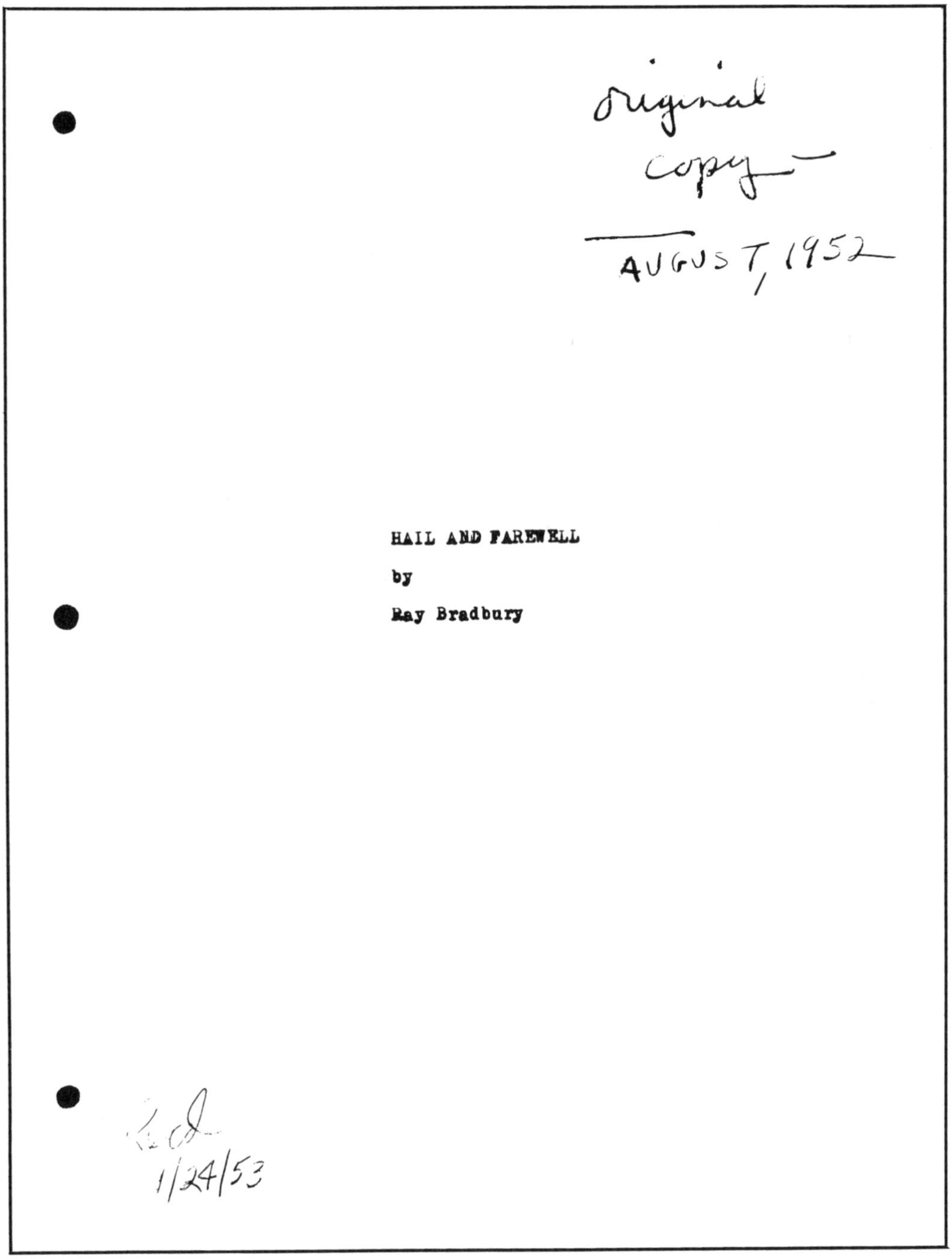

original copy —

AUGUST, 1952

HAIL AND FAREWELL

by

Ray Bradbury

Rec'd 1/24/53

Title page, and original manuscript page, from the 1952 RB short story, "Hail and Farewell."

and the brown house where he had lived, and as he turned a corner, a train whistle screamed and he began to run.

The last thing he saw and heard was a white ball tossed at the high roof of a house, back and forth, back and forth, and two voices crying as the ball pitched now up, down, and back through the sky, "Annie, Annie, over! Annie, Annie, over!" like the crying of birds flying off to the far south.

In the early morning with the smell of the mist and the dew and the cold metal, with the iron smell of the train around him and a full night of traveling shaking his bones and his body, and a smell of the sun beyond the horizon, he awoke and looked out upon a small town just arising from sleep. Lights were coming on, the sky was flushing white and pink there to the east, soft voices muttered, a red light bobbed back and forth, back and forth in the cold air. There was that sleeping hush in which echoes are dignified by clarity, in which echoes stand nakedly alone and sharp. A porter moved by, a shadow in shadows.

"Sir," said Willie.

The porter stopped.

"What town's this?" whispered the boy, in the dark.

"Mellin Town."

"How many people?"

"10,000. Why? This your stop?"

"It looks green," Willie gazed out at the cold morning town for a long time.

"This your stop, you better get off," whispered the porter.

"It looks nice and quiet. There's the school over on that hill," said Willie.

"Here There Be Tygers," first printed in *New Tales of Space and Time,* 1951. Collected in RR.

"The April Witch," *Saturday Evening Post,* April 5, 1952. Collected in GA.

"The Wilderness," *Today,* April 6, 1952. Collected in GA.

"The Lawns of Summer," *Nation's Business,* May 1952. Collected, untitled, as part of DW.

"Love Contest" (as "Leonard Douglas"), *Saturday Evening Post,* May 23, 1952.

"A Piece of Wood," *Esquire,* June 1952.

"A Sound of Thunder," *Collier's,* June 28, 1952. Collected in GA and RR.

"The Secret," ***It,* Summer 1952.

"The Smile," *Fantastic,* Summer 1952. Collected in MM and SS.

"Cora and the Great Wide World," *Maclean's* (Canada), August 15, 1952. Collected in GA, as "The Great Wide World Over There."

"The Tombling Day," *Shanandoah,* Autumn 1952. Collected in IS.

"A Flight of Ravens," *California Quarterly,* Winter 1952. Collected in MJ.

"Torrid Sacrifice," *Cavalier,* November 1952. Collected in GA, as "En la Noche."

"The Gift," *Esquire,* December 1952. Collected in MM and RR.

"Sun and Shadow," *Reporter,* March 17, 1953. Collected in GA and VB.

"Hail and Farewell," *Today,* March 29, 1953. Collected in GA, VB and SS.

"The Flying Machine," first printed in *The Golden Apples of the Sun,* [March] 1953. Collected, also, in SS.

"The Golden Apples of the Sun." First printed in *The Golden Apples of the Sun,* [March] 1953. Collected, also, in RR.

"Bullet With a Name," *Argosy,* April 1953.

"YOU'LL never come back." Hellman pared his fingernails casually. "Something frightening will happen to you, something vile and terrible. Remember the other expeditions. My God, the first Mars rocket killed off by hallucinations, the Weckner-Venus party baked alive, I hear." Hellman gestured to a three-dimensional map which hung like a dark mobile in the center of his parlor. Glittering planets floated there in a black void. "It's a hobby of mine," he said. "You see the tiny rocket ships there, on each tiny planet? I keep track, just like the government. When a particular rocket fails to return from some horrible world or other, I simply —" He twitched his hand delicately, wrist-deep, into the silent depths of the map. "— toss the rocket into the waste-basket." Something like a silver seed tinkled from his fingers into the basket. "And turn off the light in that one tiny world." *Click.* A planet stopped gleaming in the small night. "Another world investigated and found wanting, another multi-million-dollar expedition down the cosmic drain. No, my dear Forester, you'll never come back alive. Look. I've numbered this tiny new little rocket A-1000 for you and your men. You're traveling off to Planet 4 of Star System 70, right? Well, here's Planet 4; I'll switch it on for you. There. And one year from tonight, when you don't show up, I'll switch it off again and throw this little rocket of yours into the incinerator. Goodbye forever, dear friend."

Hellman smiled knowingly as he released the tiny needle-rocket at the rim of the dark galaxy. The rocket flew quietly into space leaving Hellman, the cynic, far behind. . . .

"That's it," said Forester.

He nodded out the port and the men looked with him at the beautiful globe of soil and sea and forest and cloud that swung up under their rocket. A month had passed, they had slept most of it away in the hypnotic machines and now, like children freshly wakened for their morning exercises, they waited for their ship to touch Planet Four in Star System 70.

"I keep thinking about what Hellman said." The man next to Forester rubbed his chin. "Will we come through this alive?"

Forester laughed. "Yes. Because we're *us*. I always feel that way, don't you? Bad things always happen to other people, not to us, not to *me*. I'll live forever."

"A comforting but hardly logical thought when one is impaled on a rhino-carpis."

"Rhino-carpis?"

"A terrible beast my father made up when I was a boy. He always said he'd throw me to the rhino-carpisses if I wasn't good."

The men laughed quietly. They gazed at the planet which rose softly to touch the ship. The automatic landing units functioned like the oiled machinery of a Swiss typewriter.

"Ours is a funny policy when you think of it," said Koestler, the radiologist. "We send rockets to each new world. If the rockets fail to return, we never send a second one to check the reason why. There are so many worlds we can't waste time on a hostile one, fighting futile wars, subduing natives; problems of logistics and all that."

Methods of revision are revealed by contrasting the magazine version of "Here There Be Tygers" with the book version of the same story. Even the destination is changed: from planet 4 of star system 70 to planet 7 of star system 84.

YOU HAVE TO BEAT a planet at its own game," said Chatterton. "Get in and rip it up, kill its snakes, poison its animals, dam its rivers, sow its fields, depollinate its air, mine it, nail it down, hack away at it, and get the hell out from under when you have what you want. Otherwise, a planet will fix you good. You can't trust planets. They're bound to be different, bound to be bad, bound to be out to get you, especially this far out, a billion miles from nowhere, so you get them first. Tear their skin off, I say. Drag out the minerals and run away before the damn world explodes in your face. That's the way to treat them."

The rocket ship sank down toward planet 7 of star system 84. They had traveled millions upon millions of miles; Earth was far away, her system and her sun forgotten, her system settled and investigated and profited on, and other systems rummaged through and milked and tidied up, and now the rockets of these tiny men from an impossibly remote planet were probing out to far universes. In a few months, a few years, they could travel anywhere, for the speed of their rocket was the speed of a god, and now for the ten thousandth time one of the rockets of the far-circling hunt was feathering down toward an alien world.

"No," said Captain Forester. "I have too much respect for other worlds to treat them the way you want to, Chatterton. It's not my business to rape or ruin, anyway, thank God. I'm glad I'm just a rocket man. You're the anthropologist-mineralogist. Go ahead, do your mining and ripping and scraping. I'll just watch. I'll just go around looking at this new world, whatever it is, however it seems. I like to look. All rocket men are lookers or they wouldn't be rocket men. You like to smell new airs, if you're a rocket man, and see new colors and new people if there are new people to see, and new oceans and islands."

"Take your gun along," said Chatterton.

"In my holster," said Forester.

They turned to the port together and saw the green world rising to meet their ship. "I wonder what *it* thinks of us?" said Forester.

"It won't like me," said Chatterton. "By God, I'll see to it it won't like me. And I don't care, you know, I don't give a damn. I'm out for the money. Land us over there, will you, Captain; that looks like rich country if I ever saw it."

It was the freshest green color they had seen since childhood.

Lakes lay like clear blue water droplets through the soft hills; there were no loud highways, signboards or cities. It's a sea of green golf links, thought Forester, which goes on forever. Putting greens, driving greens, you could walk ten thousand miles in any direction and never finish your game. A Sunday planet, a croquet-lawn world, where you could lie on your back, clover in your lips, eyes half shut, smiling at the sky, smelling the grass, drowse through an eternal Sabbath, rousing only on occasion to turn the Sunday paper or crack the red-striped wooden ball through the wicket.

"If ever a planet was a woman, this one is."

"Woman on the outside, man on the inside," said Chatterton. "All hard underneath, all male iron, copper, uranium, black sod. Don't let the cosmetics fool you."

He walked to the bin where the Earth Drill waited. Its great screw-snout glittered bluely, ready to stab seventy feet deep and suck out corks of earth, deeper still with extensions into the heart of the planet. Chatterton winked at it. "We'll fix your woman, Forester, but good."

"Yes, I know you will," said Forester, quietly.

The rocket landed.

"The Murderer," *Argosy* (England), June 1953. Collected in GA.

"Dandelion Wine," *Gourmet*, June 1953. Collected, untitled, as part of DW, and also collected in VB.

"And So Died Riabouchinska," *Saint Detective*, June-July 1953. Collected in MJ.

"Time in Thy Flight," *Fantastic Universe*, June-July 1953. Collected in SS.

"The Millioneth Murder," *Manhunt*, September 1953. Collected in F4 and VB, as "And the Rock Cried Out."

"Garbage Collector," *Nation*, October 10, 1953. Collected in GA.

"The Playground," *Esquire*, October 1953. Collected in F4.

Fahrenheit 451, first printed by Ballantine Books in collection of same title, in [October] 1953. Published separately thereafter. (See BOOKS AND PAMPHLETS.)

"The Golden Kite, the Silver Wind," *Epoch*, Winter 1953. Collected in GA.

"The Meadow," *Esquire*, December 1953. Collected in GA.

"A Scent of Sarsaparilla," first printed in *Star Science Fiction Stories*, 1953. Collected in MM.

"The Marriage Mender," *Collier's*, January 22, 1954. Collected in MM.

"The Dwarf," *Fantastic*, January-February 1954. Collected in OC and VB.

"Dinner at Dawn," *Everywoman's*, February 1954. Collected, untitled, as part of DW.

"All Summer in a Day," *Magazine of Fantasy and Science Fiction*, March 1954. Collected in MM.

"Interval in Sunlight," *Esquire*, March 1954.

"The Watchful Poker Chip," *Beyond*, March 1954. Collected in OC and VB, as "The Watchful Poker Chip of H. Matisse."

"Shopping for Death," *Maclean's* (Canada), June 1, 1954.

Collected in OC, as "Touched With Fire."

"At Midnight, in the Month of June," *Ellery Queen's Mystery Magazine*, June 1954.

"They Knew What They Wanted," *Saturday Evening Post*, June 26, 1954.

"The Wonderful Death of Dudley Stone," *Charm*, July 1954. Collected in OC.

"The Swan," *Cosmopolitan*, September 1954. Collected, untitled, as part of DW.

"The Strawberry Window," first printed in *Star Science Fiction Stories No. 3*, 1954. Collected in MM and RR.

Switch on the Night, first printed as a book for children, [March] 1955. (See BOOKS AND PAMPHLETS.)

"Marvels and Miracles—Pass It On!" *New York Times Magazine*, March 20, 1955. Imaginary interview with Jules Verne.

"The Last, the Very Last," *Reporter*, June 2, 1955. Collected, untitled, as part of DW—and also collected in RR, as "The Time Machine."

"The Trolley," *Good Housekeeping*, July 1955. Collected, untitled, as part of DW—and also collected in SS.

"The Dragon," *Esquire*, August 1955. Collected in MM and RR.

"The Mice," *Escapade*, October 1955. Collected in MM and VB, as "The Little Mice."

"Summer in the Air," *Saturday Evening Post*, February 18, 1956. Collected, untitled, as part of DW—and also collected in RR, as "The Sound of Summer Running."

"The First Night of Lent," *Playboy*, March 1956. Collected in MM.

"Icarus Montgolfier Wright," *Magazine of Fantasy and Science Fiction*, May 1956. Collected in MM and SS.

"Next Stop, the Stars," *Maclean's* (Canada), October 27, 1956. Collected in MM and RR, as "The End of the Beginning."

"The Time of Going Away," *Reporter*, November 29, 1956. Collected in MM.

"In a Season of Calm Weather," *Playboy,* January 1957. Collected in MM.

"Illumination," *Reporter,* May 16, 1957. Collected, untitled, as part of DW—and also collected in VB.

"Good-by, Grandma," *Saturday Evening Post,* May 25, 1957. Collected, untitled, as part of DW.

"The Day It Rained Forever," *Harper's,* July 1957. Collected in MM.

"The Happiness Machine," *Saturday Evening Post,* September 14, 1957. Collected, untitled, as part of DW.

"Green Wine for Dreaming," first printed, untitled, as part of *Dandelion Wine,* [September] 1957. Collected, under above title, in VB.

"Statues," first printed, untitled, as part of *Dandelion Wine,* [September] 1957. Collected, under above title, in VB.

"The Tarot Witch" (RB's title), first printed, untitled, as part of *Dandelion Wine,* [September] 1957.

"Magic!" (RB's title), first printed, untitled, as part of *Dandelion Wine,* [September] 1957.

Eighteen "bridge-passages" also appeared in print for the first time in *Dandelion Wine,* as chapter links, but are not complete stories.

"Almost the End of the World," *Reporter,* December 26, 1957. Collected in MJ.

"The Headpiece," *Lilliput* (England), May 1958. Collected in MM.

"The Town Where No One Got Off," *Ellery Queen's Mystery Magazine,* October 1958. Collected in MM.

"The Magic White Suit," *Saturday Evening Post,* October 4, 1958. Collected in MM and VB, as "The Wonderful Ice Cream Suit."

"The Great Collision of Monday Last," *Contact,* No. 1 (undated) 1958. Collected in MM.

"A Medicine for Melancholy," first printed in book of same title, [February] 1959. Collected, also, in VB.

"The Shoreline at Sunset," *Magazine of Fantasy and Science Fiction,* March 1959. Collected in MM, as "The Shore

Line at Sunset," and, (in England) in *The Day It Rained Forever,* as "The Sunset Harp," 1959.

"A Wild Night in Galway," *Harper's,* August 1959. Uncollected, but anthologized in (England) *The Wild Night Company,* 1970.

"Forever Voyage," *Saturday Evening Post,* January 9, 1960. Collected in MJ, as "And the Sailor, Home From the Sea."

"Death and the Maiden," *Magazine of Fantasy and Science Fiction,* March 1960. Collected in MJ.

"The Drummer Boy of Shiloh," *Saturday Evening Post,* April 30, 1960. Collected in MJ.

"The Best of All Possible Worlds," *Playboy,* August 1960. Collected in MJ.

"Very Late in the Evening," *Playboy,* December 1960. Collected in MJ, as "Some Live Like Lazarus."

"The Beggar on the Dublin Bridge," *Saturday Evening Post,* January 14, 1961. Collected in MJ, as "The Beggar on O'Connell Bridge."

"The Illustrated Woman," *Playboy,* March 1961. Collected in MJ.

"With Smiles as Wide as Summer," *Clipper,* November-December 1961.

"A Miracle of Rare Device," *Playboy,* January 1962. Collected in MJ.

"Nightmare Carousel," *Mademoiselle,* January 1962. Collected, untitled, as part of SW.

"Perhaps We Are Going Away," *Topper,* January 1962. Collected in MJ.

"The Prehistoric Producer," *Saturday Evening Post,* June 23, 1962. Collected in MJ, as "Tyrannosaurus Rex."

Something Wicked This Way Comes, first printed as a novel, [September] 1962. (See BOOKS AND PAMPHLETS.)

"Tread Lightly to the Music," *Cavalier,* October 1962.

"Come Into My Cellar," *Galaxy,* October 1962. Collected in MJ, as "Boys! Raise Giant Mushrooms in *Your* Cellar!"—and in SS under magazine title.

"The Machineries of Joy," *Playboy,* December 1962. Collected in MJ.

"The Long-After-Midnight Girl," *Eros,* Winter 1962.

"To the Chicago Abyss," *Magazine of Fantasy and Science Fiction,* May 1963. Collected in MJ.

"Bright Phoenix," *Magazine of Fantasy and Science Fiction,* May 1963.

"The Queen's Own Evaders," *Playboy,* June 1963. Collected in MJ and VB, as "The Anthem Sprinters."

"The Life Work of Juan Diaz," *Playboy,* September 1963. Collected in MJ.

"The Vacation," *Playboy,* December 1963. Collected in MJ.

"Massinello Pietro," *Connoisseur's World,* April 1964.

"The Cold Wind and the Warm," *Harper's,* July 1964. Collected in IS.

"Heavy-Set," *Playboy,* October 1964. Collected in IS.

"The Kilimanjaro Machine," *Life,* January 22, 1965. Collected in IS, as "The Kilimanjaro Device."

"The Best of Times," *McCall's,* January 1966. Collected in IS, as "Any Friend of Nicholas Nickleby's Is A Friend of Mine."

"The Blue Flag of John Folk," *Two Bells,* June 1966.

"The Year the Glop-Monster Won the Golden Lion at Cannes," *Cavalier,* July 1966.

"The Man in the Rorschach Shirt," *Playboy,* October 1966. Collected in IS.

"The Lost City of Mars," *Playboy,* January 1967. Collected in IS.

"Downwind From Gettysburg," *Playboy,* June 1969. Collected in IS.

"The Beautiful One is Here," *McCall's,* August 1969. Collected in IS, as "I Sing the Body Electric!"

"A Final Sceptre, a Lasting Crown," *Magazine of Fantasy and Science Fiction,* October 1969. Collected in IS, as "Henry the Ninth."

"The Haunting of the New," *Vogue* (England), October 1, 1969. Collected in IS.

"The Hour of Ghosts," *Saturday Review* (as an "ad-story" for A.T. and T.) October 25, 1969.

"The Terrible Conflagration up at the Place," first printed in *I Sing the Body Electric!* [October] 1969.

"Yes, We'll Gather at the River," first printed in *I Sing the Body Electric!* [October] 1969.

"The Inspired Chicken Bungalow Court," *West (Los Angeles Times)*, November 2, 1969. Collected in IS, as "The Inspired Chicken Motel."

"McGillahee's Brat," *Welcome Aboard*, Fall 1970.

"The Messiah," *Welcome Aboard*, Spring 1971.

"My Perfect Murder," *Playboy*, August 1971.

"The Parrot Who Met Papa," *Playboy*, January 1972.

The Halloween Tree, first printed as a book for children, [October] 1972. (See BOOKS AND PAMPHLETS.)

"Have I Got a Chocolate Bar for You!" *Penthouse*, October 1973.

"The Wish," *Woman's Day*, December 1973.

JUNE 15, 1938

BLUE & WHITE DAILY
LOS ANGELES HIGH SCHOOL

Editor-in-Chief
MATTHEW RAPF
Managing Editor
MORTON CAHN
Editorial Staff

Irwin Bross ---------- *Publicity*
Melvin Durslag ---------- *Boys' sports editor*
Robert Weil ---------- *News editor*
June Maseeger ---------- *Co-feature editor*
Mildred Partridge ---------- *Co-feature editor*
Jack Gleason ---------- *Art editor*
Dorothy Gardner ---------- *Girls' sports editor*
Jack Eberhardt ---------- *Mechanical adviser*

Business Staff

Marvin Saltzman ---------- *General manager*
Leonard Weil ---------- *Business manager*
Myron Dan ---------- *Advertising manager*
Neil Desmond ---------- *Subscription manager*
Jerry Jacobson ---------- *Circulation manager*
Fred Merrill ---------- *Auditor*
Ted Meiswinkel ---------- *Mailing*

The Blue and White Daily is published daily five times a week during the school year except holidays and the first seven and last four days of the semester.

Office of the publication, 4600 Olympic Blvd. Subscription price, 25c. Entered as Second Class Matter March 20, 1925, at the Post Office of Los Angeles, California, under the act of March 3, 1879.

Vacation Vagaries or Ain't Science Grand?

By Ray Bradbury

This summer many loyal Romans will head for various resorts for a few months recuperation "away from it all"

Instead of exerting yourself, just let science take care of the details. For the Roman who prefers hiking we advise old clothes, liniment, a bag of food and a stretcher on wheels. Then, when you reach the top of the mountain you can just lie back and come bounding back down again with the newly invented stretcher in three speeds.

If you're heading for the beach, many stores will be able to supply you with imitation sand made out of sugar, non squashable pies to lure the feet of bounding beach hounds. If you want to stay home instead of picnicking, electrical transcribing studios will supply you with records of cows mooing, brooks babbling, and bees stinging, (OUCH) for reasonable prices. A sprinkling system may be set up in the home to provide the very common and interesting species of rain often called the "picnic drench."

No matter what you intend doing, modern science will help you along.

MARCH 18, 1938
BLUE and WHITE DAILY

Informality Characterizes 'Town Hall Tonight' Program

By Ray Bradbury

"IT'S TOWN HALL TONIGHT FOLK!" barks Harry Vonzell, the Fred Allen program takes the air. There is no sign of Fred anywhere in the studio as we sit and wait. Harry gives his speech, the music blares, a figure bustles in from the rear of the studio, tears off a coat, puts a stick of gum in an open mouth, pushes back a hat, and hurriedly rushes up to the microphone in time to say: "This is Fred Allen, folks." in a twangy sort of voice.

He has been out prowling about the studio and has forgotten the time. He chews gum perpetually, dresses nattily, and is the soul of kindness to eager autograph fans. He is always ready with a quip when the occasion demands. Many is the time he has subtly embarrassed this writer. You see the first time I met him I mistook him for the former mayor of New York, Jimmy Walker. Ever since then, when he sees me he says drily, puckering up his thin lips: "As if it weren't bad enough, me being a comedian, but you, you have to take me for a mayor. Oh, you've struck me to the core!" Then he prances off about his business again. That is Fred Allen.

MARCH 14, 1938
BLUE and WHITE DAILY

Jack Benny Program Popular With Public

By Ray Bradbury

A well-dressed, middle-aged man strides down the sidewalk in front of the NBC Studios in Hollywood. He takes enormous steps, a big cigar in his mouth. This man is Jack Benny. Swinging along beside him comes rotund Don Wilson, bashful Kenny Baker, who is really quite shy, and a huge person in a green plaid suit, Andy Devine. Andy has a crop of reddish, curly hair, and always speaks with that same rasping clinker in his throat. Phil Harris jauntily swings among the throngs of people who come to see the program. He greets the other three and they go into a conference while resting on the lawn in front of the studio.

"FRITZ CHRYSLER" BENNY PLAYS AGAIN

Later, up in the studio, Jack gets out his violin and plays for the audience before going on the air. He usually tells a few jokes to get the audience warmed up, while Phil Harris trucks on down, Mary Livingston talks with friends, Kenny clears his throat, and Don Wilson laughs until his face is a vivid red.

The whole program is informal, which is why the audience likes to see it. You can never tell what may happen up to the time when the red light flashes on and Jack walks to the microphone, sticks out his tongue at Phil and says: "Jello again. This is Jack Benny."

Block Covers Created By Students Body Head

By Ray Bradbury

To protect Semi-annuals from destructive fingerprints when they are being signed on Semi-annual Day, a cover has been designed by Dick Fuller, Student Body president. The creation will be on sale for a nickel at all Blue and White dispensing stations and the west box office next Wednesday and Thursday.

The design was photographed on cloth with blocked letters by Dick Fuller himself, and no profit will be made from the venture.

JUNE 16, '38

Four articles by a teen-aged Bradbury from the *Blue and White Daily*, printed at Los Angeles High School in the 1930s.

ARTICLES AND MISCELLANEOUS NON-FICTION

Includes: Articles (Essays are incorporated under this heading), Commentary, Autobiographical Sketches, Guest Columns, Tributes.

Arranged in order of publication.
Minor "fanzine" humor items as well as amateur column items have been eliminated from this listing.
** denotes privately-printed amateur magazine.

For other RB non-fiction, see INTRODUCTIONS, REVIEWS, SPEECHES, INTERVIEWS, AND LETTERS.

"Jack Benny Program Popular With Public," *Blue and White Daily* (Los Angeles High School), March 14, 1938. RB's first bylined article in his high school paper.

"Informality Characterizes 'Town Hall Tonight' Program," *Blue and White Daily,* March 18, 1938. Article.

"Vacation Vagaries or Ain't Science Grand?" *Blue and White Daily,* June 15, 1938. Article.

"Block Covers Created By Students Body Head," *Blue and White Daily,* June 16, 1938. Article.

"Ray Bradbury," ***Imagination!* June 1938. Autobiographical sketch.

"What's Wrong With Scienti-Cinema?" ***Nova,* May 1939. Article.

6

And at last that final night would come, that night when you felt it was ending for the year, the other porches were emptyihg early, some had been empty for two or three nights; there were not s many people walking and tipping heir corn-flake-sounding straws under the turning elm boughs. Nights were getting a bit darker, and he lemonade was draining down and away in the pitcher. The Fourth of July squibs were shriveled away to almost nothing in the grass, and the marks where you lit the phosphorescent snakes on the concrete wiped away ERASED by many rains and suns. The night had a different, drier smell, as before a fire, and Grandma was beginning to talk of coffee instead o iced tea. The windows ere closing in the baywindows, the dinners were turning from cold cuts to hot beef. The mosquitoes were gone, too, and when they left the porch then the battle with time was over, there was nothing for it but hat the hum ns leave the battleground also.

How the LAST night was picked, I never knew. It was in the bones. It must have come first into Grandfather's b ones, for they were different kind of bone, chalk and ivory instead of peppermint and licorince whips like the children's. But the cold always touched Grandfather's bones first, like a raw hand touching a bass chord on the yellow piano IVORY mouth inside the house. And then, turning his cigar to lubricate the end in his mouth ith slow discernment he would look traight ahead into time and nod and say, "I guess we won't be coming out here tomorrow night." And in your minds eye as you sat there, you thought, enjoy this, listen to verything, for it'll be a whole winter before it comes again. And you MAKING saw tomorrow morning the CLANK chains taken down from the eyelets, the swing carried to the dusty garage, and in a few weeks, the first dried leaves blowing on the empty porch.

We would hold out until nine o'clock. I would see Grandfather unlid his gold lidded watch from his vest, note the spidery hands, click it shut and hear the ind flapping at our pant cuffs. Then at nine on a September evening, the streets dark, the porches desrted a ll down the street, we would each pick a chair, a rocker, a straightback, a cusion, and file into the house. Walking down the hall I would hear omeone poking up a fire in the library. Behind me the screen door would tap shut, and the wind might shake the windows a li tle shake. Grandfather would lock the door on the night. Summer was officially over. AND IT HAS REMAINED OVER FOR MANY YEARS

Original manuscript page from RB's first major non-fiction piece, "The Season of Sitting." Section circled in pencil dropped from printed version.

"Propaganda Via Music," *Science Fiction*, June 1939. RB's first professionally-printed article.

"Is It True What They Say About Bradbury?" (unsigned), ***Fantasy Digest*, June–July 1939. Autobiographical sketch.

"Is It True What They Say About Kuttner?" (as "Guy Amory"), ***Futuria Fantasia*, Fall 1939. Article.

"Hans Bok on the Fantasy Scene," ***Le Zombie*, December 2, 1939. Article.

"Report on the Convention," *Science Fiction*, March 1940. Article.

"Tubby, We Love You!" ***Damn Thing*, December 1940. Article.

"Of Callouses and Corns," *Script*, March 8, 1941. Article.

"Like It or Lump It!" *Script*, June 7, 1941. Article.

"Bradbury on a Bat," *Weird Tales*, November 1943. Autobiographical sketch.

"Appreciation of Paul Freehafer," ***Shangri-L'Affaires*, April 1944. Tribute.

"What Can a Writer Say?" *Weird Tales*, January 1945. Autobiographical sketch.

"Feature Flash: Ray Bradbury," *Planet Stories*, Spring 1947. Autobiographical sketch.

"Author, Author: Ray Bradbury," ***Fanscient*, Winter 1949. Autobiographical sketch—and list of printed work.

"Where Do You Get Your Ideas?" ***Etaoin Shrdlu*, April 1950. Article.

"A Few Notes on 'The Martian Chronicles,'" ***Rhodomagnetic Digest*, May 1950. Article.

"Where Do I Get My Ideas?" *Book News*, Summer 1950. Article.

"The Season of Sitting," *Charm*, August 1951. Article.

"Magic, Magicians, Carnival and Fantasy," ***Ray Bradbury Review*, [January] 1952. Article. (See ABOUT BRADBURY IN BOOKS.)

"Science and Science Fiction," ***Ray Bradbury Review*,

[January] 1952. Article. (See ABOUT BRADBURY IN BOOKS.)

"Day After Tomorrow: Why Science Fiction?" *Nation,* May 2, 1953. Article.

"Bradbury, Ray," in *Twentieth Century Authors: First Supplement,* 1955. Autobiographical sketch.

"The Joy of Writing," *Writer,* October 1956. Article.

"Words For the Times," *Los Angeles Times,* January 19, 1958. Commentary—RB's first contribution to the *Los Angeles Times.*

"Monday Night in Green Town," Mimeo-copied as part of *National Library Week Supplement Kit,* a Folder supplied to newspapers for nationwide syndication. March 16 through 22, 1958. Article.

"Hank Helped Me," ***Henry Kuttner: A Memorial Symposium.* A booklet. ed. Karen Anderson. Berkeley: Sevagram, August 1958. Tribute.

"Just For Variety," *Daily Variety,* September 4, 1958. Guest column.

"Zen and the Art of Writing," *Writer,* October 1958. Article.

"Thoughts While Sleeping at My Machine," *Daily Variety,* November 4, 1958. Article.

"In Defense of Los Angeles—After All, I Live There!" *Gentlemen's Quarterly,* March 1959. Article.

"Writer Takes Long Look Into Space," *Los Angeles Times,* January 10, 1960. Guest column.

"Paris by Stop Watch," *Mademoiselle,* March 1960. Article.

"Literature in the Space Age," *California Librarian,* July 1960. Article.

"A Serious Search for Weird Worlds," *Life,* October 24, 1960. Article.

"Novelist Appraises Himself, His Craft," *Los Angeles Times,* December 11, 1960. Commentary.

"Symposium on the Teaching of Creative Writing: Ray Bradbury," *Four Quarters,* January 1961. Commentary, as a contributor to the symposium.

"Los Angeles: Almost in Orbit," *Carte Blanche,* Spring 1961. Article.

"How to Keep and Feed a Muse," *Writer,* July 1961. Article.

"Viewing TV: Boredom as a Way of Life," *Los Angeles,* September 1962. Article.

"Cry the Cosmos," *Life,* September 14, 1962. Article.

"Writer Tries His Film Wings in Flight Saga," *Calendar (Los Angeles Times),* December 30, 1962. Article.

"Los Angeles: The Promised and Re-Promised Land," *American Home* (California Edition), July-August 1963. Article.

"Los Angeles: Orange Without a Navel," *Frontier,* February 1964. Article.

"Erv Kaplan's Little People," *Connoisseur's World,* June 1964. Commentary.

"The Fahrenheit Chronicles," *Spacemen,* June 1964. Article.

"The Last Pedestrian," *California Homeowner,* August 1964. Commentary.

"A Theater of Ideas for an Age of Ideas," *Calendar (Los Angeles Times),* October 4, 1964. Article.

"Why I Put My Children on the Stage," *Los Angeles,* October 1964. Article.

"Why Space Age Theatre?" *Playgoer* (undated) [October 1964]. Article.

"Remembrances of Things Future," *Playboy,* January 1965. Article.

"The Tailor Explains How He Made 'The Suit' " *Playgoer* (undated) [February 1965]. Article.

"What I Learned as My Own Producer," *Calendar (Los Angeles Times),* February 28, 1965. Article.

"Taming a Giant Gone Mad," *Los Angeles Times,* August 6, 1965. Article.

"The VIP Treatment for Summer Visitors: Ray Bradbury," *Los Angeles,* August 1965. Commentary.

"Ray Bradbury Replies," *Magazine of Fantasy and Science*

Fiction, October 1965. Commentary.

"The Machine-Tooled Happyland," *Holiday,* October 1965. Article.

"The Secret Mind," *Writer,* November 1965. Article.

"The Pandemonium Theatre Company Arrives," ***Trumpet,* December 1965. Article.

"At What Temperature Do Books Burn?" *New York Times,* November 13, 1966. Article.

"An Impatient Gulliver Above Our Roofs," *Life,* November 24, 1967. Article.

"Hannes Bok: A Remembrance," from ***Bokanalia,* a folio by Hannes Bok. San Francisco: Bokanalia Foundation, 1967. Tribute.

"Death Warmed Over," *Playboy,* January 1968. Article.

"Pluck of the Irish Gets to a Playwright," *Calendar (Los Angeles Times),* February 25, 1968. Article.

"About the Play," *Playgoer* (undated) [February 1968]. Article.

"Any Friend of Trains Is a Friend of Mine," *Life,* August 2, 1968. Article.

"Science Fiction: Why Bother?" *Teachers Guide Science Fiction.* A pamphlet. New York: Bantam, 1968. Article. (See also ABOUT BRADBURY IN MAGAZINES AND NEWSPAPERS, by Olfson.)

"Science-Fiction Writer Ray Bradbury's New Ending for 'Rosemary's Baby,'" *Calendar (Los Angeles Times),* January 26, 1969. Article.

"Ray Bradbury," in *Boris Karloff: The Frankenscience Monster,* ed. Forrest Ackerman. New York: Ace, 1969. Tribute.

"Comments on 'That Moon Plaque,'" in *Men on the Moon,* ed. Donald A. Wollheim. New York: Ace, 1969. Commentary.

"Dear Fred Ott: 'Gesundheit!'" *Movie,* January 23, 1970. Article.

"The Girls Walk This Way, the Boys Walk That Way—A Dream for Los Angeles in the 70s," *West (Los Angeles*

Times), April 5, 1970. Article.

"Conversations Never Finished, Films Never Made," *Producer's Journal,* June 1970. Article.

Untitled liner album note to *Songs For a Sideshow of the Mind,* 1970. Commentary. (See BRADBURY IN SOUND).

"Paying a Debt to the Gift of Being: Ray Bradbury Seeks Out God in Space," Syndicated through *Universal Science News,* April 1971. Article.

"How, Instead of Being Educated in College, I Was Graduated from Libraries or Thoughts from a Chap Who Landed on the Moon in 1932," *Wilson Library Bulletin,* May 1971. Article.

"About E.E.E.," in *Food For Demons* by E. Everett Evans. San Diego: Shroud, 1971. Tribute.

Untitled commentary on Henry Eichner in *The Atlantean Chronicles* by Henry H. Eichner. Los Angeles: Fantasy Publishing Co., 1971.

"Where Are the Golden-Eyed Martians?" *West (Los Angeles Times),* March 12, 1972. Article. (See COMIC BOOK APPEARANCES.)

"Apollo Murdered: The Sun Goes Out," *Los Angeles Times,* May 17, 1972. Commentary.

"Los Angeles is the Best Place in America," *Esquire,* October 1972. Article.

"The Playwright as Midwife to a Comet," *Calendar (Los Angeles Times),* November 19, 1972. Article.

"How Do You Swallow a Flaming Comet Whole?" Privately-printed play program for "Leviathan '99," November 1972. Article.

"From Stonehenge to Tranquillity Base," *Playboy,* December 1972. Article.

"On a Book Burning," Mimeo-prepared, by Publishers Publicity Association, 1972, for syndication to nationwide newspapers, as part of International Book Year's *Observations of American Writers.* Article.

"More SF Comments," *Writers' Yearbook,* 1972. Commentary.

"If I Were a Teacher," *Learning,* May 1973. Article/self-interview.

"W. C. Fields and the S.O.B. on Roller Skates," *Producer's Journal,* June 1973. Article.

"How to Be Madder Than Captain Ahab or Writing Explained," *Literary Cavalcade,* October 1973. Article/letter.

TRUCK DRIVER AFTER MIDNIGHT

The cars roar through the black
Of a moonless night—
Along a strip of dullness,
Over a hill of monotony,
Through the mountains of misery.
Hour after hour
Come the phantom engines
Beating a tempo with speed,
Reaming the road with whining tires.
Faces, lit by matches,
Puffs of smoke from nervous lips
Beady eyes watching,
Hands on wheels ready.
Blinking yellow circles
Probing the darkness ahead,
Eating the black with teeth of light.
Away into the distance,
They are lost.

ROY BRADBURY, AGE 17, A12

"Truck Driver After Midnight," Bradbury's poem from the 1938 anthology, *Morning Song*. Author's first name was mis-printed as "Roy" in this booklet.

Honors

The following honors in poetry have come to students of the Los Angeles High School during the past year: 1938

Poems starred are used by permission.

Honorable Mention in American Youth Forum sponsored by the *American Magazine*

* *My Hope for America* . . . Bonnie Louise Barrett

Poems published in *Morning Song,* Anthology of Los Angeles City Schools

Tonight . . . . Bonnie Louise Barrett
* *Truck Driver after Midnight* . . . Ray Bradbury
* *To Dr. Edwards* . . . . Sally Rubin
Morning Scene . . . . Ramona Stewart
* *Dust Storm at Easter* . . . . . . Betty Vellom
* *Adventurer* . . . . Robert Weil

Poems published in *The Young West Sings,* 1938 Anthology of California High School Poetry

Tonight . . . . Bonnie Louise Barrett
After the Years . . . . Freda Donahue
Wind Song . . . . Herman Fredman
The Gentle Heart . . . . Doris Maud Randall
Lyrics . . . . Sally Rubin
Mulatto . . . . Ramona Stewart
Possession . . . . Ramona Stewart

Prize-winning poems in Everett Ruess Poetry Awards

June 1938

* *To Dr. Edwards* . . . . Sally Rubin
Horizons . . . . Elna Sundquist

Honorable Mention to Floria Goldman, Patricia Geddes, Bonnie Louise Barrett.

January 1939

* *Dead Rainbow* . . . . Jane Mary Eklund
The Mirage . . . . Millicent Tag-von Stein

Honorable Mention to Elizabeth Johnston, Stellita Paniagua, Beverly Morrison.

Notice of Bradbury's first "best" selection, in May of 1938, for verse.

VERSE

Bradbury's first poem was printed in 1936. He contributed bits of verse, mostly humorous, to various fan publications and to his own fan magazine, *Futuria Fantasia,* 1938 through 1940; the west-coast magazine, *Script,* printed a few of his poems through 1941. But it was not until 1954, with "Death in Mexico," that his poetry reached professional status.

Arranged in order of publication.

Poems included in RB's book, *When Elephants Last in the Dooryard Bloomed,* are indicated WEL.

** denotes privately-printed amateur magazine.

"In Memory to Will Rogers," *Waukegan News-Sun,* August 18, 1936. RB's first appearance in print.

"Death's Voice," *Anthology of Student Verse for 1937,* ed. Snow Longley Housh. Los Angeles High School, [March] 1937. Pamphlet. RB's first book appearance.

"Truck Driver After Midnight," *Morning Song: A Book of Student Verse,* Pamphlet. Los Angeles City Schools, [May] 1938.

"Tree's a Crowd," ***Imagination!* May 1938.

"If" (as "Hollerbochen"), ***Imagaination!* June 1938.

"Tree," ***Imagination!* July 1938.

"Tis a Sinema," ***Imagination!* August 1938.

"Thought and Space," ***Futuria Fantasia,* Summer 1939.

"Satan's Mistress" (as "Doug Rogers"), ** *Futuria Fantasia,* Fall 1939.

"Tremonstrous" (as "D. Lerium Tremaine"), ** *Le Zombie,* January 30, 1940.

"Filthy Filler" (as "Guy Amory"), ** *California Mercury,* August 19, 1940.

"Hades" (anon.), ** *Futuria Fantasia,* Winter 1940.

"Stars," *Script,* December 21, 1940.

"Wilber and His Germ," *Script,* May 24, 1941.

"Thespians All!" *Script,* September 27, 1941.

"Death in Mexico," *California Quarterly,* III, 2, 1954. Collected in WEL.

"A Dublin Limerick," *Silver Treasury of Light Verse,* ed. Oscar Williams. New York: Mentor/NAL, 1957.

"Harvest," *Science Fair* [no date], 1962.

"What Age is This?" *Read,* October 15, 1963.

"Ahab at the Helm," *Connoisseur's World,* July 1964.

"Some Live Like Lazarus," ** *Ventura II,* May 1965. Collected in WEL.

"The Machines, Beyond Shylock," *Galaxy,* October 1965. Collected in WEL.

"I, Tom, and my Electric Gran," *Los Angeles,* November 1965. Collected in WEL.

"Green Remembrance," *Orange County Sun,* December 1965. Collected in WEL as "Here All Beautifully Collides."

"When Elephants Last in the Dooryard Bloomed," *P.S.,* April 1966. Collected in WEL.

"That Beast Upon the Wire," *Datamation,* December 1966. Collected in WEL.

"Dusk in the Electric Cities: And This Did Dante Do," *Florida Quarterly,* Summer 1967. Collected in WEL as "And This Did Dante Do."

"Taming the American Wilderness," *Daily Californian Weekly Magazine,* November 5, 1968. First printing of the narration RB wrote for U.S. Government Pavilion at 1964 World's Fair, where it was titled "American Journey." (See FILMS.)

"What Seems a Balm is Salt to Ancient Wounds," *Texas Quarterly,* Winter 1968. Collected in WEL.

"A Train Station Sign Viewed From An Ancient Locomotive Passing Through Long After Midnight," *Orange County Illustrated,* March 1969. Collected in WEL.

"You Can Go Home Again," *Nepenthe,* Spring 1969. Collected in WEL.

"Christus Apollo: A Cantata," *I Sing the Body Electric!* [October] 1969. (See BOOKS AND PAMPHLETS.)

"In the Year Apollo I," *Vogue* (England), December 1969. Collected in *I Sing the Body Electric!* as part of "Christus Apollo." (See BOOKS AND PAMPHLETS.)

"Boys Are Always Running Somewhere," *Newport Women's Club Magazine,* 1970. Collected in WEL.

"These Unsparked Flints, These Uncut Gravestone Brides," *Aware,* March-April 1970. Collected in WEL.

"Darwin in the Fields," *Galaxy,* April 1970. Collected in WEL as *three* poems: "Darwin, the Curious," "Darwin in the Fields," and "Darwin, Wandering Home at Dawn."

"O Give a Fig for Newton: Honor Him!" *Pawprint,* Spring 1970. Collected in WEL.

"All Flesh is One: What Matter Scores?" *Pro,* December 14, 1970. Collected in WEL.

"O To Be a Boy in a Belfry," *Agora,* March 1971. Collected in WEL.

"Old Ahab's Friend, and Friend to Noah, Speaks His Piece," Los Angeles: Roy A. Squires, May-June, 1971. Pamphlet. Collected in WEL. (See BOOKS AND PAMPHLETS.)

"Say That I Was a Teller of Tales," *Citrus College Clarion,* June 4, 1971.

"If I Were Epitaph," *Rotarian,* May 1972. Collected in WEL.

"Air to Levoisier," *Boston Review of the Arts,* July 1972. Collected in WEL.

"Christ, Old Student in a New School," *Again, Dangerous Visions,* ed. Harlan Ellison. New York: Doubleday, 1972. Collected in WEL.

"Pretend at Being Blind, Which Calls Truth Near," *Audubon,* September 1972. Collected in WEL.

"This Time of Kites," *Chicago Tribune Sunday Magazine,* September 10, 1972. Collected in WEL.

"Remembrance," *Ladies Home Journal,* September 1972. Collected in WEL.

"That Stranger on the Lawn," *Woman's Day,* May 1973. Collected in WEL as "That Woman on the Lawn."

Two RB poems, untitled, formed part of the text in *Mars and the Mind of Man,* ed. Bruce C. Murray. New York: Harper & Row, 1973. Both were collected in WEL as "That is Our Eden's Spring, Once Promised," and "If Only We Had Taller Been." (See INTRODUCTIONS. See PUBLISHED SPEECHES.)

"Ode to Electric Ben," *Galaxy,* October 1973. Collected in WEL.

The following twenty-one poems, hitherto unpublished, are collected in *When Elephants Last in the Dooryard Bloomed* (1973). (See BOOKS AND PAMPHLETS.)

"The Boys Across the Street Are Driving My Young Daughter Mad"
"Evidence"
"Telling Where the Sweet Gums Are"
"Emily Dickinson, Where Are You? Herman Melville Called Your Name Last Night in His Sleep!"
"I Was the Last, the Very Last"
"Man Is the Animal That Cries"
"N"
"Women Know Themselves; All Men Wonder"
"If You Wait Just Long Enough, All Goes"
"For a Daughter, Traveling"

"Old Mars, Then Be a Hearth to Us"
"The Thing That Goes By Night; The Self That Lazes Sun"
"Groon"
"Please to Remember the Fifth of November: A Birthday Poem for Susan Marguerite"
"The Fathers and Sons Banquet"
"Touch Your Solitude to Mine"
"God is a Child; Put Toys in the Tomb"
"And Dark Our Celebration Was"
"Mrs. Harriet Hadden Attwood, Who Played the Piano for Thomas A. Edison for the World's First Phonograph Record, is Dead at 105"
"God for a Chimney Sweep"
"To Prove That Cowards Do Speak Best and True and Well"

INTRODUCTIONS

Includes: Forewords, Afterwords, Story Prefaces, Production Notes.

Arranged in chronological order. All are first book appearances.

"Introduction." Dated by RB: March 16, 1948. *Without Sorcery,* by Theodore Sturgeon. Philadelphia: Prime Press, 1948.

Story Preface: "Why I Selected 'Zero Hour.'" *My Best Science Fiction Story,* ed. Leo Margulies and Oscar J. Friend. New York: Merlin Press, 1949. (See ANTHOLOGY APPEARANCES.)

Untitled Story Preface to RB story, "Ylla." *The Outer Reaches,* ed. August Derleth. New York: Pellegrini & Cudahy, 1951. (See ANTHOLOGY APPEARANCES.)

"Introduction." Dated by RB: July 1, 1951. *Timeless Stories For Today and Tomorrow,* ed. Ray Bradbury. New York: Bantam, 1952. (See BOOKS AND PAMPHLETS.)

"Introduction." Dated by RB: February 5, 1956. *The Circus of Dr. Lao and Other Improbable Stories,* ed. Ray Bradbury. New York: Bantam, 1956. (See BOOKS AND PAMPHLETS.)

"Introduction." *The Mysterious Island,* by Jules Verne. New York: Heritage Press, 1959.

"Introduction: The Ardent Blasphemers." Dated by RB: September 15, 1961. *20,000 Leagues Under the Sea,* by Jules Verne. New York: Bantam, 1962.

"Introduction." *Around the World in 80 Days,* by Jules Verne. New York: Heritage Press, 1962.

Introduction. Dated by RB: March 28, 1962. *R is For Rocket,* by Ray Bradbury. New York: Doubleday, 1962. (See BOOKS AND PAMPHLETS.)

"Afterword: The Queen's Own Evaders." Dated by RB: July 31, 1962. *The Anthem Sprinters and Other Antics,* by Ray Bradbury. New York: Dial Press, 1963. (See BOOKS AND PAMPHLETS.)

"Introduction." Dated by RB: September 1962. *In Memoriam: Clark Ashton Smith,* ed. Jack Chalker. Baltimore: Chalker and Associates.

"Introduction: About Bill Nolan." Dated by RB: April 1963. *Impact 20,* by William F. Nolan. New York: Paperback Library, 1963.

Untitled Story Preface to RB story, "A Miracle of Rare Device." *The Worlds of Science Fiction,* ed. Robert P. Mills. New York: Dial Press, 1963. (See ANTHOLOGY APPEARANCES.)

Untitled Story Preface to RB story, "The Wilderness." *Exploring Life Through Literature,* ed. Robert C. Pooley, Lillian Z. White, Edmund J. Farrell, Joseph Mersand. Glenview, Illinois: Scott, Foresman, 1964.

Introduction. Dated by RB: December 19, 1964. *The Autumn People,* by Ray Bradbury. New York: Ballantine, 1965. (See BOOKS AND PAMPHLETS.)

"Foreword." Dated by RB: April 20, 1965. *The Magic Man,* by Charles Beaumont. New York: Gold Medal, 1965.

"Foreword: Prelude to Bach." Dated by RB: May 17, 1965. *Biplane,* by Richard Bach. New York: Harper and Row, 1966.

Afterword: "Seeds of Three Stories." *On Writing By Writers,* ed. William W. West. Boston: Ginn, 1966. (See ANTHOLOGY APPEARANCES.)

"Introduction." Dated by RB: October 25, 1965. *Tomorrow Midnight,* by Ray Bradbury. New York: Ballantine, 1966. (See BOOKS AND PAMPHLETS.)

"Introduction." Dated by RB: December 1, 1965. *S is For Space,* by Ray Bradbury. New York: Doubleday, 1966. (See BOOKS AND PAMPHLETS.)

"Production Note." *The Pedestrian,* by Ray Bradbury. New York: Samuel French, 1966. (See BOOKS AND PAMPHLETS.) (See PUBLISHED PLAYS.)

"Author's Production Note." *The Day It Rained Forever,* by Ray Bradbury. New York: Samuel French, 1966. (See BOOKS AND PAMPHLETS.) (See PUBLISHED PLAYS.)

"Introduction." Dated by RB: 1966. *Fahrenheit 451,* by Ray Bradbury. New York: Simon and Schuster, 1967. (See BOOKS AND PAMPHLETS.)

Story Preface: "Ray Bradbury Comments on 'The Flying Machine.'" *Counterpoint in Literature,* ed. Robert C. Pooley, Edythe Daniel, Edmund J. Farrell, Alfred H. Grommon, Olive S. Niles. Glenview, Illinois: Scott, Foresman, 1967.

Untitled Story Preface to RB story, "The Life Work of Juan Diaz." *The Playboy Book of Horror and the Supernatural.* Chicago: Playboy Press, 1967. (See ANTHOLOGY APPEARANCES.)

"Introduction: To Windowpanes." *Windowpanes* (Loyola High School literary magazine), 1969.

"Foreword." Dated by RB: August 29, 1969. *The Wild Night Company,* ed. Peter Haining. London: Gollancz, 1970.

"Introduction: Buck Rogers in Apollo Year 1." Dated by RB: October 18, 1969. *The Collected Works of Buck Rogers in the 25th Century,* ed. Robert C. Dille. New York: Chelsea House, 1969.

Untitled Story Preface to RB story, "The Fire Balloons." *Special Wonder,* ed. J. Francis McComas. New York: Random House, 1970. (See ANTHOLOGY APPEARANCES.)

"Introduction: Night Travel on the Orient Express. Destination: Avram." Dated by RB: November 18, Apollo Year Two [1970]. *Strange Seas and Shores,* by Avram Davidson. New York: Doubleday, 1971.

"Introduction: The Happy Pornographer. Erv Kaplan: A Portrait." Dated by RB: November 18, Apollo Year Two [1970]. *Ob-Scenes,* by Erv Kaplan. Los Angeles: Melrose Square, 1972.

"Introduction (in Spanish)." Dated by RB: April 28, 1971. *Ray Bradbury, Humanista Del Futuro,* a biography by Jose Luis Garci. Madrid: Helios, 1971. (See ABOUT BRADBURY IN BOOKS.)

"Introduction: With Notes on Staging." Dated by RB: August 22, 1971. *The Wonderful Ice Cream Suit and Other Plays,* by Ray Bradbury. New York: Bantam, 1972. (See BOOKS AND PAMPHLETS.) (See PUBLISHED PLAYS.)

"Foreword: Remembrance of Things Present, or Vic and Sade Are Still Alive and Well and Living in Orwell-Huxley Vista." Dated by RB: May 20, 1972. *The Small House Halfway Up in the Next Block,* by Paul Rhymer. New York: McGraw-Hill, 1972.

"Introduction." *Film Fantasy Scrapbook,* by Ray Harryhausen. New York: A. S. Barnes, 1972.

"Foreword: On Going a Journey." *Mars and the Mind of Man,* ed. Bruce C. Murray. New York: Harper & Row, 1973. Also contains section by RB in "Afterthoughts." (See VERSE.) (See PUBLISHED SPEECHES.)

REVIEWS

Bradbury first functioned as a reviewer for his high school newspaper, writing film reviews in the 1930s. These were unbylined, and are impossible to identify. Arranged in order of publication.

**denotes privately-printed amateur magazine or "fanzine."

Film Reviews:

"The Doctor and the Snowbank," *Orange County Sun,* March 1966. *Dr. Zhivago.*

"The Ghost of Fellini's Wife," *Orange County Sun,* April 1966. *Juliet of the Spirits.*

"'Fahrenheit' on Film," *Calendar (Los Angeles Times),* November 20, 1966. *Fahrenheit 451.*

"Space Odyssey 2001," *Psychology Today,* May 1968. *2001: A Space Odyssey.*

Book Reviews:

"The Jester's Reign," ***Novacious,* No. 4, 1939. *The Jester's Reign,* by Boyne Grainger.

"The Stray Lamb," ***Novacious,* No. 7, 1939. *The Stray Lamb,* by Thorne Smith.

"Man Stumbles Into Odd Secret," [unlocated newspaper clipping, 1953]. *Adventures in Dimension,* ed. Groff Conklin.

"'Music of Spheres'—Fiction Into Fact," *Calendar (Los Angeles Times),* September 10, 1961. *Music of the*

Spheres, by Guy Murchie.

"The Man Who Tried Everything," *Life,* February 11, 1966. *Aldous Huxley 1894-1963,* ed. Julian Huxley.

"Macdonald . . . the Sadness of Murder," *Calendar (Los Angeles Times),* June 8, 1969. *The Goodbye Look,* by Ross Macdonald.

"Anthropologist's Magic Vision of Nature," *Book Review (Los Angeles Times),* December 14, 1969. *The Unexpected Universe,* by Loren Eiseley.

"Ross Macdonald Socks It to the Eastern Mob," *Book Review (Los Angeles Times),* July 5, 1970. *Archer at Large,* by Ross Macdonald.

"Looking Into the Future—Good or Bad," *Book Review (Los Angeles Times),* October 25, 1970. *Looking Forward,* ed. Ray Brosseau.

"Trailing the Clouds of Glory Into the Age of Apollo," *Book Review (Los Angeles Times),* January 24, 1971. *Moon: Man's Greatest Adventure,* ed. David Thomas.

"An Art's-Eye View of Space Renaissance," *Book Review (Los Angeles Times),* October 24, 1971. *Eyewitness to Space,* by H. L. Cooke and James H. Dean.

"240-Page Poem of Simmering Life Vibrartions," *Book Review (Los Angeles Times),* December 12, 1971. *The Night Country,* by Loren Eiseley.

"A Handbook to Bicycle Byways in Los Angeles," *Book Review (Los Angeles Times),* May 21, 1972. *Bicycle Touring in Los Angeles,* by G. Weltman and E. Dubin.

"John Collier Probes the Darker Regions," *Book Review (Los Angeles Times),* December 10, 1972. *The John Collier Reader,* by John Collier.

"Walt Disney, His Beauties and Beasts," *Calendar (Los Angeles Times),* October 21, 1973. *The Art of Walt Disney,* by Christopher Finch.

PUBLISHED SPEECHES

Bradbury has delivered many hundreds of speeches over the past twenty years. He now lectures regularly at high schools, colleges, clubs, libraries—and often speaks to creative writing groups in the greater Los Angeles area. The listing of printed speeches which follows reflects his range and subject matter.

Arranged by year of publication.

**denotes privately-printed amateur magazine or "fanzine."

"The 'Invisible Little Man' Award Dinner." ***Rhodomagnetic Digest,* June 1950. Speech delivered May 22, 1950 in San Francisco to a science fiction group at Berkeley on the occasion of his winning an award for *The Martian Chronicles.*

"No Man is an Island." Printed as a pamphlet under this title by the National Women's Committee of Brandeis University, Los Angeles Chapter, 1952. Speech delivered November 7, 1952. (See BOOKS AND PAMPHLETS.)

"A Writers Symposium." *Television Quarterly,* Spring 1963. Discussion panel, RB and three other TV/film writers, on KPFK-FM early in 1963.

"Creativity in the Space Age." *California Institute of Technology Quarterly,* Fall 1963. Speech delivered in the spring of 1963 at a campus assembly.

 "Literature and Science." *The Cultural Arts,* University of

California, 1964. Booklet. Discussion panel, with Aldous Huxley and others, at a conference on cultural arts in April 1963 at Royce Hall, U.C.L.A.

"Ray Bradbury Speaks on 'Film in the Space Age,'" *American Cinematographer,* January 1967. Speech delivered in late 1966 at a dinner meeting of the American Society of Cinematographers in Los Angeles.

"Creative Man Among His Servant Machines." Printed in mimeo format by Vacation Village, Mission Bay, San Diego, 1966. Speech delivered November 2, 1966 in San Diego, California, to the Users of Automatic Display Equipment. (See BOOKS AND PAMPHLETS.)

"Unthinking Man and His Thinking Machines." *Computer Group News,* May 1968. Speech delivered in November of 1967 at the Joint Computer Conference in Los Angeles.

"Watcher of the Runners and Jumpers." *Life,* June 14, 1968. Speech written in May of 1968 in acceptance of Aviation-Space Writers Association Award for his article "An Impatient Gulliver Above Our Roofs."

"Reflections From the Man Who Landed on the Moon in 1929." *Engineering and Science,* October 1970. Speech delivered on Alumni Seminar Day, 1970, at the California Institute of Technology in Los Angeles.

"Bradbury Speaks." ** *Train of Thought,* July–August 1971. Speech delivered at the San Diego Golden State Comic Convention in 1970.

"I'll Be Damned If I'll Be Bullied by Bright Children," *Mars and the Mind of Man,* ed. Bruce C. Murray. New York: Harper & Row, 1973. Discussion panel, November 1971, with Arthur C. Clarke and others, at California Institute of Technology. (See VERSE.)(See INTRODUCTIONS.)

the
essence
of creative
writing
The Pedestrian
A FANTASY IN ONE ACT
By Ray Bradbury
The Day
it Rained Forever
A COMEDY IN ONE ACT
By Ray Bradbury
Samuel French, Inc.
FOR
BILL NOLAN—
WITH THE FRIENDLIEST
WISHES OF THIS FELLOW WHO
TRIED HIS BEST TO PUT HIS SMALL
FEET INTO MELVILLE'S
TITANIC SHOES—
BEST ALWAYS
FROM
RAY BRADBURY
— DEC. 3, 1954 —
"MOBY DICK"
CONTAINING REVISIONS MADE
DURING JULY-AUGUST-SEPTEMBER, 1954
[redacted]
The Phi Mu Alpha
SINFONIA SERIES
Madrigals
for the
Space Age
FOR MIXED CHORUS AND NARRATOR
WITH PIANO ACCOMPANIMENT
Music by
LALO SCHIFRIN
Text by
RAY BRADBURY
ASSOCIATED MUSIC PUBLISHERS New York/London
SUN AND SHADOW
YES! CAPRA CHAPBOOK SERIES
Zen & the Art of Writing
by Ray Bradbury
No Man Is An Island
by
RAY BRADBURY
Old Ahab's Friend,
and Friend to Noah,
Speaks His Piece
"CREATIVE MAN AMONG HIS SERVANT MACHINES"
by Ray Bradbury
A Luncheon Address at the 5th Annual Meeting of
Users of Automatic Information Display Equipment
Vacation Village, Mission Bay
San Diego, California
Wednesday, November 2, 1966
Copyright 1967 by Ray Bradbury
RAY BRADBURY

Bradbury pamphlets—with unpublished screenplay of *Moby Dick,* inscribed and dated 1954 by RB. Untitled item on bottom right is Squires edition of *The Pedestrian.*

PUBLISHED PLAYS

Arranged in order of publication.

"The Meadow." First printed in *Best One-Act Plays of 1947–1948*, ed. Margaret Mayorga. New York: Dodd, Mead, 1948. (See BOOKS AND PAMPHLETS.) (See STAGE PRODUCTIONS.)

"The Great Collision of Monday Last, The First Night of Lent, A Clear View of all Irish Mist, The Anthem Sprinters." Collected as *The Anthem Sprinters and Other Antics*, by Ray Bradbury. New York: Dial, 1963. (See BOOKS AND PAMPHLETS.) (See INTRODUCTIONS.)

"The Day It Rained Forever." Printed as pamphlet of same title. New York: Samuel French, 1966. (See BOOKS AND PAMPHLETS.) (See INTRODUCTIONS.)

"The Pedestrian." Printed as pamphlet of same title. New York: Samuel French, 1966. (See BOOKS AND PAMPHLETS.) (See INTRODUCTIONS.)

"The Wonderful Ice Cream Suit, The Veldt, To the Chicago Abyss." Collected as *The Wonderful Ice Cream Suit and Other Plays*, by Ray Bradbury. New York: Bantam, 1972. (See BOOKS AND PAMPHLETS.) (See INTRODUCTIONS.)

STAGE PRODUCTIONS

Bradbury's stage career began in Waukegan, Illinois, when he performed magic shows as a boy. He was active in dramatics at Los Angeles High School until the summer of 1938, and in 1939 joined the Wilshire Players Guild as an actor, remaining with this group into 1941. In the 1950s he wrote three unpublished dramas, all unstaged:

A three-act play based on *Fahrenheit 451* for Charles Laughton—1955.

A short operetta, *Happy Anniversary, 2116 A.D.* for Elsa Lanchester—1956.

A musical based on *The Martian Chronicles* for David Susskind, *Rocket Summer*—1957.

The following productions are arranged by date staged.

The 1937 Roman Revue. Staged at Los Angeles High in June 1937. In addition to scripting the *Revue,* RB was assistant producer/director.

The Meadow. Staged at the Huntington Hartford Theatre, Hollywood, in March 1960. RB's play was part of an overall presentation by a trio of writers: RB, Donald Dunlavey, and Willard L. Wiener, as *Three For Today.* (See PUBLISHED PLAYS.)

Way in the Middle of the Air. Staged at the Desilu Gower

2-14

The cellar appears, GRANDFATHER capping bottles, singing)

GRANDPA

AUGUST 2ND, 1928 ...

LAURA (Muses over label; speaks)

The night ~~Ann~~ Barclay went, forever ... Don't know where, but ... Gone forever ...

(Writes)

"Lost But Never Found Day."

(FORRESTER has appeared, near DOUGLAS, but does not touch him. HE would like to, but knows no way.

GRANDFATHER begins to call off other days, and THEY begin to wax and wane. The light goes green and yellow and then dark, green and yellow and then dark; the music ascends and descends through a multiplicity of noons and midnights. Days are passing, GRANDPA is filling the bottles)

GRANDPA

(Chanting)

AUGUST 7TH, 1928 ... 2-19

AUGUST 13TH, 1928 ...

AUGUST 16TH, 1928 ...

AUGUST 19TH, 1928 ...

(And, as HE does so, the porch appears. And, on the porch are all the people who are going, and a few who are staying. Pieces of luggage stand around and about.

There is JOHN HUFF in his Sunday best, small suitcase in hand, wearing a neat cap.

And there is MR. TRIDDEN in his Sunday suit, with the conductor's cap on his head, punching his own tickets, yellow, green, pink, from which flow confetti's of punched-out paper.

COLONEL FREELEIGH, dressed for his own funeral, crepe on his left arm in a band, carrying his own black wreath.

FERN and ROBERTA, dressed in fluttered summer fineries.

Unpublished mimeo-page from the New York stage presentation at Lincoln Center in 1967 of RB's musical drama, *Dandelion Wine.*

Studios, Hollywood, in August 1962.

Yesterday, Today and Tomorrow. A presentation of three short plays: *A Medicine For Melancholy, The Wonderful Ice Cream Suit,* and *The Pedestrian.* Staged at the Desilu Gower Studios, Hollywood, in June 1963.

The World of Ray Bradbury. A presentation of three short plays: *The Veldt, The Pedestrian,* and *To The Chicago Abyss.* Staged and produced by RB at the Coronet Theater, Hollywood, over a five-month period from October 1964 into February 1965. This presentation was also staged, for three nights in New York, at the Orpheum Theater in October 1965.

The Wonderful Ice Cream Suit. A presentation of three short plays: *A Device Out of Time, The Wonderful Ice Cream Suit,* and *The Day It Rained Forever.* Staged and produced by RB at the Coronet Theater, Hollywood, over a six-month period from February into mid-August 1965. (See BOOKS AND PAMPHLETS.)

Dandelion Wine. Staged as a full-length musical drama at Lincoln Center, New York, in April 1967, with music by Billy Goldenberg, lyrics by Larry Alexander. This presentation was also staged, revised by RB, and with three new lyrics by RB, at California State College, Fullerton, in March 1972. Adapted from the RB book. (See BOOKS AND PAMPHLETS.)

The Anthem Sprinters. Staged at the Beverly Hills Playhouse in October 1967, and at the Coronet Theater in late February 1968. RB combined four of his one-act Irish plays: *The Great Collision of Monday Last, The First Night of Lent, A Clear View of an Irish Mist,* and *The Anthem Sprinters,* into this unified production. (See BOOKS AND PAMPHLETS.)

Any Friend of Nicholas Nickleby's is a Friend of Mine. Staged at the Actor's Studio West, Hollywood, in August 1968, and at Rio Hondo College in 1969.

Christus Apollo. Staged at Royce Hall, U.C.L.A., in December 1969 as a cantata, with music by Jerry Goldsmith, lyrics by RB. (See *I Sing the Body Electric!* in

BOOKS AND PAMPHLETS.) (See VERSE.)

Leviathan '99. Staged at Samuel Goldwyn Studio Stage 9 Theater, Hollywood, in November 1972. Adapted by RB from his radio play. (See RADIO.)

Madrigals For the Space Age. Staged at Los Angeles Music Center, Dorothy Chandler Pavilion, in February 1973, with music by Lalo Schifrin, lyrics by RB. (See BOOKS AND PAMPHLETS.)

Pillar of Fire. Staged at the Little Theatre, California State College, Fullerton, in December 1973.

CLARIDGE'S *typed by Bradbury*

TELEGRAMS Claridge's London TELEPHONE Mayfair 8860

AHAB

Yes, the same, ~~the~~ same as I, when I struck my first whale forty, forty, ~~forty~~ years ago. When I think of this life I have led; forty years, and only three ~~spent~~ ashore; forty years I have fed on dry salted fare and loneliness. The madness, the frenzy, the boiling blood and the smoking brow with which, for a thousand lowerings, I have chased my prey--more a demon than a man. What a forty years fool--old fool--I have been. Why this chase? why weary my arm at the oar, and the iron, and the lance? How much richer or better am I for it? Is there joy enough at the end of it? Oh, the sea's highway is long and nowhere in the world will you find print of where I passed. The sea ~~wkpkkkOhfkyfokkkpkkk~~ washes your path away behind you. ~~Forty years ago I started out as young as you, and all that time and traveling have brought me to this place and this hour.~~

~~Now the time is at hand. This is the moment for which I have lived.~~

(CONT.)

Original typed manuscript page from screenplay of *Moby Dick,* written in London in April of 1954.

rewrite July 28, 1954 Shot 596 Pg. 96 mimeo'd script

596 M. S. QUARTERDECK OF "PEQUOD"

AHAB looks after STARBUCK. From afar there is a faint peal that grows louder and louder, until AHAB recognizes it for what it is - the sound of thunder emerging from the heavy silence. AHAB'S gaze flickers to the darkening horizon. The thunder fades.

One man pours his grog out on the deck.

AHAB

Captain Gardiner's ship is named well. RACHEL weeping for her children, because they were not.

The other men stand silently, the untouched grog in their hands.

AHAB looks them over.

AHAB

(Solemnly) Harpooners - your weapons, break them.

The harpooners obey slowly. AHAB pours the sockets full.

AHAB

Five minutes ago - I promised if we killed Moby Dick you should have my share of the profits from this voyage.

The men stand waiting for him to go on.

AHAB

Now I'll give ye a greater profit.

AHAB peers into each face near him.

AHAB

It was a hard thing to turn away from the RACHEL. But with a murderer loose on the world, then we be murderers, too. Oh, men, have ye not had nights when you doubted the sanity of this world? When friends die on each side of ye and ye are helpless? Yet where to strike? how revenge yourself? Where in the world can man take hold of Fate to wring its neck? Nowhere, nowhere. How kill the wind? how burn the sea? disembowel the heavens of their lightning? how make Death die? Must we stand patient by waiting for our heads to be chopped off? No, no, I say; I will not stand like an animal for slaughter. I will roll all the evil of this world into one great hill of snow, one great cold body. That Fate which nuzzles me, and thee, and the RACHEL, I'll nuzzle with my steel. Some small part of death will die, some small part of this universal horror lie cold in my hands when I lay hold on Moby Dick.

Unpublished revision page from *Moby Dick* screenplay, written by RB in California in July of 1954.

FILMS

Bradbury has been involved with film work since the early 1950s. In all, nine properties have reached the screen.

Arranged in order of release.

It Came From Outer Space. Universal, 1953. RB wrote this as an original screen story, "The Meteor," at the studio. The shooting script by Harry Essex was based directly on his 110-page treatment and incorporated dialogue from it. Released as "the world's first 3-D science fiction film."

The Beast From 20,000 Fathoms. Warner Brothers, 1953. Based on RB's short story from the *Saturday Evening Post.* Bradbury did not work on the screenplay.

Moby Dick. Warner Brothers, 1956. Based on the Melville novel. RB shared final screenplay credit with director John Huston.

King of Kings. M.G.M., 1961. RB wrote the voice-over narration for this film, but no screen credit was given for narration. He did not work on the screenplay.

Icarus Montgolfier Wright. Format Films, 1962. Based on RB's short story. Bradbury shared screenplay credit with George C. Johnson on this 18-minute animated film, with artwork by Joseph Mugnaini. It was nominated for an Academy Award as best animated short subject of the year.

So at last America stands lit upon
the ancient wilds, one huge electric
city facing the Future. You have
been part of three motions of Weather.
A wind of change that blew across
oceans. A weather of need that strewed
wildflower human seed to populate the
four corners of Nowhere and make it Somewhere. And the Boy Mechanics who flew
the kites and lit July Fourth rockets,
who now grown men, make ready for the
time of your final voyaging.

You look away from the seas of Earth,
the seas of grass, and the lights in
your constellation cities toward the
lights in the sky which are stars. The
weather of change is eternal. The
warm American climate carries
its momentum...UP!

Melted and fused by new desire, hoping
to become one race, you build a Giant's
eye to stare unblinking upon Truth, gone
infinite, in Space.

Mimeo-page from RB's film narration, *American Journey*, as presented during the World's Fair at the U.S. Government Pavilion in 1964.

1-16-61 P.117

WILDER speaks to himself.

WILDER
He's making a target of himself.
Does he trust me to do the job?
Can he trust me? Spender, get
down, I don't want to do this...

He aims the gun.

We see what he sees, SPENDER above in the open, firing.

CLOSEUP with SPENDER. We see him sweating, firing, firing, swaying there.

WILDER presses the trigger of his rifle.

WILDER
Spender, go on!

SPENDER fires.

WILDER waits.

WILDER
Your last chance.

He fires.

The men quiver at the shot.

SPENDER above, pauses a moment.

WILDER looks up, waiting.

SPENDER falls.

The men yell.

WILDER rises slowly. The wind is blowing.

WILDER bolts up the hill, running fast.

The men stand up and look after him, not moving.

WILDER reaches the rock-ledge and comes over. He looks down at the body of SPENDER. The wind blows dust; it mourns through the books.

WILDER looks at the books.

The wind blows the pages. The harp-voices sing softly.

WILDER remembers what the words are.

Two versions of Jeff Spender's death: (left) Unpublished RB screenplay of *The Martian Chronicles,* written at M.G.M. in 1961. (right) Unpublished mimeo-page from unproduced RB screenplay of same book, written in 1964, showing concept revision.

WILDER and his men, silent, guns holstered, can only watch as:

SPENDER breathes slowly, then opens his fists as if to free himself of life.

Slowly he sinks, as his power dies, down along the cliff-side, down along the immense faces and bas-reliefs. He starts his descent in the last rays of the sun which strike into the fiord from a long distance.

WILDER watches, cold and alone.

The others see:

A long ribbon of red unwind from the sliding distant moth-like body of SPENDER as it sinks and slithers down and down the side of the cliff. The rubbon unwinds very bright. By the time SPENDER has sunk from sight in the dark at the base of the cliff, the scarlet sash, the bright path of red, stretches fifty of sixty yards from start to obscured finish.

WILDER hovers for a long moment.

The men hover, staring at that empty cliff face.

Then, with one mind, they all fly down into the dusk.

WILDER stands over!

The crumpled shape at the base of the cliff.

The other men are behind him.

WILDER bends to take one arm.

PARKHILL hesitates, then bends to take the other.

The other men crouch.

And silently they are airbourne. The CAMERA drifts up with them as they rise high along the blue shadowed stone precipices where stranger creatures than themselves fly sculpted in old symboled pictures.

And their funeral procession, their airbourne cortege, flies quietly higher, SPENDER's body carried among the stunned men into the air of evening where the first stars are coming out.

An American Journey. U.S. Government, 1964. RB was commissioned to write this special film for the U.S. Government Pavilion at the New York World's Fair. It ran for 13 1/2 minutes and was projected on 130 separate screens. (See VERSE.)

Fahrenheit 451. Universal, 1966. Based on RB's novel. Bradbury did not work on the screenplay. (For full details, see "Journal of Fahrenheit 451," by Francois Truffaut in *Cahiers du Cinema,* Numbers 5, 6, and 7, in 1966.)

The Illustrated Man. Warners/Seven Arts, 1969. Based on three RB stories from the book: "The Veldt," "The Long Rain," and "The Last Night of the World." Plus his Prologue/Epilogue, used to frame the stories. Bradbury did not work on the screenplay.

Picasso Summer. Warners/Seven Arts, 1972. Based on RB's short story, "In a Season of Calm Weather." RB used pseudonym "Douglas Spaulding" in final screenplay co-credit with "Edwin Boyd" (Ed Weinberger). Released in U.S. as an original film for television.

Bradbury has worked on many film projects which remain unproduced: a screenplay based on his short story, "The Fox and the Forest," a film treatment titled "Dark Carnival," a screen version of "The Wonderful Ice Cream Suit," a screenplay based on *Something Wicked This Way Comes,* and a treatment melding a trio of his short stories, "The Rocket," "King of the Gray Spaces," and "The Rocket Man," into a unified production. He was also paid to develop the following unproduced screen properties:

"The Face in the Deep." An original screen treatment in 1952 for 20th Century-Fox.

"And the Rock Cried Out." A screenplay based on his story, which he wrote in London for Carol Reed in 1957.

"The Dreamers." A screenplay for Hecht-Hill-Lancaster in 1958, based on the novel by Roger Manvell.

"White Hunter, Black Heart." A screenplay for Hecht-Hill-

Lancaster in 1959, based on the novel by Peter Viertel.

"The Martian Chronicles." A screenplay written at M.G.M. in 1960–1961, for Julian Blaustein.

"The Martian Chronicles." A screenplay for Robert Mulligan and Alan Pakula in 1964.

"The Halloween Tree." A screenplay for animation, with Chuck Jones, for M.G.M. in 1968.

TELEVISION

Bradbury has sold sixteen teleplays since 1955. Six were originals, eight were adaptations of his own stories, and two were adapted from the work of other writers. Twelve of these were produced and are here arranged by date of telecast.

"Shopping For Death." Telecast January 29, 1956 on *Alfred Hitchcock* (CBS). Based on his story, "Touched With Fire."

"The Marked Bullet." Telecast November 20, 1956 on *Jane Wyman's Fireside Theater* (NBC). Original for TV.

"The Wonderful Ice Cream Suit." Telecast during 1958 on *Rendezvous* (CBS). Based on his story.

"Design For Loving." Telecast November 9, 1958 on *Alfred Hitchcock* (CBS). Based on his story, "Marionettes, Inc."

"The Gift." Telecast December 20, 1958 on *Steve Canyon* (NBC). Original for TV.

"Special Delivery." Telecast November 29, 1959 on *Alfred Hitchcock* (CBS). Based on his story, "Come Into My Cellar."

"The Tunnel to Yesterday." Telecast May 13, 1960 on *Trouble Shooters* (ABC). Original for TV.

"The Faith of Aaron Menefee." Telecast January 30, 1962 on *Alfred Hitchcock* (CBS). Based on a story by Stanley Ellin.

"REPORT FROM SPACE"

FADE IN

1 THE NIGHT SKY - MILLIONS OF BRIGHT STARS

Silence. We hear only the crickets and frogs and the blowing of the wind, as if we were out in night country. After a moment, the wind rises slightly, breathing.

2 OVER SCENE DISSOLVE THE WORDS:

Bryna Productions Presents

Ray Bradbury's

REPORT FROM SPACE

In the few seconds it takes to read these words, the wind blows very quietly, the crickets chirp. Then the words blow on out into space and vanish among the million stars. We see the night sky again, absolutely clear.

CAMERA PANS slowly down to:

3 EXT. SUBURBAN STREET - NIGHT

A quiet, tree-lined residential area.

NARRATOR'S VOICE
The time . . . tomorrow morning.

Silence for a beat. Then:

NARRATOR'S VOICE
It must be morning . . .

4 CAMERA PANS SLIGHTLY UP

to horizon showing over the rooftops.

NARRATOR'S VOICE
. . . for look.

A light glows on the dark horizon. It builds slowly in an enlarging mushroom.

NARRATOR'S VOICE
No, wait. Not the sun. What, then?

The light glows intently. Suddenly it detaches itself, flings itself up, taking shape as a pencil of light in the sky, to run off in a path of light among the stars.

The night is quiet again after the brief thunder. We hear the crickets.

Cont.

994-T - 1 -

Opening of unpublished television series-concept, *Report From Space,* written in 1955 and based on *The Martian Chronicles.* Optioned but unproduced.

4 Cont.

NARRATOR'S VOICE
A rocket heading for outer space.

5 & 6 LONG SHOT

CAMERA PANS slowly down from the star-filled sky to the houses on the tree-lined avenue.

NARRATOR'S VOICE
And the men who dream and build and fly such rockets live here on Chestnut Street in a green and shady town near a big American city.

The CAMERA PANS from one side of the street to the other, stops on a house.

NARRATOR'S VOICE
This is the house of the Captain of the first rocket ship outward bound for Mars.

The figure of the Captain moves in from CAMERA LEFT, his back to the CAMERA, strolling idly.

NARRATOR'S VOICE
The Captain's name . . .

The Captain turns easily, to look into the CAMERA.

WILDER
Jonathan Wilder.

He strolls again, the CAMERA with him.

WILDER
Just out for a walk. Don't get much chance in my business.

He touches a lawnmower on the lawn, gives it a push.

WILDER
Here's my lawnmower, my lawn, which I never quite finish up because -

He glances at the sky as a rocket roars off on the horizon.

WILDER
I'm always going somewhere.

Cont.

994-T

"The Jail." Telecast February 6, 1962 on *Alcoa Premiere* (ABC). Original for TV.

"I Sing the Body Electric!" Telecast May 8, 1962 on *Twilight Zone* (ABC). Original for TV, later developed into short story.

"The Life Work of Juan Diaz." Telecast October 26, 1964 on *Alfred Hitchcock* (NBC). Based on his story.

"The Groon." Telecast October 30, 1971 on *Curiosity Shop* (ABC). Original for TV.

Four of Bradbury's teleplays remain unproduced:

"And the Moon Be Still as Bright." Optioned in 1955 by Bryna Productions as first show in potential TV series created by RB, *Report From Space,* based on his *Martian Chronicles.*

"The Veldt." Purchased for *Seven Lively Arts* in 1957. Based on his story.

"The Rocket." Purchased for *Shirley Temple Storybook* in 1960. Based on his two stories, "The Rocket" and "King of the Grey Spaces."

"To Build a Fire." Purchased for a TV anthology series in 1961. Based on the story by Jack London.

Several Bradbury stories have been adapted for television by other writers. These include:

"Zero Hour." Adapted for *Tales of Tomorrow* (ABC) in 1951.

"Marionettes, Inc." Adapted for *Tales of Tomorrow* (ABC) in 1951.

"Zero Hour." Adapted for *Lights Out* (NBC) on July 23, 1951.

"The Man." Adapted for *Out There* (CBS) on December 23, 1951.

"Summer Night." Adapted for *Suspense* (CBS) on February 19, 1952.

"The Rocket." Adapted for *CBS Television Workshop* in 1952.

RAY BRADBURY - *The Story of a Writer*

KCOP T-V - Channel 13

Wednesday Night, November 20th, 9:00 P.M.
1963

A Wolper Production

Directed by Terry Sanders

Announcement of TV special based on RB's life and career and a reproduction of an oil painting by Bradbury.

"The Black Ferris." Adapted as series pilot for Sam Goldwyn, Jr. in 1954.

"Cora and the Great Wide World." Adapted for *G.E. Theater* (CBS) in 1955.

"And So Died Riabouchinska." Adapted for *Alfred Hitchcock* (CBS) on February 12, 1956.

"The Jar." Adapted for *Alfred Hitchcock* (CBS) on February 14, 1964.

"The Screaming Woman." Adapted as a Universal-ABC *Movie of the Week* on January 29, 1972.

An original Bradbury short story, "Dial Double Zero," was dramatized as part of the NBC-TV special, *The Story of a Writer,* based on RB's life and work. Telecast November 20, 1963 (West Coast).

878 M.C.S. ON WHALE'S BACK

AHAB hoists his harpoon high and shrieks his imprecations as he jams the weapon into the whale again and again and again.

AHAB: To the last I grapple with thee! from hell's heart I stab at thee! for hate's sake I spit my last breath at thee, thou damned whale! Thus! I give up my spear!

He thrusts mightily.

879 F.S. SECTION OF SEA

MOBY DICK thunders and shudders.

880 M.S. WHALEBOATS AND SEA

The men in the boats stand transfixed.

881 M.S. STARBUCK'S WHALEBOAT

STARBUCK stands, a cry frozen in his throat.

The men put out their hands from the boat as if to stop AHAB.

882 M.C.S. ON WHALE'S BACK

In a maniac frenzy, AHAB strikes again and again and again.

883 F.S. SECTION OF SEA

The whale quakes like a great berg in the sea.

884 M.S. WHALEBOATS AND SEA

The men stand in the boats, watching, unable to move.

885 M.S. STARBUCK'S WHALEBOAT

STARBUCK stands motionless.

ISHMAEL cries out.

886 F.S. SECTION OF SEA

Less than three feet away, in his great plunge, MOBY DICK rises up and slides down like a white avalanche sinking, falling into the terrible dark waters.

887 M.C.S. ON WHALE'S BACK

On the side of this avalanche, mouth wide, still striking in and striking in with his harpoon, clinging to the rusted weapons, AHAB is seen going down and down, vanishing, into the sea.

ISHMAEL (Cont:)
flashing meteors, eroded, baked,
swallowed, vanished in the all
encompassing light...each man
thrown to a different warp in
time...

WE HEAR THE RENDING OF THE SHIPS, MEN'S YELLS, DESTRUCTIONS, THE YAMMERING OF RADIATION.

ISHMAEL
The men in life craft one, their
weapon stilled, hurled down to
death perhaps and burials with King
Richard on his plain, the crown
lost at his feet...the men in life
craft two spun further on to drop
in open grave with Yorick's skull?
or near the tomb in Illinois where
Lincoln dreamt away? I do not know.
The Captain last! Through Quell I
heard his cry...

THE CAPTAIN
What, the weapons gone? My men
dispersed? Why then I have these
hands! Blind, I seize on you! Gone
dead, I grapple you! Where is your
heart! There! there, I'll stifle it!
O damned Leviathan, it comes to this!

A FINAL EXPLOSION, YAMMER OF SOUND, CRIES...MUSIC... SILENCE.

ISHMAEL
Ripped out, I was tossed forth
myself...alone I watched as now
at last the whiteness went its
way. With gibbering voice off
down the long black mineshaft of
the Universe, its bridal veil
trailing despairs and woes,
celebrating itself, a mindless
mystery forever in motion...
vanishing...an echo...gone...
and gone all ships, men, large,
small, sane or mad, The Captain
with them, madness maddened...
and for a billion years I knew
that Leviathan, on return, circling
round, would bring back with it
him who would have done it unto
death...the two of them were one
at last, the hunter and the hunted,
the fearer and the feared, the flesh

86-1[illegible]

Left: Unpublished mimeo-page from *Moby Dick* screenplay, describing death of Ahab. Right: Unpublished mimeo-page from *Leviathan '99* radio play, describing death of "the Captain," a character based directly on Ahab.

RADIO

Bradbury's initial work for radio consisted of nine radio "spots" written for the Red Cross, 1943–1944, soliciting blood donations. He also wrote a series of six 15-minute radio scripts for the Los Angeles Department of Civil Defense during this same period. He has written only two commercial radio plays:

"The Meadow." Original half-hour drama, broadcast January 2, 1947 on *World Security Workshop* (ABC). This radio play was anthologized in *Best One-Act Plays of 1947–1948* and was later revised into a stage play and short story. (See STAGE PRODUCTIONS.)

"Leviathan '99." Original hour drama, broadcast May 3, 1968 over the BBC in London, England. Later revised into a stage play. (See STAGE PRODUCTIONS.)

Three Bradbury stories were sold as radio originals in 1947–1948 directly to CBS, for *Suspense,* but were dramatized by other writers. For broadcast dates, see *Suspense* entry.

"Riabouchinska"—later printed as a short story, "And So Died Riabouchinska."

"Summer Night"—later printed as a short story, "The Whole Town's Sleeping."

"The Screaming Woman"—later printed as a short story, same title.

Bradbury's only other direct contribution to dramatic radio was an original narration written and spoken by RB as an introduction to two of his adapted stories, "Hail and Farewell" and "Season of Disbelief," for *CBS Radio Workshop* on February 17, 1956.

The following Bradbury stories were adapted by other writers. Arranged by program series title.

ABC Radio Workshop
"Mars is Heaven."
"The Whole Town's Sleeping." } Broadcast March 16, 1953.

CBS Radio Workshop
"Hail and Farewell."
"Season of Disbelief." } Broadcast February 17, 1956.

Dimension X (NBC)
"To the Future." Broadcast May 27, 1950.
"There Will Come Soft Rains."
"Zero Hour." } Broadcast June 17, 1950.
"Mars is Heaven." Broadcast July 7, 1950.
"The Martian Chronicles." Broadcast August 18, 1950.
"And the Moon Be Still as Bright." Broadcast September 29, 1950.
"Dwellers in Silence." Broadcast July 19, 1951.
"The Veldt." Broadcast August 9, 1951.
"Marionettes, Inc." Broadcast August 30, 1951.
"Kaleidoscope." Broadcast September 15, 1951.

Escape (CBS)
"Mars is Heaven." Broadcast June 2, 1950.
"The Earth Men." Broadcast July 25, 1951.
"Zero Hour." Broadcast October 4, 1953.

Molle Mystery Theatre (ABC)
"Killer, Come Back to Me." Broadcast during 1946.

THE CBS RADIO WORKSHOP

MUSIC: OVERTURE OR DEAD AIR

VOICE: (ON) CBS RADIO - A Division of the Columbia Broadcasting System - and its two-hundred and seventeen affiliated stations, present - THE CBS RADIO WORKSHOP - Radio's distinguished series dedicated to man's imagination; the theatre of the mind.

MUSIC: THEME AND TO B.G.

VOICE: Tonight, from Hollywood, "Season of Disbelief" - and "Hail and Farewell" - adapted and directed by Antony Ellis. Two unusual and provocative character studies by one of America's most original authors -- Ray Bradbury. Ladies and gentlemen - Mr. Bradbury.

MUSIC: HARP EFFECT AND TO B.G.

TAPE: (MR. BRADBURY) It has always seemed to me that life, to all of us, is an endless coil of rope-playing through our hands every moment of every hour of the day. The long line of the rope goes back to the time we were born and extends on out ahead to the time of our death.
In between, lies the eternal Now...the flickering moments when each of us must play the rope as best we can.
Without burning our fingers --- snarling the coils -- or breaking the line.
This is a study of one woman and her rope.

MUSIC: OUT

VOICE: "Season of Disbelief"

MUSIC: OVERTURE AND TO B.G.

DH

CBS WORKSHOP -10A-
2-17-56

VOICE: Presenting now the Second of our Duo -- and Mr. Ray Bradbury!

MUSIC: HARP EFFECT AND TO B.G.

BRADBURY: The rope of life [redacted] hisses through our fingers [redacted] WE REACH — IT'S GONE! ~~beautiful because it can not last~~. The beauty of any particular flower, song, poem or person lies often in the fact that roses must fade, songs die with the breath, poems burn in the fire, [redacted] "Golden lads and GIRLS ALL MUST AS ~~lasses~~ [redacted]t, [redacted]e chimney sweepers, come to dust." But what if beauty could be made to last? Would it still be beautiful or monstrous? Here's the study of a person who seized the travelling rope of life A MOMENT OF BEAUTY and felt it freeze in his hands.

MUSIC: OUT:

VOICE: "Hail And Farewell"

MUSIC: OVERTURE AND TO B.G.

Mimeo pages from unpublished radio play by Antony Ellis broadcast on CBS in February of 1956 with original narration written and spoken by RB for this production.

NBC Presents: Short Story
"The Rocket." Broadcast January 4, 1950.

Radio City Playhouse (NBC)
"The Lake." Broadcast October 16, 1949.
"The Wind." Broadcast October 30, 1949.

Radio Pacifica (Berkeley):
"Usher II." Broadcast during 1970.

Suspense (CBS)
"Riabouchinska." Broadcast November 13, 1947.
"Summer Night." Broadcast July 15, 1948.
"The Screaming Woman." Broadcast November 25, 1948.
"The Crowd." Broadcast September 21, 1950.
"Zero Hour." Broadcast April 5, 1955.
"The Whole Town's Sleeping." Broadcast June 14, 1955.
"Kaleidoscope." Broadcast July 12, 1955.

X Minus 1 (NBC)
"And the Moon Be Still as Bright." Broadcast April 22, 1955.
"Mars is Heaven." Broadcast May 8, 1955.
"The Veldt." Broadcast August 4, 1955.
"Dwellers in Silence." Broadcast November 10, 1955.
"To the Future." Broadcast December 14, 1955.
"Marionettes, Inc." Broadcast December 21, 1955.
"There Will Come Soft Rains." } Broadcast December 5, 1956.
"Zero Hour." }

Nelson Olmsted read four RB stories over the air during 1947-1948 on his show, *Stories By Olmsted:* "The Night." "The Miracles of Jamie." "One Timeless Spring." "Powerhouse."

 Writers in other countries have also adapted RB stories

for radio, but data is incomplete. Known titles are listed by country.

AUSTRALIA
"The Whole Town's Sleeping" (in 1952).

CANADA
"The Pedestrian," on *Theater 10:30.*
"Dandelion Wine," on *Theater 10:30* (in four parts).
"To the Chicago Abyss," on *Theatre 10:30.*
"Fahrenheit 451," on *CBS Stage* (in 1971).
"Frost and Fire," on *Vancouver Theatre* (in 1969).
"The Town Where No One Got Off," on CBS.
"The Crowd," on CBC.
"Night Call, Collect," on CBC.

DENMARK
"The Martian Chronicles."
"The Veldt."
"The Highway" (in 1952).
"The Night."
"The Wind" (in 1951).

ENGLAND
"The Flying Machine," on BBC (in 1954).
"The Golden Kite, the Silver Wind," on BBC (in 1954).
"The Meadow," on BBC (in 1954).
"The Great Wide World Over There," on BBC (in 1954).

FRANCE
"The Fox and the Forest."
"Marionettes, Inc."

GERMANY
"Leviathan '99."

SOUTH AFRICA

"A Sound of Thunder," on *SF:68* (in 1968).

"The Wind," on *SF:68* (in 1968).

"The Fox and the Forest," on *Saturday Playhouse.*

PUBLISHED LETTERS

It would be all but impossible to compile a full listing of Bradbury's letters, since so many appeared in fanzines in the 1930s. The listing which follows, arranged in order of publication, begins in the period when he wrote "fan" letters to the professional science fiction and fantasy magazines, 1939-1941, and extends through 1972.

**denotes privately-printed amateur magazine or "fanzine."

"Dear Mr. Campbell:" *Unknown*, July 1939.

"That Stellar Line-Up," *Thrilling Wonder Stories*, August 1939.

"Laid Him Low!" *Amazing Stories*, September 1939.

"Dear Mr. Campbell:" *Unknown*, March 1940.

"Fantastic Records," *Fantastic Adventures*, April 1940.

"We Have Him, in F.N." *Famous Fantastic Mysteries*, December 1940.

"Dear Mr. Campbell:" *Unknown*, February 1941, written as a "dialogue" between RB, "Guy Amory," and "Anthony Corvais"—Bradbury pen names.

Untitled, ***Shangri-L'Affaires*, April 1944.

"Dear Mrs. Wagner:" *Script*, March 3, 1945.

"Ray Bradbury," ***Fabulous Faust Fanzine*, January 1950.

"Dear Mr. Eaton:" ** *Rhodomagnetic Digest*, August 1950.

Untitled, *Argosy*, February 1952. RB comments on "The Rocket Man" in editor's column.

"Bradburiana," ***Rhodomagnetic Digest,* No. 19, 1952. Features a facsimile postcard to Anthony Boucher from RB, plus letter to RB from Boucher and long reply letter from RB dated February 18, 1952.

"Of Her We Sing," *Harper's,* September 1952.

"To the Republican Party," *Daily Variety,* November 10, 1952. An "open letter" paid for by RB.

"Dear Bill:" *Weird Science,* January-February 1953. Letter, in this comic book, refers to illustrated adaptations of his work for all E.C. comic books. (See COMIC BOOK APPEARANCES.)

"Ray Bradbury," *Weird Science,* May-June 1953. RB letter is at end of bio sketch on him—which also appeared in several other E.C. comic books. (See COMIC BOOK APPEARANCES.)

Untitled, *Ellery Queen's Mystery Magazine,* June 1954. RB letter serves as introduction to his story, "At Midnight, In the Month of June."

"A Man of Mercy," *Life,* December 6, 1954.

"To the Editor:" *Reporter,* September 6, 1956.

"Calm View," *Los Angeles Times,* October 15, 1957.

"Bradbury," *Help!* April 1961.

Untitled, *Writer,* July 1961.

Untitled, *American Artist,* March 1962. RB letter is quoted in profile of artist Joe Mugnaini.

"Letters to a Young Aspiring Author," printed as pamphlet by San Antonio Public Library, 1962, as *The Essence of Creative Writing.* (Three RB letters, slightly abridged, are printed.) (See BOOKS AND PAMPHLETS.)

"Transit Ideas Changed," *Los Angeles Times,* August 8, 1964.

"Dear Sirs:" *Hollywood Reporter,* November 10, 1964.

"Letter From Bradbury," *Helicon,* Vol. 3 #1, 1964.

"Transit Board Has Real Need," *Los Angeles Times,* May 8, 1965.

"Sirs:" *Life,* February 24, 1967.

Untitled, *Los Angeles Times,* March 4, 1967.

"To the Editors:" *New Journal,* January 21, 1968.

"Dear Leland S.:" ***Riverside Quarterly,* Vol. 3 # 4, 1968.

"Downtown Unbeautiful," *Los Angeles Times,* March 5, 1969.

Untitled, *Pen,* Spring 1969.

"Ray Bradbury," ***Squa Tront,* No. 3, 1969.

"Dear Bryan Joseph:" *Writers Guild of America Newsletter,* November 1970.

"Dear Doug:" *Forgotten Fantasy,* February 1971.

"Ray Bradbury," ***Is,* October 1971.

"The Public Speaks," *Los Angeles Times,* October 23, 1971.

"From Ray Bradbury," *Family Weekly,* February 6, 1972.

"Dear Mr. Cazedessus," ***ERB-dom,* February 1972. RB discusses influence of Edgar Rice Burroughs on his life and career.

Untitled, *Waukegan News-Sun,* June 5, 1972. RB letter is part of piece on Bradbury's early life in Waukegan. Also map drawn by RB.

"Bradbury Replies," *Calendar (Los Angeles Times),* June 18, 1972.

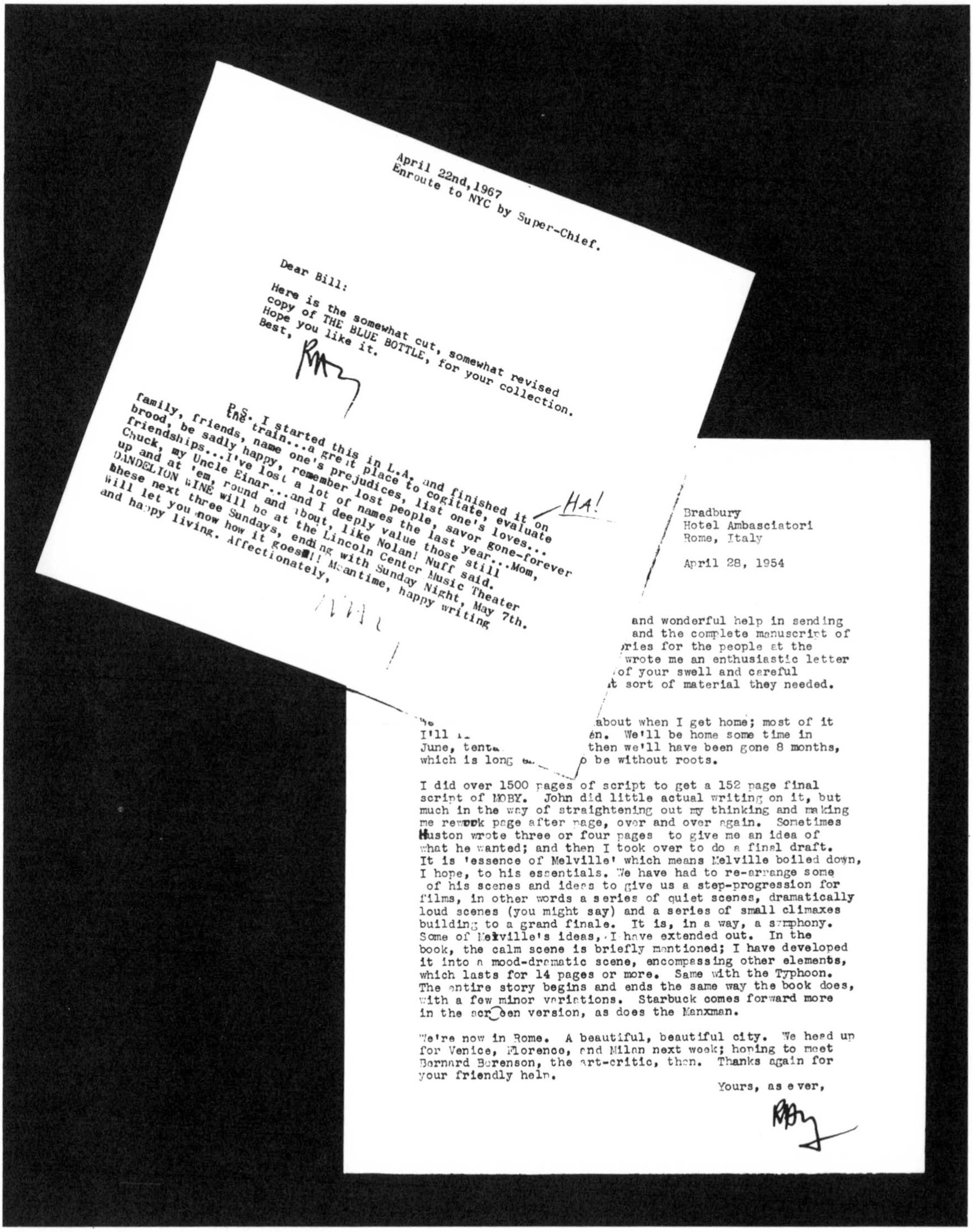

April 22nd,1967
Enroute to NYC by Super-Chief.

Dear Bill:

Here is the somewhat cut, somewhat revised copy of THE BLUE BOTTLE, for your collection. Hope you like it.

Best,

RBy

P.S. I started this in L.A. and finished it on the train...a great place to cogitate, evaluate family, friends, name one's prejudices, list one's loves... brood, be sadly happy, remember lost people, savor gone-forever friendships...I've lost a lot of names the last year...Mom, Chuck, my Uncle Einar...and I deeply value those still up and at 'em, round and about, like Nolan! Nuff said. HA! DANDELION WINE will be at the Lincoln Center Music Theater these next three Sundays, ending with Sunday Night, May 7th. Will let you know how it goes!!! Meantime, happy writing and happy living. Affectionately,

Bradbury
Hotel Ambasciatori
Rome, Italy

April 28, 1954

and wonderful help in sending
and the complete manuscript of
ries for the people at the
wrote me an enthusiastic letter
of your swell and careful
t sort of material they needed.

about when I get home; most of it
I'll ... en. We'll be home some time in
June, tenta... then we'll have been gone 8 months,
which is long ... o be without roots.

I did over 1500 pages of script to get a 152 page final script of MOBY. John did little actual writing on it, but much in the way of straightening out my thinking and making me rework page after page, over and over again. Sometimes Huston wrote three or four pages to give me an idea of what he wanted; and then I took over to do a final draft. It is 'essence of Melville' which means Melville boiled down, I hope, to his essentials. We have had to re-arrange some of his scenes and ideas to give us a step-progression for films, in other words a series of quiet scenes, dramatically loud scenes (you might say) and a series of small climaxes building to a grand finale. It is, in a way, a symphony. Some of Melville's ideas, I have extended out. In the book, the calm scene is briefly mentioned; I have developed it into a mood-dramatic scene, encompassing other elements, which lasts for 14 pages or more. Same with the Typhoon. The entire story begins and ends the same way the book does, with a few minor variations. Starbuck comes forward more in the screen version, as does the Manxman.

We're now in Rome. A beautiful, beautiful city. We head up for Venice, Florence, and Milan next week; hoping to meet Bernard Berenson, the art-critic, then. Thanks again for your friendly help.

Yours, as ever,

RBy

Two unpublished letters from RB to William F. Nolan.

INTERVIEWS

Bradbury has been interviewed many times on radio and television, but no attempt has been made here to list these appearances. The only exception to this is his interview with Pierre Berton on TV; the talk was transcribed and published in Berton's book, and is therefore included. Arranged in order of publication.

IN BOOKS:

"Ray Bradbury." Interviewed by Harvey Breit in *The Writer Observed.* New York: World, 1956. Reprints "A Talk With Mr. Bradbury" from *New York Times Book Review,* August 5, 1951. (See IN MAGAZINES AND NEWSPAPERS.)

"Ray Bradbury: Cassandra on a Bicycle." Interviewed by Pierre Berton in *Voices From the Sixties.* New York: Doubleday, 1967. Transcribed television interview.

Untitled interview. By William Melton in *I Get My Best Ideas in Bed.* Los Angeles: Nash, 1971. RB one of 190 "popular" authors interviewed for book. All interviews are broken up and spaced throughout book under varied headings.

IN MAGAZINES AND NEWSPAPERS:

**denotes privately-printed amateur magazine.

"The Market is Not the Story." Interviewed by R. Walton Willems, *Writers' Markets and Methods,* March 1948.

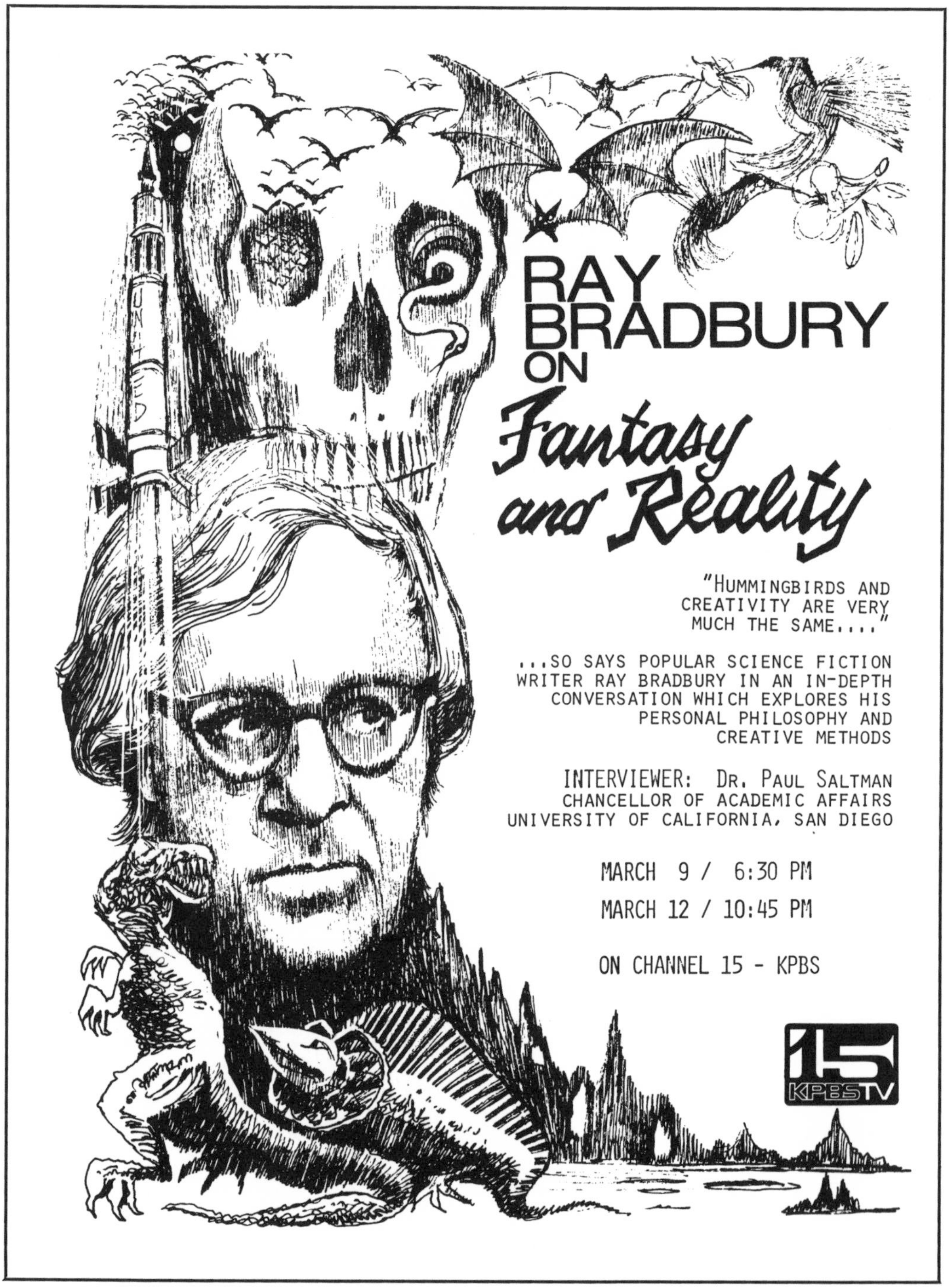
RAY BRADBURY ON
Fantasy and Reality
"HUMMINGBIRDS AND CREATIVITY ARE VERY MUCH THE SAME...."
...SO SAYS POPULAR SCIENCE FICTION WRITER RAY BRADBURY IN AN IN-DEPTH CONVERSATION WHICH EXPLORES HIS PERSONAL PHILOSOPHY AND CREATIVE METHODS
INTERVIEWER: DR. PAUL SALTMAN
CHANCELLOR OF ACADEMIC AFFAIRS
UNIVERSITY OF CALIFORNIA, SAN DIEGO
MARCH 9 / 6:30 PM
MARCH 12 / 10:45 PM
ON CHANNEL 15 - KPBS
15
KPBS TV
UNITED

Promotional leaflet announcing a Bradbury television appearance.

"An Interview With Ray Bradbury." Interview unsigned, ***Utopian,* May 1950.

"A Talk With Mr. Bradbury," Interviewed by Harvey Breit, *New York Times Book Review,* August 5, 1951. (See IN BOOKS.)

"Words on Writing—Ray Bradbury." Interviewed by Bob Rosenstone, *Westwind,* (U.C.L.A.) Fall 1957.

"Lyke Interviews Ray Bradbury." Interview unsigned, *Lyke* (San Jose State College), May 1959.

"The Editor Visits Ray Bradbury." Interviewed by Raymond Lee, *Offbeat,* I, 4, 1959.

"Off the Cuff: Ray Bradbury." Interview unsigned, ***Shangri-L'Affaires,* August 1959.

"Weave Tapestry of Truth, Author Says." Interviewed by Marylou Luther, *Los Angeles Times,* April 14, 1960.

"So You Want to be a Writer!" Interview unsigned, *Friends,* January 1961.

"A Rationale for Bookburners: A Further Word From Ray Bradbury." Interviewed by Everett T. Moore, *American Library Association Bulletin,* May 1961.

"Ray Bradbury Speaks of Writing as Self-Discovery." Interviewed by F. A. Rockwell, *Author and Journalist,* February 1962.

"An Interview With Ray Bradbury." Interviewed by Dan Yergin, *Avant Garde,* Vol. 4, 1962.

"The Playboy Panel: 1984 and Beyond." Interviewed by Playboy editors for panel discussion (with 11 other writers), *Playboy* (two parts), July and August 1963.

"A Portrait of Genius: Ray Bradbury." Interview unsigned, *Show,* December 1964.

"Predicting the Future is an Art as Old as Plato." Interviewed by Kitte Turmell, *Youth,* January 17, 1965.

"The World of Ray Bradbury." Interviewed by Thomas Schulz, *Knight,* May 1966.

"Ray Bradbury." Interviewed by Mike Rose, *El Playano* (Loyola University), Summer 1966.

"Los Angeles—A Discussion in Depth With Ray Bradbury." Interviewed by John Bryan, *California Living,* December 4, 1966.

"An Exclusive Interview With Ray Bradbury." Interviewed by Frank Roberts, *Writer's Digest* (two parts), February and March 1967.

"Ray Bradbury and Tom Wolfe on Pop Culture." Interviewed by Shelly Burton, *Cavalier,* April 1967.

"The Fantasy Makers: A Conversation with Ray Bradbury and Chuck Jones." Interviewed by Mary Harrington Hall, *Psychology Today,* April 1968.

"Ray Bradbury." Interviewed by Shelly Burton, *Actress,* November 1968.

"An Interview With Ray Bradbury." Interviewed by William B. Allen, *Phalanx* (Journal of Southern California Collegiate Studies Conference), Winter 1968.

"An Interview With Ray Bradbury." Interviewed by John Stanley, *Castle of Frankenstein* (two parts), Spring and Summer 1969.

"What on Earth Can You Do in Space?" Interviewed (as part of group) by Susan Vibert and Meema Keene, *Pace,* August 1969.

"The Illustrated Fan: A Day With Ray Bradbury." Interviewed by Greg Bear, ** *Luna,* November 1969.

"Encore: Ray Bradbury." Interviewed by Lois Nemcik, *Royal Purple* (Cypress College), January 1970.

"Martian Advisor." Interview unsigned, *Century City Centurion,* July-August 1970.

"An Informal Interview With Ray Bradbury." Interviewed by Greg Orfalea, *Courier* (Georgetown University), November 1970.

"Ray Bradbury: High Priest of Sci-Fi." Interviewed by William Hall, *Rex* (England), No. 28, 1971.

"Collision of Minds Generate Dialog on America's Future." Interviewed by Digby Diehl, *Calendar (Los Angeles Times),* October 24, 1971.

"King of the Science Fiction Writers." Interviewed by Jeff

Hansen, *Scene (Torrence Daily Breeze)*, March 26, 1972.

"Rituals Important Claims Writer Bradbury." Interviewed by Judi Roski, *Register*, April 2, 1972.

"Ray Bradbury: Space Age Moralist." Interviewed by William F. Nolan, *Unity*, April 1972.

"Ray Bradbury Launches Powerful Criticism at 'Ignorant' Apollo Critics." Interviewed by Steve Siebig, *Campus News* (East Los Angeles College), May 3, 1972.

"An Interview With Ray Bradbury." Interviewed by Marc Shapiro, *Los Angeles Free Press*, September 15, 1972.

"Ray Bradbury." Interviewed by Edward Gerson, *Hyde Parker*, February-March 1973.

"Interview With Ray Bradbury." Interviewed by Paul Turner and Dorothy Simon, *Vertex*, April 1973.

"Ray Bradbury on Hitchcock, Huston and Other Magic of the Screen." Interviewed by Arnold R. Kunert, *Take One* (Canada), September 26, 1973.

ANTHOLOGY APPEARANCES

It is doubtful that the work of any American author has approached the remarkable anthology exposure achieved by Bradbury. For example, in her comprehensive bibliography of Ernest Hemingway's work, Audre Hanneman lists 351 anthologies extending over forty-three years and including foreign-language volumes. In just twenty-eight years Bradbury's anthology sales number above two thousand. His sales to grade, high school and college textbooks continue to mount. In 1972 alone his work appeared in over thirty of these, and the total is now well above 200. One RB story, "There Will Come Soft Rains," has appeared in eighteen textbooks since 1955.

Considering these facts, a complete anthology listing is not within the scope of this checklist. It has therefore been limited to a chronological listing of 156 volumes, concentrating on first book appearances (FBA). Often it is all but impossible to determine exactly when a Bradbury story was first collected in book form due to its having been selected for several volumes within the *same* year. One would have to have complete data on the month of publication for each of these volumes in order to determine which one appeared first. However, I have listed as many first book appearances as possible within the scope of my knowledge and research. I have attempted to include all "best" or prize anthologies as well as a representative sampling of textbooks and science fiction volumes (since his reputation was built in this genre).

Within each year the books are arranged alphabetically by story title.

1946

"The Big Black and White Game" (FBA) in: *The Best American Short Stories 1946,* ed. Martha Foley. Boston: Houghton Mifflin.

"The Lake" (FBA) in: *Who Knocks? Twenty Masterpieces of the Spectral For the Connoisseur,* ed. August Derleth. New York: Rinehart. RB's first anthology sale.

"The Watchers" (FBA) in: *Rue Morgue No. 1,* ed. Rex Stout and Louis Greenfield. New York: Creative Age Press.

1947

"Homecoming" (FBA) in: *Prize Stories of 1947: The O. Henry Awards,* ed. Herschel Brickell. New York: Doubleday.

"The Smiling People" (FBA) in: *The Night Side: Masterpieces of the Strange & Terrible,* ed. August Derleth. New York: Rinehart.

1948

"I See You Never" (FBA) in: *The Best American Short Stories 1948,* ed. Martha Foley. Boston: Houghton Mifflin.

"The Jar" in: *Fear and Trembling: Shivery Stories,* ed. Alfred Hitchcock. New York: Dell.

"The Meadow" (FBA) in: *The Best One-Act Plays of 1947–1948,* ed. Margaret Mayorga. New York: Dodd, Mead. RB radio play.

"The Million Year Picnic" (FBA) in: *Strange Ports of Call: 20 Masterpieces of Science Fiction,* ed. August Derleth. New York: Pellegrini & Cudahy. RB's first appearance in a science fiction anthology.

"Powerhouse" (FBA) in: *Prize Stories of 1948: The O. Henry Awards,* ed. Herschel Brickell. New York: Doubleday. Third-prize winner.

1949

"Mars is Heaven!" (FBA) and "And the Moon Be Still as Bright" (FBA) in: *The Best Science Fiction Stories: 1949,* ed. Everett F. Bleiler and T. E. Dikty. New York: Frederick Fell.

"Pillar of Fire" (FBA) and "The Earth Men" (FBA) in: *The Other Side of the Moon,* ed. August Derleth. New York: Pellegrini & Cudahy.

"Zero Hour" (FBA) and "The Million Year Picnic" in: *Invasion From Mars: Interplanetary Stories,* ed. Orson Welles. New York: Dell.

"Zero Hour" in: *My Best Science Fiction Story: As Selected by 25 Outstanding Authors,* ed. Leo Margulies and Oscar J. Friend. New York: Merlin Press. (See INTRODUCTIONS.)

1950

"Dwellers in Silence" and "The Man" (FBA) in: *The Best Science Fiction Stories: 1950,* ed. Everett F. Bleiler and T. E. Dikty. New York: Frederick Fell.

"The Exiles" (FBA) in: *Beyond Time & Space: A Compendium of Science Fiction Through the Ages,* ed. August Derleth. New York: Pellegrini & Cudahy.

"Forever and the Earth" (FBA) in: *Big Book of Science Fiction,* ed. Groff Conklin. New York: Crown.

"The Great Fire" (FBA) in: *The Best Humor of 1949–1950,* ed. Louis Untermeyer and Ralph E. Shikes. New York: Henry Holt.

"King of the Grey Spaces" (FBA) in: *The Science Fiction Galaxy,* ed. Groff Conklin. New York: Permabooks.

1951

"Asleep in Armageddon" (FBA) in: *Possible Worlds of Science Fiction,* ed. Groff Conklin. New York: Vanguard Press.

"The Fox in the Forest" in: *The Best Science Fiction Stories: 1951,* ed. Everett F. Bleiler and T. E. Dikty. New York: Frederick Fell.

"Here There Be Tygers" (FBA) in: *New Tales of Space and Time,* ed. Raymond J. Healy. New York: Henry Holt.

"The Highway" in: *Stories For Here and Now,* eds. Joseph Greene and Elizabeth Abell. New York: Bantam.

"Holiday" (FBA) and "The One Who Waits" (FBA) in: *Far Boundaries: 20 Science Fiction Stories,* ed. August Derleth. New York: Pellegrini & Cudahy.

"The Illustrated Man" (FBA) in: *In the Grip of Terror,* ed. Groff Conklin. New York: Permabooks.

"The Shape of Things" (FBA) in: *Travelers of Space,* ed. Martin Greenberg. New York: Gnome Press.

"Ylla" in: *The Outer Reaches: Favorite Science Fiction Tales Chosen By Their Authors,* ed. August Derleth. New York: Pellegrini & Cudahy. (See INTRODUCTIONS.)

1952

"A Little Journey" (FBA) in: *Galaxy Reader of Science Fiction,* ed. H. L. Gold. New York: Crown.

"The Other Foot" in: *The Best American Short Stories 1952,* ed. Martha Foley. Boston: Houghton Mifflin.

"The Pedestrian" (FBA) in: *The Best Science Fiction Stories: 1952,* ed. Everett F. Bleiler and T. E. Dikty. New York: Frederick Fell.

"Referent" (FBA) in: *Imagination Unlimited: Science Fiction and Science,* ed. Everett F. Bleiler and T. E. Dikty. New York: Farrar, Straus and Young. First appearance of this story under RB byline.

1953

"The Illustrated Man" in: *The Esquire Treasury,* ed. Arnold Gingrich. New York: Simon and Schuster.

"The Man Upstairs" in: *Harper's Magazine Reader.* New York: Bantam.

"The Naming of Names" (FBA) in: *The Best From Startling Stories,* ed. Samuel Mines. New York: Henry Holt.

"A Scent of Sarsaparilla" (FBA) in: *Star Science Fiction Stories*, ed. Frederik Pohl. New York: Ballantine.

"Small Assassin" in: *Children of Wonder: 21 Remarkable and Fantastic Tales*, ed. William Tenn. New York: Simon and Schuster.

"The Smile" (FBA) in: *Worlds of Tomorrow: Science Fiction With a Difference*, ed. August Derleth. New York: Pellegrini & Cudahy.

"The Tombling Day" (FBA) in: *The Supernatural Reader*, ed. Groff and Lucy Conklin. New York & Philadelphia: Lippincott.

1954

"The Playground" in: *Portals of Tomorrow: The Best Tales of Science Fiction and Other Fantasy*, ed. August Derleth. New York: Rinehart.

"The Strawberry Window" (FBA) in: *Star Science Fiction Stories No. 3*, ed. Frederik Pohl. New York: Ballantine.

"Subterfuge" (FBA) in: *Assignment in Tomorrow*, ed. Frederik Pohl. New York: Hanover House.

"Sun and Shadow" in: *Prize Articles 1954: The Benjamin Franklin Magazine Awards*, ed. Llewellyn Miller. New York: Ballantine. RB wins award for "the best short story published in an American magazine during 1953."

1955

"All Summer in a Day" (FBA) in: *The Best From Fantasy and Science Fiction: Fourth Series*, ed. Anthony Boucher. New York: Doubleday.

"The Fire Balloons" in: *Best SF: Science Fiction Stories*, ed. Edmund Crispin. London: Faber & Faber.

"Punishment Without Crime" (FBA) in: *Science Fiction Terror Tales*, ed. Groff Conklin. New York: Gnome Press.

"Shopping For Death" (FBA) in: *Best Detective Stories of the Year—1955*, ed. David C. Cooke. New York: E. P. Dutton.

1956

"En La Noche" in: *A Treasury of Ribaldry*, ed. Louis Untermeyer. New York: Hanover House.

"Garbage Collector" in: *Current Thinking and Writing: Third Series*, ed. Joseph M. Bachelor, Ralph L. Henry, and Rachel Salisbury. New York: Appleton-Century-Crofts. Textbook.

"The Last, the Very Last" (FBA) in: *The Reporter Reader*, ed. Max Ascoli. New York: Doubleday.

"Zero Hour" in: *Best SF Two: Science Fiction Stories*, ed. Edmund Crispin. London: Faber & Faber.

1957

"The Fog Horn" "Sun and Shadow" and "The Fox and the Forest" in: *Tell Me a Story*, ed. Charles Laughton. New York: McGraw-Hill.

"Icarus Montgolfier Wright" (FBA) in: *The Best From Fantasy and Science Fiction: Sixth Series*, ed. Anthony Boucher. New York: Doubleday.

"The Illustrated Man" in: *Great Stories About Show Business*, ed. Jerry D. Lewis. New York: Coward-McCann.

"The Marriage Mender" (FBA) in: *The Wild Sweet Wine: Superb Stories of Sensual Love*, ed. Don Congdon. New York: Ballantine.

"The October Game" (FBA) in: *Alfred Hitchcock Presents: Stories They Wouldn't Let Me Do on TV*, ed. Alfred Hitchcock. New York: Simon and Schuster.

"Sneakers" in: *Anthology of Best Short-Short Stories: Vol. 5*, ed. Robert Oberfirst. New York: Frederick Fell.

"The World the Children Made," in: *Reading For Pleasure*, ed. Bennett Cerf. New York: Harper & Brothers.

1958

"The Day It Rained Forever" (FBA) in: *The Best American Short Stories 1958*, ed. Martha Foley and David Burnett. Boston: Houghton Mifflin.

"Good-by, Grandma" in: *Anthology of Best Short-Short*

Stories: Vol. 6, ed. Robert Oberfirst. New York: Frederick Fell.

"The Screaming Woman" (FBA) in: *The Graveyard Reader*, ed. Groff Conklin. New York: Ballantine.

"The Town Where No One Got Off" (FBA) in: *Ellery Queen's 14th Mystery Annual*, ed. Ellery Queen. New York: Random House.

1959

"In a Season of Calm Weather" in: *The Permanent Playboy*, ed. Ray Russell. New York: Crown.

"I See You Never" in: *Understanding Fiction*, 2nd edition, ed. Cleanth Brooks and Robert Penn Warren. New York: Appleton-Century-Crofts. Textbook.

"The Magic White Suit" (FBA) in: *The Saturday Evening Post Stories 1958.* New York: Doubleday.

"Pillar of Fire" in: *A Treasury of Great Science Fiction*, ed. Anthony Boucher. Volume 1. New York: Doubleday.

1960

"Invisible Boy" in: *40 Best Stories From Mademoiselle 1935–1960*, ed. Cyrilly Abels and Margarita G. Smith. New York: Harper & Brothers.

"The Marriage Mender" in: *Anthology of Best Short-Short Stories: Vol. 7*, ed. Robert Oberfirst. New York: Frederick Fell.

"The Shoreline at Sunset" in: *The Year's Best S-F: 5th Annual Edition*, ed. Judith Merril. New York: Simon and Schuster.

"The Veldt" in: *The Britannica Library of Great American Writing*, ed. Louis Untermeyer. Volume 2. Chicago: Britannica Press.

1961

"I See You Never" in: *75 Short Masterpieces: Stories From the World's Literature*, ed. Roger B. Goodman. New York: Bantam.

"A Serious Search For Weird Worlds" (FBA) in: *6th Annual Edition: The Year's Best S-F,* ed. Judith Merril. New York: Simon and Schuster. Non-fiction.

"The Whole Town's Sleeping" in: *Alfred Hitchcock Presents: Stories For Late at Night,* ed. Alfred Hitchcock. New York: Random House.

1962

"The Emissary" in: *Best Tales of Terror,* ed. Edmund Crispin. London: Faber & Faber.

"In a Season of Calm Weather" in: *Best Fantasy Stories,* ed. Brian W. Aldiss. London: Faber & Faber.

"Royal Crown Cream-Sponge Para Litefoot Tennis Shoes" in: *Teen-Age Treasury of Imagination and Discovery,* ed. Seon Manley and Gogo Lewis. New York: Funk & Wagnalls.

"Thoughts While Sleeping at My Machine" (FBA) in: *Hello, Hollywood! A Book About the Movies by the People Who Make Them,* ed. Allen Rivkin and Laura Kerr. New York: Doubleday. Non-fiction.

"The Women" (FBA) in: *The Fiend in You,* ed. Charles Beaumont. New York: Ballantine.

1963

"Come Into My Cellar" (FBA) in: *17 X Infinity,* ed. Groff Conklin. New York: Dell.

"Kaleidoscope" in: *Great Stories of Space Travel,* ed. Groff Conklin. New York: Grosset and Dunlap.

"The Man Upstairs" in: *The Vampire,* ed. Ornella Volta and Valeria Riva. London: Neville Spearman.

"A Miracle of Rare Device" (FBA) in: *The Worlds of Science Fiction,* ed. Robert P. Mills. New York: Dial Press. (See INTRODUCTIONS.)

"A Miracle of Rare Device" in: *8th Annual Edition: The Year's Best S-F,* ed. Judith Merril. New York: Simon and Schuster.

"There Will Come Soft Rains" in: *Of Men and Machines,*

ed. Arthur O. Lewis, Jr. New York: Dutton.

1964

"Cry the Cosmos" (FBA) in: *College English: The First Year,* Fourth Edition, ed. Alton C. Morris, Biron Walker, Philip Bradshaw, John C. Hodges and Mary E. Whitten. New York: Harcourt, Brace & World. Textbook. Non-fiction.

"No Strings Attached" in: *The Hilton Bedside Book, Volume Six.* Chicago: Hilton Hotels Corporation.

1965

"The Beggar on the Dublin Bridge" in: *Short Story: A Thematic Anthology,* ed. Dorothy Parker and Frederick B. Shroyer. New York: Scribners.

"The Black Ferris" (FBA) in: *The Dark Side,* ed. Damon Knight. New York: Doubleday.

"Changeling" (FBA) in: *The Pseudo-People: Androids in Science Fiction,* ed. William F. Nolan. Los Angeles: Sherbourne Press.

"Dark They Were, and Golden-Eyed" in: *Accent: U.S.A.,* ed. Robert C. Pooley, Alfred H. Grommon, Virginia B. Lowers, Elsie Katterjohn, and Olive S. Niles. Glenview, Ill.: Scott, Foresman. Textbook.

"The Other Foot" in: *Fifty Best American Short Stories: 1915–1965,* ed. Martha Foley. Boston: Houghton Mifflin.

"Payment in Full" (FBA) in: *Man Against Tomorrow,* ed. William F. Nolan. New York: Avon.

"Small Assassin" in: *Best Terror Tales 2,* ed. Edmund Crispin. London: Faber & Faber.

"The Veldt" in: *Second Orbit: A New Science Fiction Anthology For Schools,* ed. G. D. Doherty. London: John Murray. Textbook.

"Wake for the Living" in: *Modern Masterpieces of Science Fiction,* ed. Sam Moskowitz. New York: World.

1966

"All Summer in a Day" in: *Tomorrow's Children: 18 Tales of Fantasy and Science Fiction*, ed. Isaac Asimov. New York: Doubleday.

"August 2026: There Will Come Soft Rains" "Forever and the Earth" "I See You Never" "How to Keep and Feed a Muse" (FBA) "Seeds of Three Stories" (FBA) in: *On Writing By Writers*, ed. William W. West. Boston: Ginn. Textbook. The last two items are non-fiction. (See INTRODUCTIONS.)

"Doodad" (FBA) in: *Strange Signposts: An Anthology of the Fantastic*, ed. Sam Moskowitz and Roger Elwood. New York: Holt, Rinehart and Winston.

"Kaleidoscope" in: *Best SF Six: Science Fiction Stories*, ed. Edmund Crispin. London: Faber & Faber.

"The Sound of Summer Running" in: *Bold Journeys*, ed. Marion Gartler, Caryl Roman, and Marcella Benditt. New York: Macmillan. Textbook.

"There Will Come Soft Rains" in: *The Vintage Anthology of Science Fantasy: Twenty Stories in the Modern Manner*, ed. Christopher Cerf. New York: Vintage.

"The Veldt" in: *Masters' Choice: The Best Science Fiction Stories of All Time Chosen by the Masters of Science Fiction*, ed. Laurence M. Janifer. New York: Simon and Schuster.

1967

"Heavy Set" (FBA) and "The Life Work of Juan Diaz" in: *The Playboy Book of Horror and the Supernatural*. Chicago: Playboy Press. (See INTRODUCTIONS.)

"I, Rocket" (FBA) in: *The Human Zero and Other Science Fiction Masterpieces*, ed. Sam Moskowitz and Roger Elwood. New York: Tower.

"The Last Night of the World" in: *The Edge of the Chair*, ed. Joan Kahn. New York: Harper & Row.

"The Scythe" in: *The Discovery of Fiction*, ed. Thomas E. Sanders. Glenview, Ill.: Scott, Foresman. Textbook.

"Skeleton" in: *Famous Monster Tales,* ed. Basil Davenport. Princeton: Van Nostrand.

"Tomorrow and Tomorrow" (FBA) in: *Untamed.* New York: Belmont.

"The Trunk Lady" (FBA) in: *Horror Times Ten,* ed. Alden H. Norton. New York: Berkley.

1968

"The Candy Skull" (FBA) in: *Masters of Horror,* ed. Alden H. Norton. New York: Berkley.

"The Day It Rained Forever" in: *Literature for Listening: An Oral Interpreter's Anthology,* ed. Keith Brooks, Eugene Bahn, and L. LaMont Okey. Boston: Allyn and Bacon. Textbook.

"Dwellers in Silence" in: *Fiction for Composition,* ed. Bert C. Bach and Gordon Browning. Glenview, Ill.: Scott, Foresman. Textbook.

"The Fog Horn" in: *The Best of Both Worlds: An Anthology of Stories for All Ages,* ed. Georges McHargue. New York: Doubleday.

"The Lost City of Mars" (FBA) in: *3 To the Highest Power,* ed. William F. Nolan. New York: Avon.

"The Piper" (FBA) in: *The Future Makers: Tales of Fantasy,* ed. Peter Haining. London: Sidgwick & Jackson.

"There Will Come Soft Rains" in: *Prose For Discussion,* ed. E. W. Buxton. Toronto: Gage. Textbook.

"There Will Come Soft Rains" in: *Utopian Literature,* ed. J. W. Johnson. New York: Modern Library.

1969

"I, Mars" (FBA) in: *A Wilderness of Stars: Stories of Man in Conflict With Space,* ed. William F. Nolan. Los Angeles: Sherbourne Press.

"It Burns Me Up!" (FBA) in: *Hauntings and Horrors: Ten Grisly Tales,* ed. Alden H. Norton. New York: Berkley.

"There Will Come Soft Rains" in: *21 Great Stories,* ed. Abraham H. Lass and Norma L. Tasman. New York: Mentor.

"The Watchers" "Fever Dream" "The Dead Man" "The Handler" in: *Bloch and Bradbury,* ed. Kurt Singer. New York: Tower. RB did not collaborate in editing this collection.

1970

"All Summer in a Day" in: *Teacher's Edition of The World of Language, Book 6: A Guide and Resource Book,* ed. Muriel Crosby. Chicago: Follett. Textbook.

"And This Did Dante Do" (FBA) in: *Nova One: An Anthology of Original Science Fiction Stories,* ed. Harry Harrison. New York: Delacorte Press. Verse.

"The Blue Bottle" (FBA) in: *A Sea of Space,* ed. William F. Nolan. New York: Bantam.

"A Final Sceptre, a Lasting Crown" in: *Twenty Years of the Magazine of Fantasy and Science Fiction,* ed. Edward L. Ferman and Robert P. Mills. New York: Putnam & Sons.

"The Fire Balloons" in: *Special Wonder: The Anthony Boucher Memorial Anthology of Fantasy and Science Fiction,* ed. J. Francis McComas. New York: Random House. (See INTRODUCTIONS.)

"The Fog Horn" in: *Anatomy of Reading,* ed. Laura Hackett and Richard Williamson. New York: McGraw-Hill. Textbook.

"The Last Night of the World" in: *The Voices of Man Literature Series: A Man of His Own,* ed. Bethel Bodine, Tom Finn, Ellen Newman, Helen Rosenblum and Barbara Dodds Stanford. Menlo Park, Calif.: Addison-Wesley. Textbook.

"Mars is Heaven!" in: *The Science Fiction Hall of Fame: The Greatest Science Fiction Stories of All Time,* ed. Robert Silverberg. Volume 1. New York: Doubleday.

"The Pedestrian" in: *The Curious Eye,* ed. Walden Leecing and James L. Armstrong. New York: McGraw-Hill. Textbook.

"The Piper" (FBA) in: *Futures to Infinity,* ed. Sam Moskowitz. New York: Pyramid. This early fan magazine version of the RB story is not to be confused with later version, same title, in Haining's *The Future Makers.*

"A Wild Night in Galway" (FBA) in: *The Wild Night Company: Irish Stories of Fantasy and Horror,* ed. Peter Haining. London: Victor Gollancz.

1971

"All Summer in a Day" in: *Voyages: Scenarios For a Ship Called Earth,* ed. Rob Sauer. New York: Ballantine.

"The Crowd" in: *Impact: Short Stories for Pleasure,* ed. Donald L. Stansbury. Englewood Cliffs, N.J.: Prentice-Hall.

"Lorelei of the Red Mist" (with Leigh Brackett) in: *The Human Equation: Four Science Fiction Novels of Tomorrow,* ed. William F. Nolan. Los Angeles: Sherbourne Press. Although not a FBA, this is the story's first book appearance in unabridged form. (See ABOUT BRADBURY IN BOOKS.)

"Pendulum" (with Henry Hasse) (FBA) and "The Pendulum" (FBA) in: *Horrors Unknown: Newly Discovered Masterpieces by Great Names in Fantastic Terror,* ed. Sam Moskowitz. New York: Walker. Both RB's original fan magazine version and the later professional version, written with Hasse, are presented here.

"The Prehistoric Producer" and "Death Warmed Over" (FBA) in: *The Hollywood Nightmare: Tales of Fantasy and Horror From the Film World,* ed. Peter Haining. New York: Taplinger. The latter RB item is non-fiction.

"A Sound of Thunder" in: *Eco-Fiction,* ed. John Stadler. New York: Washington Square Press.

"There Will Come Soft Rains" in: *Literary Types and Themes,* Second Edition, ed. Maurice B. McNamee, James E. Cronin, and Joseph A. Rogers. New York: Holt, Rinehart & Winston. Textbook.

"The Vacation" in: *Voices of Concern: The Playboy College Reader.* New York: Harcourt Brace Jovanovich.

1972

"All Summer in a Day" in: *Moments in Literature,* ed. Philip McFarland, Melinda Kavanagh, William Jamison, and Morse Peckham. Boston: Houghton Mifflin. Textbook.

"And the Rock Cried Out" and "There Will Come Soft Rains" in: *Coming Together: Modern Stories by Black and White Americans,* ed. Adam A. Casmier and Sally Souder. Encino, Calif.: Dickenson. Textbook.

"Apollo Murdered" (FBA) in: *Perry Rhodan 18: Menace of the Mutant Master,* ed. Forrest Ackerman. New York: Ace. Non-fiction.

"August 2002: Night Meeting" in: *Crossroads: Quality of Life Through Rhetorical Modes,* ed. Tom E. Kakonis and James C. Wilcox. Lexington, Mass.: Heath. Textbook.

"August 2002: Night Meeting" and "February 2002: The Locusts" in: *From Experience: A Basic Rhetoric and Reader,* ed. Monte M. Hart and Benson R. Schulman. Dubuque, Iowa: Brown. Textbook.

"Christ, Old Student in a New School" (FBA) in: *Again, Dangerous Visions,* ed. Harlan Ellison. New York: Doubleday. Verse.

"The Dragon" in: *Writer's Journal: Explorations,* ed. Dalton H. McBee. New York: Harcourt Brace Jovanovich. Textbook.

"I See You Never" in: *Growth in English: Experiences in Language,* ed. John S. Hand, Wayne Harsh, James W. Ney, and Benarr Folta. River Forest, Ill.: Laidlaw Brothers. Textbook.

"A New Ending to Rosemary's Baby" (FBA) in: *Focus on the Horror Film,* ed. Roy Huss and T. J. Ross. Englewood Cliffs, N.J.: Prentice-Hall. Non-fiction.

"The Pedestrian" and "Dark They Were, and Golden-Eyed" in: *Explorations in Literature,* ed. Philip McFarland, Linda Konichek, Jeanne King, William Jamison, and Morse Peckham. Boston: Houghton Mifflin. Textbook.

"A Sound of Thunder" in: *Futures Conditional,* ed. Robert Theobald. New York: Bobbs-Merrill. Textbook.

"There Will Come Soft Rains" in: *Perceptions in Literature,* ed. Philip McFarland, Allen Kirschner, and Morse Peckham. Boston: Houghton Mifflin. Textbook.

"Time in Thy Flight" in: *The Young America Basic Reading Program,* ed. Leo Fay and Myron L. Coulter. Chicago: Lyons & Carnahan. Textbook.

"The Vacation" in: *Reflections in Literature,* ed. Philip McFarland, Sharon Breakstone, and Morse Peckham. Boston: Houghton Mifflin. Textbook.

"The Whole Town's Sleeping" in: *Best Horror Stories 3,* ed. Alex Hamilton. London: Faber & Faber.

1973

"Luana the Living" (FBA) in: *Horrors in Hiding,* ed. Sam Moskowitz and Alden H. Norton. New York: Berkley. This fan magazine story was first printed when RB was nineteen.

1974

"Hollerbochen's Dilemma" (FBA) in: *Horrors Unseen,* ed. Sam Moskowitz. New York: Berkley. RB's first story, printed when he was seventeen.

COMIC BOOK APPEARANCES

Bradbury's only work in the field of illustrated drama involves his attempt to syndicate *The Martian Chronicles* as a newspaper strip in collaboration with artist Joseph Mugnaini. It remains unsold, although a section of this strip was printed in the March 12, 1972 issue of *West,* a *Los Angeles Times* Sunday supplement. RB did the text, with artwork by Doug Wildey and John Cassone from Mugnaini's concept. Parts of "Ylla" and "Mars is Heaven" were incorporated into the feature. (For RB article accompanying this, see ARTICLES AND MISCELLANEOUS NON-FICTION.)

Bradbury has never adapted his own work for comic book publication. The May–June 1952 issue of *Weird Fantasy* comics contained "Home to Stay," which had been adapted from two RB stories, "The Rocket Man" and "Kaleidoscope." This had been done without Bradbury's knowledge, although when he contacted the publisher he was paid for use of his work. He subsequently granted permission for twenty-four more of his stories to be adapted by Albert B. Feldstein into comic book format for the E.C. line of magazines published out of New York. Sixteen of these were later collected into two Ballantine pocket editions. (See BOOKS AND PAMPHLETS.)

Arranged by title of magazine. All are E.C. publications.

*denotes stories not collected into book format.

Unprinted ink sketch by Joe Mugnaini prepared as guide to the final artwork on *The Martian Chronicles* comic strip.

 Unprinted ink sketch by Joe Mugnaini.

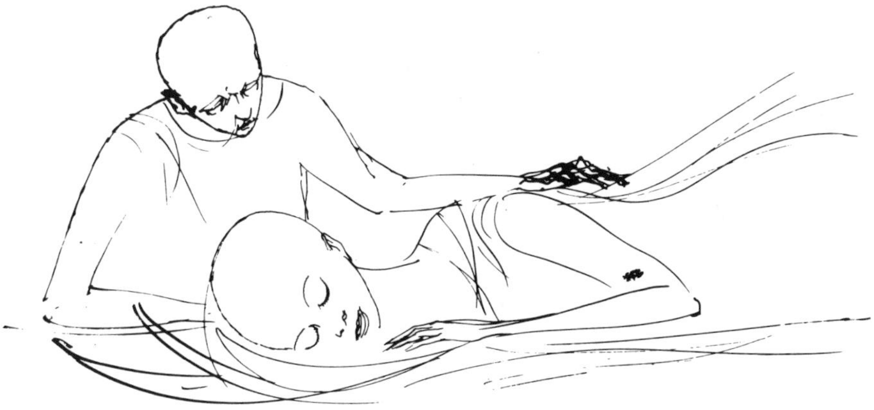

Unprinted ink sketch by Joe Mugnaini.

Unprinted ink sketch by Joe Mugnaini.

Crime SuspenStories

"The Screaming Woman," February-March 1953. Illustrator: Kamen

"Touch and Go," June-July 1953. Illustrator: Craig.

Haunt of Fear

"The Coffin," November-December 1952. Illustrator: Davis.

*"The Black Ferris," March-April 1953. Illustrator: Davis.

Shock SuspenStories

"The Small Assassin," February-March 1953. Illustrator: Evans.

*"The October Game," June-July 1953. Illustrator: Kamen.

Tales From the Crypt

"There Was an Old Woman," February-March 1953. Illustrator: Ingels.

"The Handler," June-July 1953. Illustrator: Ingels.

Vault of Horror

"Let's Play Poison," February-March 1953. Illustrator: Davis.

"The Lake," June-July 1953. Illustrator: Orlando.

Weird Fantasy

"There Will Come Soft Rains," January-February 1953. Illustrator: Wood.

*"Zero Hour," March-April 1953. Illustrator: Kamen.

"King of the Grey Spaces," May-June 1953. Illustrator: Elder.

"I, Rocket," July-August 1953. Illustrator: Williamson.

*"The Million Year Picnic," September-October 1953. Illustrator: Elder.

EACH MAN SEES A FAMILIAR HOUSE AND RUSHES TO KNOCK AND RING BELLS. ALL THROUGH THE TOWN DOORS OPEN. THE ROCKET MEN CRY OUT, FINDING LONG DEAD, LOST, AND LOVED FATHERS, MOTHERS, ENTIRE FAMILIES!
IN DOZENS OF OLD HOMES THAT NIGHT, BANQUETS ARE SPREAD, RELATIVES GATHER, LEMONADE POURS, PIANOS PLAY "BEAUTIFUL OHIO." THE ROCKET MEN, STUNNED WITH JOY, DOUBT BUT FINALLY ACCEPT THESE REBORN FAMILIES.
ON HIS WAY TO BED, THE CAPTAIN ASKS HIS MOTHER, "HOW DID YOU GET HERE?" "DON'T QUESTION FINE MIRACLES," SHE SAYS. "ENJOY THIS WARM REUNION. GOOD NIGHT."
UPSTAIRS WITH HIS NEW-FOUND YOUNGER BROTHER, THE CAPTAIN FINDS THE SAME FOOTBALL PENNANTS, THE SAME BRASS BED THEY SLEPT IN AS BOYS!
BUT, NEAR SLEEP, THE CAPTAIN THINKS: IF I WERE MARTIAN AND SAW EARTHMEN INVADING, WHAT WOULD I DO? FOOL THEM WITH TELE-PATHIC ILLUSIONS? YES! WHAT IF THIS TOWN, THEN, IS ONLY A HYPNOTIC MIRAGE PUT IN MY HEAD? WHAT IF MY BROTHER HERE IN THIS BED, IS REALLY A... MARTIAN?!
SOFTLY, THE CAPTAIN GETS OUT OF BED. HIS BROTHER STIRS: "WHERE ARE YOU GOING?" HE ASKS.
THE CAPTAIN BREAKS, RUNS. HE YELLS. BUT HE NEVER MAKES IT TO THE DOOR...
THE TWIN MOONS GO DOWN. AND IN HOUSES ALL AROUND TOWN, THE OTHER ROCKET MEN, SURROUNDED BY DEAR RELATIVES, GO UP TO BED. "GOOD NIGHTS," ARE CALLED. RADIOS SHUT UP. A LAST PIANO PLAYS AN OLD AND FADING TUNE, AND ONE BY ONE, THE LAST LIGHTS GO OUT AND OUT AND OUT...
THE END.

From RB's comic-strip version of "Mars is Heaven!"

*"The Silent Towns," November-December 1953. Illustrator: Crandall

Weird Science

"The Long Years," January-February 1953. Illustrator: Orlando.

"Mars is Heaven!" March-April 1953. Illustrator: Wood.

"The One Who Waits," May-June 1953. Illustrator: Williamson.

*"Surprise Package," July-August 1953. Illustrator: Kamen.

"Punishment Without Crime," September-October 1953. Illustrator: Kamen.

"Outcasts of the Stars," November-December 1953. Illustrator: Orlando.

Weird Science-Fantasy

*"The Flying Machine," March 1954. Illustrator: Krigstein.

*"A Sound of Thunder," September 1954. Illustrator: Williamson.

At least two amateur fanzines have adapted Bradbury stories into comic format:

Kaleidoscope

"The Man," No. 1, 1967. Illustrator: Taylor.

Xanadu

"The Gift," Summer 1970. Illustrator: Fritz.

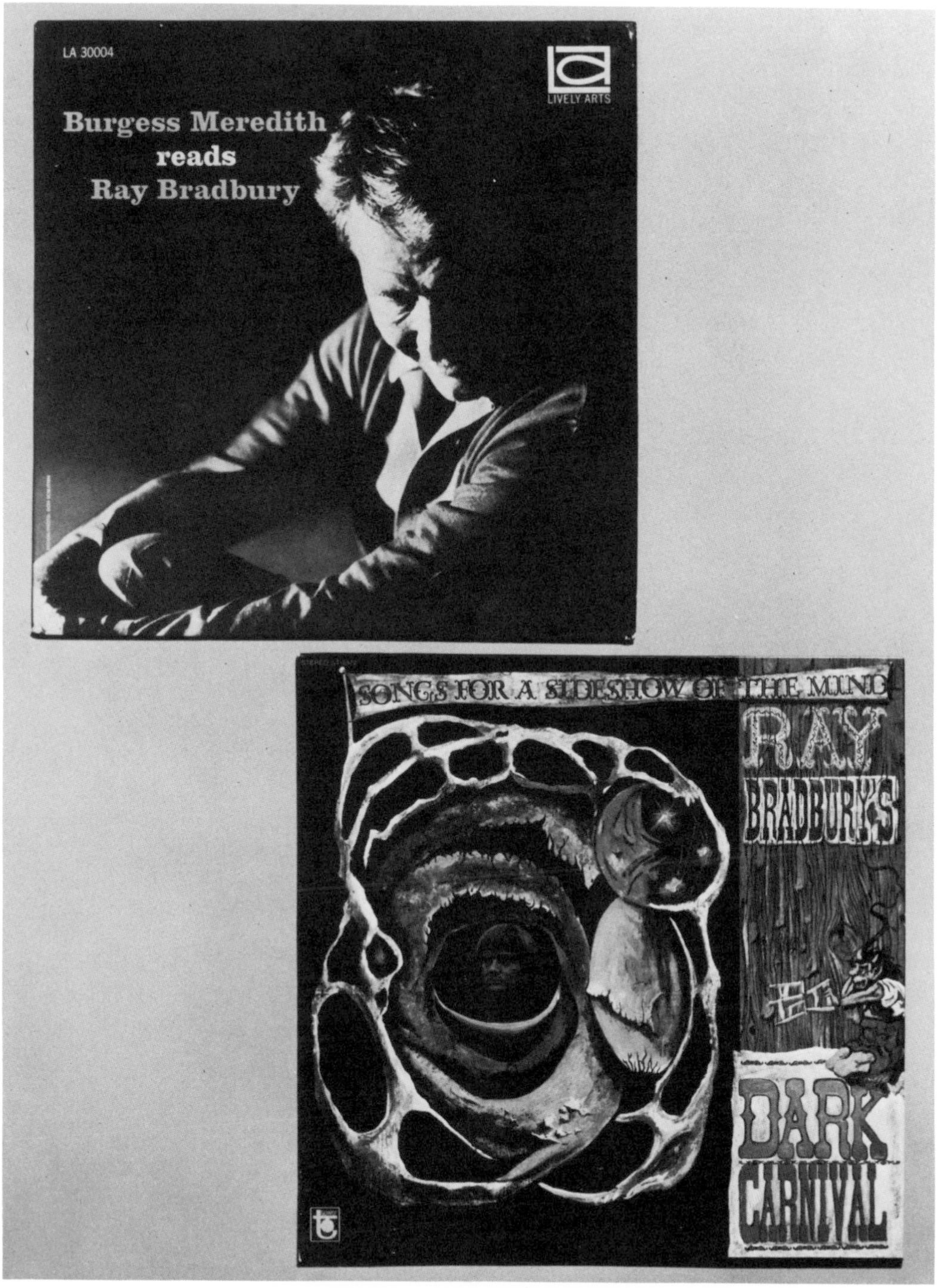
LA 30004
LIVELY ARTS
Burgess Meredith
reads
Ray Bradbury
SONGS FOR A SIDESHOW OF THE MIND
RAY
BRADBURY'S
DARK
CARNIVAL

Two commercial LP records dealing with Bradbury.
Record below features narrative songs from RB stories.

BRADBURY IN SOUND

Reflecting the wide popularity of RB, at least eight separate rock groups have named themselves after Bradbury books and stories (including "The Autumn People," "The October Country," and "The Strawberry Window"). Other groups have recorded their versions of RB stories (including "Rocket Man").

Bradbury has issued, privately, two LP records:

Icarus Montgolfier Wright and *An American Journey.* Sound tracks of RB films. (See FILMS.)

Christus Apollo. The recorded presentation of his cantata as performed at Royce Hall, U.C.L.A. (See STAGE PRODUCTIONS.)

These were distributed to friends of the author.

The following long-playing-records are arranged by date of release:

The Martian Chronicles. On eight LP records, as "A Talking Book." From American Printing House for the Blind, 1958. Reading by Milton Metz.

Burgess Meredith Reads Ray Bradbury. On one LP record. From Lively Arts, 1962. The actor reads two RB stories: "Marionettes, Inc." and "There Will Come Soft Rains."

Sum and Substance. On one LP record. From Modern Learning Aids, 1963. RB is interviewed as aid to students.

The Martian Chronicles. On five LP records, as "A Talking

Book." From American Foundation for the Blind, 1967.

Teaching Guide. On one LP record. From Ginn, 1969. RB's story, "The Smile," is dramatized for students.

Songs For a Sideshow of the Mind. Sub-titled: *Ray Bradbury's Dark Carnival.* On one LP record. From Tower, 1970. Bob Jacobs adapts eight RB stories into narrative songs: "The Emissary," "The Wind," "The Small Assassin," "Homecoming," "The Illustrated Man," "The Dwarf," "The Jar," and "There Was An Old Woman." RB liner note. (See ARTICLES AND MISCELLANEOUS NON-FICTION.)

Film:

The Story of a Writer. A learning-aid film for students. Originally presented on TV in 1963 as a documentary on RB's life and work, with Bradbury narrating portions of the film. (See TELEVISION.)

Note: Through their "Beyond Tomorrow Record Club," Renaissance Radio Production (Box 377, Seymour, Connecticut) is making available, on records and casette tapes, transcriptions of several Bradbury radio shows from *X Minus 1,* broadcast over NBC in the 1950s. (See RADIO.) Each record will contain two shows.

BOOK DEDICATIONS

For Bradbury, each book dedication pays an emotional debt. Spaced through two and a half decades, these dedications celebrate family ties, old friendships, and major career influences.

DARK CARNIVAL (1947)
"To GRANT M. BEACH"

THE MARTIAN CHRONICLES (1950)
"for my wife MARGUERITE with all of my love"*

THE ILLUSTRATED MAN (1951)
"This book is for FATHER, MOTHER and SKIP, with love"

THE GOLDEN APPLES OF THE SUN (1953)
"And this one, with love, is for Neva, daughter of Glinda the Good Witch of the South"

FAHRENHEIT 451 (1953)
"This one, with gratitude, is for DON CONGDON"

SWITCH ON THE NIGHT (1955)
"for SUSAN MARGUERITE and RAMONA ANNE with love"

THE OCTOBER COUNTRY (1955)
"For who else but August Derleth"

*RB extended this dedication for the 1973 illustrated edition, as follows: "And for Walter I. Bradbury, editor and friend, who was midwife to this book, a long time ago . . . with gratitude"

THE CIRCUS OF DR. LAO AND OTHER IMPOSSIBLE STORIES (1956)

"This collection is dedicated to Saul David, of Bantam Books, who waited three years for the mountain to deliver forth the mouse; and to William F. Nolan, for suggestions and help all down the line. Because of them, the show is on the road."

DANDELION WINE (1957)

"For Walter I. Bradbury neither uncle nor cousin but most decidedly editor and friend"

A MEDICINE FOR MELANCHOLY (1959)

"For Dad, whose love, very late in life, surprised his son. And for Bernard Berenson and Nicky Mariano, who gave me a new world."

THE DAY IT RAINED FOREVER (1959)

"For RUPERT HART-DAVIS in memory of the terrible skirmish the temporary loss but our inevitable victory at the Mirabelle"

SOMETHING WICKED THIS WAY COMES (1962)

"With gratitude to JENNET JOHNSON, who taught me how to write the short story, and to SNOW LONGLEY HOUSH, who taught me poetry at Los Angeles High School a long time ago, and to JACK GUSS, who helped with this novel not so long ago"

R IS FOR ROCKET (1962)

"I dedicate these stories to all boys who wonder about the Past, run swiftly in the Present, and have high hopes for our Future. The stars are yours, if you have the head, the hands, and the heart for them."

THE ANTHEM SPRINTERS AND OTHER ANTICS (1963)

"To John Huston, who sent me after the White Whale; To Nick, the cab-driver of Kilcock, who helped me in my Search; To Len and Beth Probst, who found me when I was lost; and to Maggie, who brought me safely home."

THE MACHINERIES OF JOY (1964)

"For Ramona, who cried when she heard that the Hound

of the Baskervilles was dead . . . For Susan, who snorted at the same news . . . For Bettina, who laughed . . . And for Alexandra, who told everyone to just get out of the way . . . This book, dear daughters, with four different kinds of love, for you."

S IS FOR SPACE (1966)

"For Charles Beaumont who lived in that little house halfway up in the next block most of my life. And for Bill Nolan and Bill Idelson, friend of Rush Gook, and for Paul Condylis . . . Because . . ."

I SING THE BODY ELECTRIC! (1969)

"This book, a bit late in the day, but with admiration, affection, and friendship, is for NORMAN CORWIN."

THE WONDERFUL ICE CREAM SUIT AND OTHER PLAYS (1972)

"This book is dedicated to Charles Rome Smith, who has directed all of my work for the theater so far, and who will, God allowing, direct more in the years ahead."

THE HALLOWEEN TREE (1972)

"With love for MADAME MAN'HA GARREAU-DOMBASLE met twenty-seven years ago in the graveyard at midnight on the Island of Janitzio at Lake Patzcuaro, Mexico, and remembered on each anniversary of The Day of the Dead."

WHEN ELEPHANTS LAST IN THE DOORYARD BLOOMED (1973)

"THIS ONE TO THE MEMORY OF my grandmother Minnie Davis Bradbury and my grandfather Samuel Hinkston Bradbury, and my brother Samuel and my sister Elizabeth Jane, long lost in the years but now remembered."

BRADBURY PSEUDONYMS

The bulk of Bradbury's work has appeared under his own name, but a number of early fanzine items and several professional pieces were printed under pen names, often because two of his stories were scheduled for the same issue of a magazine.

Beginning in the late 1930s (into the early 1940s) Bradbury appeared in "fanzines" (including his own—see BRADBURY'S MAGAZINE) under a variety of pseudonyms. The following names were used during this period:

"Doug Rogers"	"E. Cunningham"
"Ron Reynolds"	"Brian Eldred"
"Guy Amory"	"Cecil Claybourne Cunningham"
"Anthony Corvais"	"D. Lerium Tremaine"

Professionally, Bradbury's work has been released under the following seven pen names:

"Edward Banks"—used once, in a Canadian edition of *Weird Tales,* July 1945—for a Bradbury reprint. Pseudonym chosen by editor.

"D. R. Banet"—used once, for a story in *Dime Mystery,* July 1945.

"William Elliott"—used twice, for work in the *Californian,* June 1946 and August 1946.

"Brett Sterling"—a "house name" assigned to a Bradbury story in *Thrilling Wonder Stories,* October 1948.

"Leonard Spaulding"—used once, on a story in *Copy,* Spring 1950. RB chose his father's first and middle names as the basis for this pseudonym.

"Leonard Douglas"—used once, on a story in *Saturday Evening Post,* May 23, 1952. Basis: his father's first name and RB's middle name.

"Douglas Spaulding"—used, for co-credit, on the screenplay of *Picasso Summer* in 1972. Basis: RB's middle name and his father's middle name.

WRITINGS ABOUT RAY BRADBURY

ABOUT BRADBURY IN BOOKS

Reference volumes, such as *Who's Who* and *Contemporary Authors,* are not included in this listing.

Arranged by year of publication, within each section.

Book About:

Ray Bradbury, Humanista Del Futuro, by Jose Luis Garci. Madrid: Helios, 1971.

This 372-page paperback volume is basically a career biography, yet it also contains analysis of RB's fiction, a checklist of his work in Spanish translation, film listings, and other data. The introduction is by RB, in Spanish. (See INTRODUCTIONS.)

Booklet About:

Ray Bradbury Review, ed. William F. Nolan. San Diego: Nolan, 1952.

This 64-page photo-offset publication, illustrated by the editor, was released in a limited edition of 1200 copies. It contains critical and biographical articles on RB*, plus book reviews, parodies, and a checklist of his work through 1951. Bradbury wrote two articles for the *Review*† and a third is reprinted. A Bradbury short story, reprinted, is also included.

*(See ABOUT BRADBURY IN MAGAZINES AND NEWSPAPERS)
†(See ARTICLES AND MISCELLANEOUS NON-FICTION)

Biographical Material:

Science Fiction Handbook, by L. Sprague De Camp. New York: Hermitage House, 1953.

This book, written as a guide in writing sf, is also a history of the genre—and contains a short career sketch of RB by the author.

The Immortal Storm, by Sam Moskowitz. Atlanta: Atlanta SF Organization Press, 1954.

Brief references to RB as a teenaged sf fan in this history of science fiction fandom. Also photos of RB taken in the late 1930s.

Living Like a Lord, by John Godley, Lord Kilbracken. Boston: Houghton Mifflin, 1956.

An autobiography with chapters on the making of *Moby Dick.* Contains account of RB in Ireland when he worked on the screenplay of this film with John Huston.

Sinners and Supermen, by William F. Nolan. Los Angeles: All Star, 1965.

A collection of profiles, including "Ray Bradbury, Space Age Storyteller," a revised and expanded version of the author's profile of RB from the *Magazine of Fantasy and Science Fiction.* (See ABOUT BRADBURY IN MAGAZINES AND NEWSPAPERS.)

If the Sun Dies, by Oriana Fallaci. New York: Atheneum, 1965.

A book on the space effort dealing, in large part, with the author's life among the astronauts. Contains an account of the author's visit to RB's home in California.

John Huston: King Rebel, by William F. Nolan. Los Angeles: Sherbourne Press, 1965.

A biography of the film director with a chapter on *Moby Dick,* involving Bradbury as writer.

Seekers of Tomorrow, by Sam Moskowitz. New York: World, 1966.

A collection of profiles of major science fiction

writers, updated and revised from the series first printed in *Amazing.* Contains "Ray Bradbury," revised from the author's article on RB in 1961. (See "What Makes Bradbury 'Burn'?" in ABOUT BRADBURY IN MAGAZINES AND NEWSPAPERS.)

In Search of Wonder, by Damon Knight. Chicago: Advent, 1967. Revised edition.

Contains an article by the author, "When I Was in Knee Pants: Ray Bradbury."

3 to the Highest Power, ed. William F. Nolan. New York: Avon, 1968.

Contains profile, "Ray Bradbury," by the editor—plus a checklist of RB's fantasy and science fiction work. (See ANTHOLOGY APPEARANCES.)

Enemies of the Permanent Things, by Russell Kirk. New Rochelle, N.Y.: Arlington House, 1969.

Contains a chapter by the author on RB, "The World of Ray Bradbury."

All Our Yesterdays, by Harry Warner, Jr. Chicago: Advent, 1969.

A history of science fiction fandom up to the 1950s. The section of fans-turned-professionals contains a profile by the author, "Ray Bradbury."

The Human Equation, ed. William F. Nolan. Los Angeles: Sherbourne Press, 1971.

Contains a full biographical preface by the editor, "Leigh Brackett and Ray Bradbury," discussing background of their story "Lorelei of the Red Mist." (See ANTHOLOGY APPEARANCES.)

The Martian Chronicles, by Ray Bradbury. New York: Doubleday, 1973. Revised edition.

This special illustrated and expanded edition of RB's book contains "Ray Bradbury, A Biographical Sketch"—and a checklist of RB's books and short stories, both by William F. Nolan. (See BOOKS AND PAMPHLETS.)

Critical Material:

Modern Science Fiction: Its Meaning and Its Future, ed. Reginald Bretnor. New York: Coward-McCann, 1953.

RB's work is discussed in several of the essays on sf in this volume.

A Clerk at Oxenford, by Gilbert Highet. New York: Oxford University Press, 1954.

RB is discussed.

The Martian Chronicles, by Ray Bradbury. New York: Doubleday, 1958. New edition.

Contains "Prefatory Note" by Clifton Fadiman. (See BOOKS AND PAMPHLETS.)

New Maps of Hell, by Kingsley Amis. New York: Harcourt, Brace, 1960.

In this discussion of the science fiction field RB's work is covered, particularly *Fahrenheit 451.*

The Martian Chronicles, by Ray Bradbury. New York: Time/Life, 1963. Revised edition.

This edition contains "Editors' Preface" by Time/Life editors and "Introduction" by Fred Hoyle. (See BOOKS AND PAMPHLETS.)

The American Short Story, by William Peden. Boston: Houghton Mifflin, 1964.

Contains references to RB and includes him in checklist of "One Hundred Notable American Short Story Writers, 1940–1963."

The Issue at Hand: Studies in Contemporary Science Fiction, by "William Atheling, Jr." (James Blish). Chicago: Advent, 1964.

Contains review-discussions of RB's work.

The Vintage Bradbury, by Ray Bradbury. New York: Vintage, 1965.

Contains "Introduction" by Gilbert Highet. (See BOOKS AND PAMPHLETS.)

The Future as Nightmare, by Mark R. Hillegas. New York: Oxford University Press, 1967.

Contains references to RB.

Fahrenheit 451, by Ray Bradbury. New York: Ballantine "Bal-Hi" school edition, 1967.

Contains "A Note to Teachers and Parents" by Richard H. Tyre. (See BOOKS AND PAMPHLETS.)

More Issues at Hand, by "William Atheling, Jr." (James Blish). Chicago: Advent, 1970.

Contains review-discussions of RB's work.

Science Fiction: What It's All About," by Sam J. Lundwall. New York: Ace, 1971.

Contains discussion of RB.

SF: The Other Side of Realism, ed. Thomas D. Clareson. Bowling Green, Ohio: Bowling Green University Press, 1971.

Several of the essays on science fiction refer to RB.

The Universe Makers, by Donald A. Wollheim. New York: Harper and Row, 1971.

This history of modern sf contains references to RB.

Science Fiction Criticism, by Thomas Clareson. Kent, Ohio: Kent State University Press, 1972.

A checklist of 800 books and articles dealing with science fiction, many of which include discussion of RB.

Billion Year Spree: The True History of Science Fiction, by Brian W. Aldiss. New York: Doubleday, 1973.

Contains references to RB.

ABOUT BRADBURY IN MAGAZINES AND NEWSPAPERS

An effort has been made to include all profiles, sketches and articles dealing directly with RB—but the listing *is* selective with regard to reviews of his books and films, since many review pieces contribute little or nothing to an understanding of Bradbury and/or his work. Arranged in order of publication.
**denotes privately-printed amateur magazine or "fanzine."

"L.A. High Student Editor of Magazine," Anon. *Blue and White Daily* (Los Angeles High School), December 13, 1937. Refers to his co-editing duties on the sf club magazine, *Imagination!*

"Bradbury, Ray Douglas," Anon. ***Who's Who in Fandom*, 1939.

"Fantasy's Prodigy," by "Geoffrey Giles" (pseud. for Walt Gillings and Forrest Ackerman), ***Fantasy Review* (England), Summer 1949.

"Masters of Fantasy: Ray Bradbury—The October Man," Anon. (Forrest Ackerman), *Famous Fantastic Mysteries,* October 1949.

"Author, 29, Hits Jackpot With Grisly Chiller Tales," Anon. *Santa Monica Evening Outlook,* February 8, 1950.

"Christopher Isherwood Reviews 'The Martian Chronicles'," by Christopher Isherwood, *Tomorrow,* October 1950.

"Morals From Mars," by Richard Donovan, *Reporter,* June 26, 1951.

"The Case Against Bradbury," by Edward Wood, ***Journal of Science Fiction,* Fall 1951.

"Contemporary Science-Fiction," by August Derleth, *English Journal,* January 1952.

The following 12 pieces were all printed in the same issue of ***Ray Bradbury Review,* [January] 1952:

"R.B.: A Biographical Sketch," by "Frank Anmar" (William F. Nolan)

"The Rebel," by Lasca Huebner

"Ray Bradbury: Beginner," by Anthony Boucher

"Ray Bradbury's Themes," by Henry Kuttner

"The Fireman, You and I," by Roger Nelson

"Ray Bradbury: Humanist," by Marilyn Venable

"This Monster Bradbury," by Sam Sackett

"A Writer in Three Dimensions," by William F. Nolan

"Ray Bradbury: The Martian Chronicler," by Chad Oliver

"A Comment on Mr. B.," by Jack Traub

"A Note to the Critics," by Ian Macauley

"Ray Bradbury Index," by William F. Nolan

(See ABOUT BRADBURY IN BOOKS.)

"The Illustrative Man," by Charles Freudenthal, ***Journal of Science Fiction,* Fall 1952.

"Mr. Bradbury Talks Back," Anon. *Nation,* November 29, 1952.

"Poet of the Pulps," Anon. *Time,* March 23, 1953.

"Social Content of Science Fiction," by Oscar Shaftel, *Science and Society,* Spring 1953.

"About Ray Bradbury," by Arthur C. Clarke, *Science Fiction News* (England), March–April 1953.

"Ray Bradbury," Anon. *Weird Science,* May–June 1953. This same profile also appeared in several other E.C. comic books.

"Angus Wilson Writes [About] 'The Martian Chronicles,'" *Science Fiction News* (England), May–June 1953.

"Science, Yes—Fiction, Maybe," by Joseph Kostolefsky, *Antioch Review,* June 1953.

"Bradbury, Ray (Douglas)," Anon. *Current Biography,* June 1953.

"Reactors of the Imagination," by Reuel Denney, *Bulletin of Atomic Scientists,* July 1953.

"Scientifiction," by Alan Devoe, *American Mercury,* August 1953.

"The Bradbury Years," by William F. Nolan, ***Inside,* September 1953.

"Ray Bradbury Index Supplement," by William F. Nolan, ***Shangri-La,* Fall–Winter 1953.

"Books of Our Times," by Orville Prescott, *New York Times,* October 21, 1953.

"They came From Inner Space," by J. B. Priestley, *New Statesman and Nation* (England), December 5, 1953.

"Terror and Satire: Fahrenheit 451," Anon. *Nation,* December 19, 1953.

"The Fiction in Science Fiction," by William Tenn, *Science Fiction Adventures,* March 1954.

"The Rocket Ship Man Has Never Left the Ground," by Charles Fox, *Recorder* (England), April 10, 1954.

"Social Criticism in Science Fiction," by L. W. Michaelson, *Antioch Review,* December 1954.

"The World of Science Fiction," by Sidney Finkelstein, *Masses and Mainstream,* April 1955.

"Space Author Trades Rockets for Harpoons," by Cecil Smith, *Los Angeles Times,* August 21, 1955.

"That Thing From Another World," by Peter Fison, *Twentieth Century,* September 1955.

"Ray Bradbury's World of Reasonable Bogeymen," by William Hogan, *San Francisco Chronicle,* November 16, 1955.

"A Chamber or Horrors: The October Country," by Carlos Baker, *New York Times Book Review,* December 11, 1955.

"Recommended Reading," by Anthony Boucher, *Magazine of Fantasy and Science Fiction,* February 1956.

"The Quest for Captain Ahab," by Hollis Alpert, *Saturday Review,* June 9, 1956.

"Thar She Blows!" by Robert Bingham, *Reporter,* August 9, 1956.

"Summer of Innocence," by Robert O. Bowen, *Saturday Review,* September 7, 1957.

"Trade Winds," by Jerome Beatty, Jr., *Saturday Review,* October 12, 1957.

"Visions of Childhood," Anon. *Times Literary Supplement* (England), November 8, 1957.

"Books and People," by Robert Kirsch, *Los Angeles Times,* November 17, 1957.

"Bradbury Sees Moon Conquest in 10 Years," by Dorothy Townsend, *Los Angeles Times,* November 21, 1957.

"Ray Bradbury Pities Unprepared Humans Who Must Explore Space," by Richard Donovan, *Los Angeles Times,* August 22, 1958.

"Science Fiction," by Kenneth Methold, *Contemporary Review,* March 1959.

"Ray Bradbury," by William F. Nolan, *Rogue,* October 1961.

"What Makes Bradbury 'Burn?'" by Sam Moskowitz, *Amazing Stories,* October 1961. (See ABOUT BRADBURY IN BOOKS.)

"The Magic World of Ray Bradbury," by "Charles Davenport" (Charles Champlin), *Los Angeles,* March 1962.

"Space Age Baffles TV—Bradbury," by Hal Humphrey, *Los Angeles Times,* May 4, 1962.

"Bradbury: Prose Poet in the Age of Space," and "An Index to the Works of Ray Bradbury," by William F. Nolan, (Special Bradbury Issue) *Magazine of Fantasy and Science Fiction,* May 1963. (See "Sinners and Supermen" in ABOUT BRADBURY IN BOOKS.)

"A Soviet View of American Science Fiction," by Alexander Kazantsev, *Amazing Stories,* May 1963.

"Writers' Garbo Complex: They Want to Be Alone," by Art Seidenbaum, *Calendar (Los Angeles Times),* May 26, 1963.

"Film to Mix Fact in Space Fiction," by Murray Schumach, *New York Times,* June 10, 1963.

"The Writers Who Revived America's Own Literary Form, the Short Story," by Douglas M. Davis, *National Observer,* March 23, 1964.

"Outer Space Finds Inner Place," by Art Seidenbaum, *Los Angeles Times,* July 20, 1964.

"Science Fiction Writer Sees Smog as Killer," Anon., *Los Angeles Times,* July 30, 1964.

"Writer to Stage Science Fiction," by Peter Bart, *New York Times,* August 1, 1964.

"Bradburies," by Stephen Hugh-Jones, *New Statesman* (England), September 18, 1964.

"The World of Ray Bradbury" (5 parts), by Hy Hyberger, *Canyon Crier,* October 1 through November, 1964.

"The Other World of Ray Bradbury," by Cecil Smith, *Los Angeles Times,* October 26, 1964.

"Playwrights: Allegory of Any Place," Anon., *Time,* October 30, 1964.

"Bradbury Demands Certain Filming Rights for Yarns," Anon. *Hollywood Reporter,* November 6, 1964.

"Future on Tap," by Peter Bart, *New York Times,* November 8, 1964.

"TV Writer Finding Success in Theatre," by Cecil Smith, *Washington Post,* November 12, 1964.

"WLB Biography: Ray Bradbury," by Lee Ash, *Wilson Library Bulletin,* November 1964.

"A Taste for Pandemonium," by Arthur Knight, *Saturday Review,* December 5, 1964.

"Ray Bradbury and the Irish," by Bruce Cook, *Catholic World,* January 1965.

"The Man Who Drives the Kilimanjaro Machine," by George P. Hunt, *Life*, January 22, 1965.

"Science Fiction Theatre," by John J. McLaughlin, *Nation*, January 25, 1965.

"Books," by Virginia Kidd, *Magazine of Fantasy and Science Fiction*, October 1965.

"Ray Bradbury: A Short Critique," by Bob Parkinson,** *Vector* (England), April 1966.

"The Best of Ray Bradbury," by William F. Nolan, *Calendar (Los Angeles Times)*, April 3, 1966.

"Beginning With the 19th Century," by Theodore Sturgeon, *National Review*, April 5, 1966.

"Small Science and Less Technology: A Close Dialogue With a Science Fiction Addict on the Problems of Ray Bradbury," by George Plimpton, *Book Week (Washington Post)*, June 26, 1966.

"Letter From Paris," by Jean Genet, *New Yorker*, October 1, 1966.

"Bradbury Outlines Shape of Future," by Ann Sonne, *Los Angeles Times*, October 3, 1966.

"Shades of Orwell," by Arthur Knight, *Saturday Review*, December 3, 1966.

"Author Happy With Film Version of Book," Anon., *Washington Post*, December 15, 1966.

"Count Dracula and Mr. Ray Bradbury," by Russell Kirk, *National Review*, April 4, 1967.

"Truffaut and Dickens: Fahrenheit 451," by Donald Federman, *Florida Quarterly*, Summer 1967.

"Science Fiction: The Crisis of Its Growth," by Michel Butor, *Partisan Review*, Autumn 1967.

"Space Flights Called Religious by Bradbury," Anon., *Los Angeles Times*, December 4, 1967.

"The Gents at Heeber Finn's: A Memoir," by Laurence DeVine, *Los Angeles Herald-Examiner*, March 3, 1968.

"Ray Bradbury and Science Fiction," by David Wade, *London Times Saturday Review* (England), May 11, 1968.

"Revival of Fantasy," by Russell Kirk, *Triumph,* May 1968.

"On Ray Bradbury," by Kirill Andreyev, *Soviet Literature,* May 1968.

"A Prose Poet in the Age of Space," by John Stanley, *San Francisco Examiner and Chronicle,* August 18, 1968.

"Bradbury's 'Fahrenheit 451' in the Classroom," by Charles F. Hamblen, *English Journal,* September 1968.

"The Case for Bradbury," by Lewy Olfson, *Teachers Guide Science Fiction.* A pamphlet. New York: Bantam, 1968. (See ARTICLES AND MISCELLANEOUS NON-FICTION.)

"Of Hammett, Chandler, Brand and Bradbury . . ." by William F. Nolan, *Armchair Detective,* January 1969.

"Bradbury Revisited," by Willis E. McNelly, *CEA Critic,* March 1969.

"The Novels of Ray Bradbury," by Justin St. John, ***Green Town Review,* Spring 1969.

"Bradbury and Freberg vs. the Prune People," Anon., *Nepenthe,* Spring 1969.

"Ray Bradbury's Song of Experience," by L. T. Biddison, *New Orleans Review,* Spring 1969.

"Science Fiction for College Libraries," by Dorothy W. Bowers, *Choice,* June 1969.

"Ray Bradbury's 'The Illustrated Man,'" by Joe Dante, *Castle of Frankenstein,* Summer 1969.

"Bradbury on Screen: A Saga of Perseverance," by "F. E. Edwards" (William F. Nolan), *Venture SF,* August 1969.

"In the Picture: The Illustrated Man," by Philip Strick, *Sight and Sound* (England), Autumn 1969.

"L.A.: Space Age Center of Arts?" Anon. *Los Angeles Times,* December 7, 1969.

"A Study of Allusions in Bradbury's 'Fahrenheit 451,'" by Peter Sisario, *English Journal,* February 1970.

"Ray Bradbury Keeping Eye on Cloud IX," by Maggie Savoy, *Los Angeles Times,* March 15, 1970.

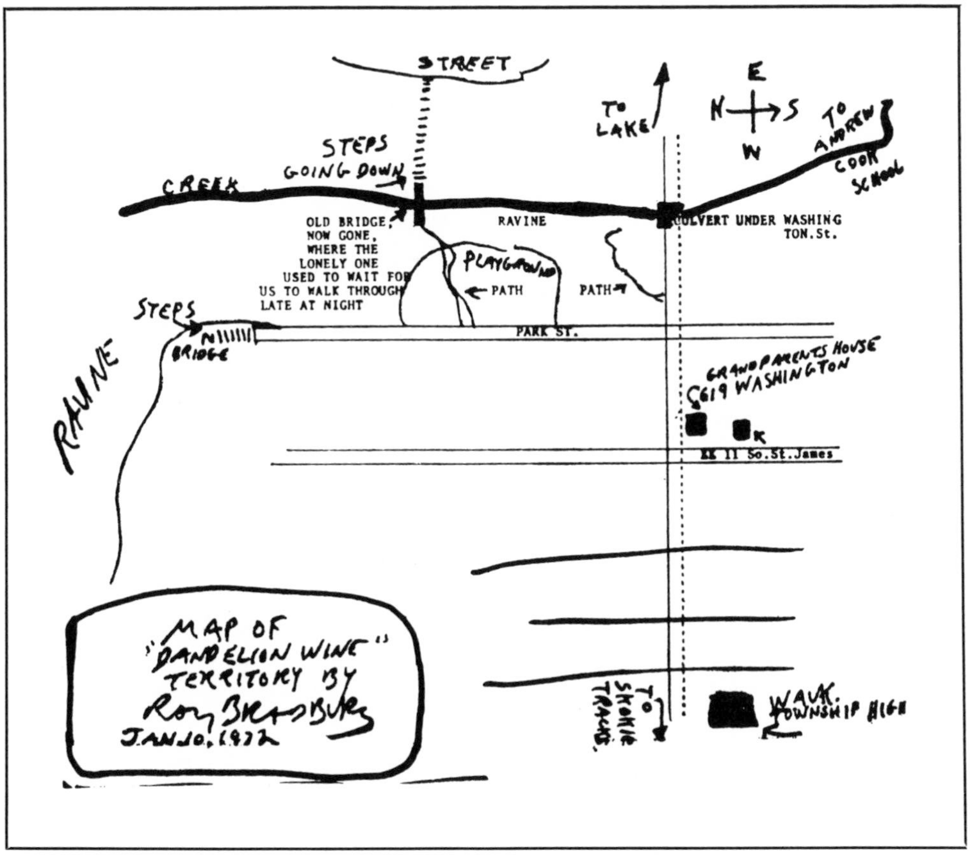
STREET
TO LAKE
E
N
S
W
TO ANDREW COOK SCHOOL
STEPS GOING DOWN
CREEK
OLD BRIDGE, NOW GONE, WHERE THE LONELY ONE USED TO WAIT FOR US TO WALK THROUGH LATE AT NIGHT
RAVINE
CULVERT UNDER WASHINGTON.St.
PLAYGROUND
PATH
PATH
STEPS
BRIDGE
PARK ST.
RAVINE
GRANDPARENTS HOUSE
619 WASHINGTON
11 So.St.James
MAP OF "DANDELION WINE" TERRITORY BY
Ray Bradbury
JAN 10, 1972
TO SKOKIE TRACKS
WAUK. TOWNSHIP HIGH

Map of his home-town neighborhood drawn by RB for the *Waukegan News-Sun* in 1972.

"Ray Bradbury: The Incredible Thinking Man," by Gene Baley, *TWA Ambassador,* July-August 1970.

"Ray Bradbury: Prose Painter of the Mind," by Richard S. Dimeo, *Perihelion,* Fall 1970.

"Homage to Bradbury," by David Dortort, *Hollywood Reporter*(40th Anniversary Edition), December 4, 1970.

" 'The Martian Chronicles': A Provocative Study," by Juliet Grimsley, *English Journal,* December 1970.

"Bradbury Illustrated," by Donald J. Brown, ***Fantasy Collector,* 1970 (Annual Edition).

"Ray Bradbury." Anon. ***Static, Flutter and Pop,* No. 2, 1970.

"What Were the Waukegan Haunts of Ray Bradbury's Early Shocker?" by Rex Knauer, *Waukegan News-Sun,* January 23, 1971.

"Dandelion Wine," by Tom Bradford, *Chicago Review,* January-February 1971.

"The Crime / Suspense Fiction of Ray Bradbury: A Listing," by William F. Nolan, *Armchair Detective,* April 1971.

"Ray Bradbury: A Checklist of First Editions and Some Others," compiled by Mary Crofts and Phil Garland, ***Presenting Moonshine,* August 7, 1971.

"Ray Bradbury's 'Dandelion Wine': Themes, Sources and Style," by Marvin E. Mengeling, *English Journal,* October 1971.

"The Artistry of Ray Bradbury," by Robert Reilly, ***Extrapolation,* December 1971.

"Man and Apollo: A Look at Religion in the Science Fantasies of Ray Bradbury," by Steven Dimeo, *Journal of Popular Culture,* Spring 1972.

"Very Much Like Waukegan—But Not Any More," by Linda P. Hansen, *Waukegan News-Sun,* June 5, 1972.

"Ray Bradbury: A Series," by Phil Garland, ***Presenting Moonshine,* September, October, December 1972; January, March, April, May, July, August, September, October, 1973. To be continued.

"Bradbury Writes Children's Fantasy," by Jerome Cushman, *Calendar* (*Los Angeles Times*), October 29, 1972.

"Ray Bradbury and Fantasy," by Anita T. Sullivan, *English Journal*, December 1972.

"Bradbury's Closing Night," by Jim Moore, *Los Angeles Herald-Examiner*, December 15, 1972.

"The Drama of Ray Bradbury," by Ben P. Indick, ***Huitloxopetl*, #8, 1972.

"Birds of a Different Feather Nest Under Bradbury Wing," by S. L. Stebel, *Calendar* (*Los Angeles Times*), June 24, 1973.

GRADUATE STUDENT WORK ON BRADBURY

Many school papers have been written on Ray Bradbury; it was not until the late 1960s that students began to study Bradbury's work in depth. The six graduate studies cited here reflect this study. There will obviously be more.

"An Examination of Some Aspects of the Writing of Ray Bradbury."

MA Thesis: Rodger Lee Pettichord, Washington State University, 1967.

"Ray Bradbury."

MA Thesis: Joseph W. Dauben, Harvard University, 1967.

"Ray Bradbury: A Vision Into the Future."

MA Thesis: Maria Del Rosario Briones Gutierrez, Instituto Techologico De Estudios Superiores De Monterrey, 1970.

"The Mind and Fantasies of Ray Bradbury."

Ph.D. Dissertation: Richard Steven Dimeo, University of Utah, 1970.

"Write the Other Way: The Correlation of Style and Theme in Selected Prose Fiction of Ray Bradbury."

Ph.D. Dissertation. Mark A. Foster, Florida State University, 1973.

In Progress: "Ray Bradbury: Portrait of a Popular Writer." Ph.D. Dissertation: Edward L. Gerson, University of Chicago.

Graduate Student Work on Bradbury

INDEX

To the Writings of
Ray Bradbury

Index to the Writings of Ray Bradbury

Index to the Writings of Ray Bradbury

DARK CARNIVAL
RAY BRADBURY
RAY BRADBURY THE MARTIAN CHRONICLES
RAY BRADBURY
THE ILLUSTRATED MAN
A BANTAM GIANT
RAY BRADBURY
Timeless Stories
FOR TODAY AND TOMORROW
STEINBECK
KAFKA
E. B. WHITE
ISHERWOOD
and others
RAY BRADBURY
THE GOLDEN APPLES OF THE SUN
RAY BRADBURY
FAHRENHEIT 451
BALLANTINE BOOKS
Switch on the Night
Ray Bradbury
THE OCTOBER COUNTRY
Ray Bradbury
A MEDICINE FOR MELANCHOLY
RAY BRADBURY
ray bradbury
the circus of dr. lao
and other improbable stories
DANDELION WINE
A NOVEL BY
RAY BRADBURY
Ray Bradbury